REVOLUTION!

REVOLUTION!

SOUTH AMERICA
AND THE RISE OF
THE NEW LEFT

NIKOLAS KOZLOFF

palgrave
macmillan

First published in 2008 by
PALGRAVE MACMILLAN™
175 Fifth Avenue, New York, N.Y. 10010 and
Houndmills, Basingstoke, Hampshire, England RG21 6XS.
Companies and representatives throughout the world.

PALGRAVE MACMILLAN is the global academic imprint of the
Palgrave Macmillan division of St. Martin's Press, LLC and of Palgrave
Macmillan Ltd. Macmillan® is a registered trademark in the United
States, United Kingdom and other countries. Palgrave is a registered
trademark in the European Union and other countries.

ISBN-13: 978-0-230-60057-7
ISBN-10: 0-230-60057-3

Kozloff, Nikolas.
   Revolution! : South America and the rise of the new left / Nikolas
Kozloff.
      p.   cm.
   Includes bibliographical references and index.
   ISBN 0-230-60057-3
   1. South America—Politics and government—21st century. 2. New
Left—South America.   3. Revolutions—South America.   4. Social
movements—South America.   5. Political participation—South
America.   6. Political culture—South America.   7. Natural
resources—Government policy—South America.   I. Title.
   JL1860.K69   2008
   980.04—dc22
                                                              2007041907

A catalogue record of the book is available from the British Library.

Design by Letra Libre

First edition: April 2008
10 9 8 7 6 5 4 3 2 1
Printed in the United States of America.

CONTENTS

INTRODUCTION

SOUTH AMERICA TURNS A CRITICAL PAGE

For Americans who take pride in their country's institutions and democratic traditions, the idea that the United States may have an overseas "empire" can come as something of a surprise. Since World War II the United States has enjoyed an enormous amount of political, economic, and military leverage in South America. By backing compliant elites and militaries, the United States was able to secure raw natural resources and other vital interests in the region. While U.S. influence remains strong throughout much of the region today, many South American nations are now asserting a more independent course free of Washington's control. What are the contours of this political earthquake that has spread throughout the hemisphere, and what are its larger implications? These are the questions that I seek to take up in my book.

Traditionally, many South American countries have been known for their turbulent and volatile politics. Up until the recent past, the region was characterized by unstable democracies that were constantly vulnerable to military coups. After World War II, the United States allied itself to the armed forces in South America in an effort to bolster right-wing governments. But recently South America, far from fitting its stereotype as a region of "banana republics," seems to have turned a critical page in its political history. While the military remains strong, there is little risk that the armed forces will overthrow civilian democracies. Even more noteworthy, in some cases the military has even allied itself to newly elected, left-leaning regimes and severed military ties to the United States.

Diminished control over the military is perhaps the most glaring manifestation of the decline in U.S. influence, but it is by no means the only example of the dramatic political shift. Today, South America is a potent symbol to many in the Third World because it has managed to challenge the capitalist system. While South American countries have certainly not overturned capitalism, their governments have neverthe-less been able to resist some of its more extreme characteristics and even to set up innovative economic arrangements outside of formal market strictures. For years, the United States has sought to compel South American countries to submit to unfettered market policies. Indeed, Washington long backed the implementation of so-called "neo-liberal" policies in South America stressing maximum and efficient exploitation of the region's resources, including labor, raw materials, and markets. Under "structural adjustment" policies favored by the United States and the International Monetary Fund, countries were obliged to remove ob-stacles to foreign investment and compelled to raise exports. Most of the time, such exports were produced or sold to multinational corporations. Today however, South American nations are resisting the pressure, and their governments have assumed a much greater role in the economy. If the region continues its present political drift to the left over the long term, it could constitute a significant ideological challenge to the United States.

What's more, with left-leaning governments sweeping to power, the United States is losing its ability to secure advantage for American busi-ness. Across the region, governments have held U.S. oil companies to greater account and control. Moreover, corporations have been forced to hand over a greater share of profits to the state and in some cases have been obliged to enter into joint ventures with national govern-ments. Today, it would appear as if the heady days when U.S. business called the shots are at an end. Indeed, a whole new generation of tough and idealistic government officials is determined to secure a fair deal with the companies and gain the revenue needed to tackle grinding poverty and inequality, which still affect millions. Since the U.S. gov-ernment has much less diplomatic clout in the region than it once had, American corporations have little choice but to adapt to the new politi-cal milieu.

The engine driving governments to adopt a more nationalistic and progressive agenda is civil society, which, after decades of political repression, has now come to the fore. Hardly content to merely stand by and vote, many across South America have helped to organize dynamic social movements. While the movements differ in many respects from country to country, they all share antipathy towards U.S. political, economic, and military control. Though many social movements pressure governments from without, some have also merged with political parties themselves, creating a potent coalition to spearhead social change. It may be said that South American societies are now trying to reconfigure politics and actually rethink the role of the state and its relationship to the people. If social movements continue to grow in power and influence, it would undoubtedly represent an enormous ideological setback for the United States.

The first big blow against U.S. influence came in 1998 when, taking the world by surprise, Hugo Chávez won Venezuela's presidential election handily. Chávez himself came up through poverty. The son of schoolteachers, he grew up in a small village on the Venezuelan Plain in the west of the country. Chávez, who had formed his own party, the MVR or Fifth Republic Movement, blew apart Venezuela's corrupt two-party system and won the election with 56 percent of the vote. Like other South American regimes that would later seek to reconfigure politics and the relationship between state and society, Chávez quickly convened a new National Constituent Assembly. The Venezuelan president hoped that the new body would end the isolation between the political system and the Venezuelan masses. Venezuelans voted to give all but six seats in the new assembly to legislators associated with Chávez's movement. Once elected, the legislators set about writing a new constitution.

Galvanizing the people around him, Chávez frequently derided the so-called neo-liberal policies pushed by his predecessors. A phenomenon that largely slipped under the radar of the mainstream U.S. media, neo-liberalism, with its stress on deregulation, privatization of state-run industry, implementation of fiscal austerity plans, and trade liberalization, hit South America hard. In line with International Monetary Fund (IMF) recommendations, debt-ridden nations slashed government spending, leading to a popular backlash. Venezuela was hit particularly hard: following a crash in world oil prices, successive governments led by Venezuela's corrupt two parties sought to deal with the debt problem

in the 1980s by cutting social spending. In 1989, when the government
of Carlos Andrés Pérez announced that it would implement neo-liberal
restructuring in accordance with IMF guidelines as well as raise fuel
prices, residents in the capital city of Caracas protested and rioted.
Chávez, then a young military officer, was repulsed by the government's
decision to send in the army in an effort to put down the uprising in
poor neighborhoods. On the presidential campaign trail in 1998,
Chávez pledged to increase social spending in opposition to the IMF.[1]
Buoyed by higher oil prices, Chávez went on to challenge the neo-liberal order by increasing social spending and carrying out reciprocal
trading schemes with Cuba.

In many ways, Chávez inspired much of the resource nationalism
that has taken root in South America today. Today, oil plays a huge economic role in Venezuela. Oil accounted for 90 percent of the country's
export earnings and about half the government's revenue in 2005.
Venezuela is the fourth-largest exporter of crude to the Unites States.[2]
For years, U.S. oil companies such as Standard Oil and Gulf had dominated the local industry, setting up a massive petroleum infrastructure in
the Lake Maracaibo region. Relations between local communities and
the oil companies were not always amicable, and industrial accidents, oil
blow-outs, and environmental pollution were common.[3] Meanwhile,
labor strife plagued the Maracaibo oil fields, and Venezuelans smarted
under the racist practices of the companies.[4] During his first, more nationalist presidential term in office in 1975–76, Carlos Andrés Pérez nationalized the oil industry and created a new state oil company, PdVSA.
However, under successive administrations the government began to
lose its control, and a smaller percentage of oil earnings wound up in
state coffers. Meanwhile, company managers, who were setting oil
policy independent of the national government, earned huge salaries
and enjoyed large expense accounts. On the campaign trail, Chávez ex-
coriated PdVSA and pledged to assert more government control over
the company. Having consolidated his political victory, Chávez set about
reining in PdVSA's independence by asserting more government control
over the state oil sector. He also enacted a new Hydrocarbons Law,
mandating that no private company could own more than 50 percent
stock in joint oil ventures with the state.

Chávez's election stood to upset other traditional interests such as
the military. Since Venezuela's war of independence against Spain in the

first decades of the nineteenth century, the armed forces have played a crucial role in the nation's political affairs, not always for the good. In the nineteenth century, regional strongmen prevailed, and for much of the twentieth, Venezuela was plagued by brutal military rule. Chávez had joined the military in an effort to get out of poverty. Touring the country as a young soldier, he was moved by the plight of Venezuela's dirt-poor Indians and the rampant social injustice he saw. In 1992, he organized a coup d'état against Carlos Andrés Pérez, in an effort to overturn rampant corruption and the "dictatorship of the International Monetary Fund." Though the coup was a failure, it established Chávez as a prominent figure and underscored growing political tension within the ranks.[5] Cruising to victory in 1998, this time as a civilian, Chávez broke military ties with the United States. He also had the armed forces carry out public works projects.

For a brief moment, however, it looked as if Chávez's so-called "Bolivarian Revolution" might be snuffed out before it could exert much influence on the rest of South America. The Venezuelan opposition, led by wealthy globalizing magnates, conservative army officers, and oil industry executives opposed to Chávez's nationalistic petroleum policy, rebelled. In April 2002 the opposition, which had been receiving money from the United States through the taxpayer-funded National Endowment for Democracy, took to the streets of Caracas to demand Chávez's resignation. Taking advantage of street violence and political confusion, dissident officers kidnapped Chávez. Pedro Carmona, a former petrochemical executive, took power, dissolving the Supreme Court and eliminating the country's constitution. However, officers loyal to Chávez, aided by massive street protests by pro-Chávez demonstrators, soon returned the president to power. Chávez's return came as a stinging rebuff to Washington and allowed the Venezuelan president to consolidate his position over the state oil company. With the money from the petroleum industry, Chávez has been able to deepen the Bolivarian Revolution by undertaking ambitious programs in such areas as health and education.[6]

The watershed April 2002 coup proved important on a psychological level. In 1998, Chávez seemed a living anachronism, somehow out of step with the neo-liberal regimes in power throughout the region. But Chávez demonstrated that a government could indeed resist the United States as well as the trend towards unfettered, market-driven globalization. For years, South America had seen social revolt against neo-liberal reforms. Now, inspired by Chávez's example, people throughout the region finally voted the governments implementing those reforms out of power. An apparent political throwback when he was first elected in 1998, the new Venezuelan president was quickly joined by a whole host of other leaders who provided key diplomatic support. One such leader was Luiz Inácio "Lula" da Silva, of the Brazilian Workers' Party. Like Chávez, Lula was born into poverty and as a boy sold peanuts and shined shoes. Lula's political trial by fire, however, came not through military service but rather labor-union organizing. During the 1980s, the young man organized key strikes against foreign businesses in the industrial ABC region of São Paulo, Brazil's largest city.

The rise of Lula was significant, in that it raised the prospect of a larger axis opposed to free market reforms. Like Venezuela, Brazil had undergone its own history of following neo-liberal proscriptions. While such policies made the country appealing to foreign investors and helped stave off inflation, they also left Brazil vulnerable to financial shocks on the world market. In the late 1990s, when a financial crisis hit Asia and Russia, stocks plunged in Brazil as investors rushed to pull their money out of the South American nation. When billions poured out of Brazil, the government devalued the currency, the *real*. Even with an International Monetary Fund bailout, the government was obliged to freeze wages and cut jobs in the state sector.[7] With the public now souring on globalization as a panacea to the country's problems, the country was looking for a change. Lula, who had helped to launch the Workers' Party or PT, a dynamic organization comprised of his old labor colleagues as well as other social activists, was now on the verge of achieving true national status.

In 2002, voters long disgusted with corrupt party politics and neo-liberal experiments handed Lula the presidency with more than 60 percent of the vote. Would the region now move sharply to the left? Brazil, a much larger and more populous nation than Venezuela, raised the possibility. Lula, a politician who had himself grown up poor, pledged to transform Brazil's highly unequal society by expanding education and redistributing land. He sought to finance his social reform by redirecting funds earmarked for debt repayment. He also promised to invest more money in social welfare programs. "For many Brazilians," writes the Council on Hemispheric Affairs, "the October 2002 election of President Luiz Inácio Lula da Silva symbolized the ascendance to power of a leftist prodigal son."[8] While that's surely what many activists within the Workers' Party had hoped for, they have been sorely disappointed by Lula. Investors who might have been alarmed that this nation of 188 million would undergo economic and political radicalization turned out to have little to fear: despite his rhetoric, Lula refused to stand up to the IMF, instead presiding over huge cuts in public spending and deteriorating living conditions.[9] Certainly no Chávez, Lula has continued to pursue market-oriented policies, to the dismay of many of his staunch party followers. On the other hand, he has opposed George Bush's Free Trade Area of the Americas or FTAA and spurred the creation of anti-poverty programs. Although today's Lula hardly resembles the radical labor organizer from São Paulo, he has given Chávez some breathing room by refusing to isolate Venezuela diplomatically.

While Chávez and Lula have put on a public show of solidarity, it's clear that the two differ somewhat in their political and economic orientation. Hoping to shore up his international standing, Chávez needed a true ally. But where could he look? In 2003, the Venezuelan leader got his answer. In Argentina, the revolt against neo-liberal policies seemed to be taking a dramatic and violent turn. For years, the Argentine political class had followed globalization's dictates by dismantling protectionist trade and business regulations and embarking on an ambitious wave of privatizations. During the Asian economic crisis of 1998, a huge outflow of capital gradually led to a painful four-year depression. In November 2001 a financial panic ensued, and in December bloody riots shook the capital of Buenos Aires, forcing President De la Rúa's resignation.[10]

With the election of Néstor Kirchner, however, Chávez could take some solace that a sympathetic politician was now coming to the fore. Coming to power in 2003 in the midst of a social and political collapse, Kirchner was not entering a promising milieu. A former governor of the province of Santa Cruz, he hardly enjoyed a strong popular mandate: he received the second-largest number of votes in the first round of the presidential election but won his office only by default when his challenger, Carlos Menem, who had won the first round but feared being trounced in the second, declined to participate in the run-off . Though many of Kirchner's associates in government come from the traditional political class, he has done much to create a sense of political renewal.[11]

In an effort to build up his standing with the public and his party, Kirchner sought to differentiate his administration from those of his predecessors by challenging neo-liberalism. The president adopted fiery rhetoric, which he deployed to great effect against the likes of the IMF, foreign investors, and parts of the business community. But Kirchner has gone beyond mere rhetoric, bolstering his support by raising wages and pensions for the neediest. On energy policy, he has bucked neo-liberal logic by creating a new state-run oil company; he has also sealed energy deals with Venezuela.

Like Chávez, Kirchner also undertook a major overhaul of military policy. During the military dictatorship of 1976–83, at least 13,000 people, and perhaps as many as 30,000, were killed by the armed forces. Most of them were "disappeared," their bodies never found.[12] Through the so-called "Dirty War," the military hunted down those it viewed as subversives—not only leftist guerrillas, but also union activists, university students, and even Jewish psychiatrists.[13] The security forces disposed of the bodies of the disappeared in ingenious ways, such as dumping them into the Atlantic Ocean from air force planes. The United States welcomed the military takeover in Argentina. When a deputy warned Henry Kissinger that repression and "a good deal of blood" would likely follow the military coup, the then-secretary of state ordered that the United States support the new regime. "I do want to encourage them," he said. "I don't want to give the sense that they're harassed by the United States."[14] Argentina's military government collapsed in disarray following defeat in the Falklands War. Initial attempts to bring human rights violators faltered in the midst of repeated barrack rebellion. However, Kirchner has now charged or investigated hundreds of the perpetrators. According to *The Economist*, Kirchner, whose government comprises a number of former followers of the Montonero guerrillas, was personally in favor of the prosecutions. In carrying out his policy, Kirchner had public opinion behind him: according to polls, 70 percent of the Argentine population favored the Supreme Court's decision to annul amnesty laws for the military.[15]

The tectonic shift away from repressive militaries seemed to come full circle two years after Kirchner's election, when nearby Chile underwent its own kind of political renewal. In January 2005, after running as the candidate of the center-left governing coalition, Michele Bachelet was elected Chile's first woman president. Bachelet's election underscored the nation's attempt to come to terms with its brutal military past going back more than thirty years.

In 1970, Salvador Allende, a Marxist and a member of Chile's Socialist Party, won the country's presidential election with only 36 percent of the vote and a plurality of only 36,000 votes. Allende's program included land expropriation and nationalization of private industry, which happened to include U.S. interests in Chile's major copper mines. On September 11, 1973, General Augusto Pinochet overthrew the Allende government. The Nixon administration, the Central Intelligence Agency, and big metal and telecommunications companies backed Pinochet. Over the next seventeen years, more than 3,000 Chileans were disappeared by the Pinochet regime, while tens of thousands were tortured, imprisoned, or driven into exile. Bachelet, who was an opponent of the regime, was one of the torture victims herself.[16] But at least she survived; her father, a general in the air force who had refused to collaborate with the coup, was not as fortunate. In 1974 he was tortured to death at a military academy. Bachelet and her mother were able to escape the clutches of the Pinochet government through military contacts. Michele fled to Australia, and later traveled to East Germany. When Pinochet came up for reelection in 1989, he lost a popular referendum by a wide 14 percent margin, which paved the way for democratic elections and the return of civilian government.[17] Shortly afterwards, Chile returned to democracy with the election of Patricio Aylwin, who led a coalition of parties called the Concertación. Under the Aylwin government, the authorities set up an independent inquiry into the disappeared. But the perpetrators could not be brought to justice: the Pinochet dictatorship, in an effort to cover its tracks, had already declared amnesty for crimes committed under the military regime. Bachelet, who had become a pediatrician and a socialist, was appointed the country's first female minister of defense, taking up her duties under the regime of Ricardo Lagos. Pinochet died in December 2006. Though he was never brought to justice, the former dictator had become totally disgraced at home and abroad. In response to an extradition request from Spain, Pinochet was arrested in London in 1998. The British House of Lords ruled that he lacked immunity under international law, and though he was subsequently let go, the ex-dictator was under almost constant threat of arrest in his last years. When he died at age 91, he was facing trial on various charges including murder, torture, and tax evasion. Since becoming

president herself as a member of the Socialist Party and a representative
of the center-left Concertación, Bachelet has sought to come to terms
with Chile's military past. Indeed, since 1999 the Supreme Court has removed most of the obstacles to trying crimes committed during the
Pinochet years; 148 people, including 50 military officers, have already
been convicted of human rights violations. Over 400 more, almost all
from the military, have been indicted or are under investigation.[18]

In taking on the military, Bachelet was confronting an institution
that historically had warm ties with the United States. But the question
remained whether the Chilean president would challenge the United
States in other respects. As president, Bachelet would have to come to
terms with Chile's gruesome military past but also the legacy of neo-liberalism. Despite its military authoritarianism, the Pinochet regime pursued market-friendly economic policies, selling off many state-owned
companies.[19] When Pinochet's neo-liberal reforms faltered during the
debt crisis of the early 1980s, fault lines began to appear in the military
regime, and calls for greater political openness gained momentum.[20]
Nevertheless, Bachelet has continued many of the free-market policies
of the past; in this sense, she is little different from the three democratic
regimes that preceded her, all of which continued the privatization of
the Pinochet years, but at a slower pace.[21] Perhaps Bachelet is more akin
to Lula in terms of overall economic orientation. Nevertheless, Chávez
has said that he considers Chile to be an ally in the wider region, certainly an unpleasing development for Washington.[22]

Already diplomatically weakened in the region, the United States
was soon dealt a further blow when Bolivia underwent a major political
renewal under its newly elected president, Evo Morales. An Aymara Indian, Morales is the first president in Bolivian history to come from the
country's ethnic majority. An impoverished and politically unstable
country, Bolivia was long ruled by military governments. In 1964, General René Barrientos seized the government, initiating a long string of
military regimes. The country only returned to civilian democracy in
1985. In Bolivia, two thirds of the people are indigenous. The country's
population comprises 37 ethnic groups, including Aymaras, Quechuas,
and Guaraníes. The Aymaras currently number almost two million, 80
percent of whom reside in Bolivia, with the rest living in neighboring
Peru and Chile. The overwhelming majority of the Aymara is poor and
ekes out a living from the land as *campesino* peasants. Morales was born

in Isallavi, an Andean community in the western province of Oruro. The area is firmly rooted in Aymara culture. Though the future president later emigrated to the central semitropical area of Chapare, Morales still keeps to the customs, language, and traditions of Isallavi.

Taking his cue from the Chávez script, Morales sought to revamp the government's relationship to society. Morales's secret weapon is the MAS, a loose conglomeration of leftist labor unions and social interest groups that has campaigned on a platform of coca decriminalization and nationalization of natural resources. Bolivia's Vice President Álvaro García Linera has described MAS as a "confederation of social movements" lacking a monolithic or even vertical structure.[23] Hardly a party in the traditional sense, MAS can best be summed up as "a political instrument" of social organizations. What essentially happened, writes Judy Rebick of the *Toronto Star*, was that indigenous organizations got together to form a political organization that could contest elections. The Indians were joined by various elements of the middle class, as well as intellectuals and figures from the urban left. While most of the membership of MAS is male, the party has taken significant steps towards gender equality. Morales's cabinet consists of 25 percent women, including the ministers of health, interior, and justice.[24] In an effort to transform the relationship between the state and indigenous peoples, Morales opened the new Constituent Assembly in 2006. In his own words, the new body was designed to "re-found" Bolivia on an entirely new basis. The president of the new Assembly was an indigenous *campesina* woman, and Indian women have proposed to the Assembly that all 50 percent of officials elected and appointed to the new body be female. With grit and determination, Morales and the MAS sought to rip down the sacrosanct structure of Bolivian society. The president himself remarked that the challenge for the new body would be to "finish" with the colonial state. Once the old state machinery was sloughed off, the government would then proceed to eradicate neo-liberalism once and for all. "A peaceful revolution is happening in Bolivia," remarks Rebick. "The indigenous majority has taken over the government and is beginning a profound transformation of the country."[25]

Morales's electoral victory also underscored the lack of popularity for Washington's militarized policy throughout the Andes, which is predicated on fighting the so-called drug war. In Bolivia and the Andes, coca leaf or *Erythroxylon coca* is legally used as an infusion to make tea.

The leaf, which was domesticated over 4,000 years ago, is usually chewed with a bitter wood-ash paste to bring out the stimulant properties, which are similar to caffeine or nicotine. In the Andes, visitors are commonly offered coca tea to combat *soroche* or altitude sickness, which can cause headache and vertigo. Coca is also used for cosmetic products such as skin cream and toothpaste. Outside the region, however, coca is classified as a prohibited drug. In order to convert coca leaf into cocaine, it must be combined with other ingredients and subjected to a complex chemical process. Morales, a former leader of the coca-growers federation, has sought to allow the free cultivation of the coca plant, which is the most lucrative cash crop for indigenous peasants. Thumbing his nose at Washington's drug war in the Andes, Morales raised the ceiling for licit coca cultivation from 12,000 hectares to 20,000 hectares.[26] Morales's stand on coca production has been a critical factor in explaining his rising political popularity. Morales even displayed a coca leaf before the General Assembly of the United Nations in New York in September 2006. Coca, he said, has therapeutic uses and should not be criminalized. The prohibition of coca was "an historic injustice . . .the United Nations has to know that scientifically, it has been demonstrated that coca does not harm human health." Morales agreed that it was necessary to fight drug smuggling but said that criminalizing coca was a strategy by the great powers to re-colonize the Andean nations.[27]

Morales's election and the rise of MAS marked the culmination of long years of bitter struggles against the neo-liberal state, including the famous "water wars" of 1992 against the privatization of water in Cochabamba; Morales's own struggle to protect traditional coca growers against U.S attempts to eradicate the plant; and the brutal "gas wars" of 2003, when residents of El Alto fought to prevent the selling off of natural gas. In this last struggle, the protesters won but at the cost of 70 dead and 200 wounded.[28] Morales himself has branded George Bush a terrorist and argues that capitalism is a global blight. "The worst enemy of humanity is capitalism," Morales has said. "That is what provokes uprisings like our own, a rebellion against a system, against a neo-liberal model, which is the representation of a savage capitalism. If the entire world doesn't acknowledge this reality, that the national states are not providing even minimally for health, education and nourishment, then each day the most fundamental human rights are being violated." What's more,

Morales has described the U.S.-driven Free Trade Area of the Americas as "an agreement to legalize the colonization of the Americas," adding that Bolivia, Cuba, and Venezuela might constitute an "axis of good" in contrast to the "axis of evil" comprising the United States and its allies.[29] In line with his anti-neo-liberal bent, Morales "nationalized" Bolivia's hydrocarbons sector and eventually signed new contracts with the gas companies, which is likely to result in higher revenue for the government. According to the U.S. State Department, "These policies have pleased Morales' supporters, but have complicated Bolivia's relations with some of its neighboring countries, foreign investors, and members of the international community."[30]

With willing allies in Kirchner and Morales, and friendly ties to Brazil and Chile, Chávez's political star was already on the rise in the new, left-leaning South America when another potential ally, Rafael Correa, was elected president of Ecuador in 2006. Correa is Ecuador's eighth president in 10 years. Like Bolivia, the country has been beset by political instability since it returned to democracy in 1979. Lawmakers have dismissed the last three elected presidents in response to huge protests demanding their ousters. According to the 2001 census, Indians number some 800,000, or just under 7 percent of the population,[31] though CONAIE, or Confederación de Nacionalidades Indígenas del Ecuador, the main indigenous federation, claims that they account for 45 percent of the country's people.[32] The government's own bilingual education agency estimates that the Quichua Indians alone number 3.9 million out of the total Ecuadoran population of some 13 million.[33] Currently, 3 million Ecuadorans live abroad as a result of economic crisis,[34] and more than 60 percent of the people within Ecuador live in poverty.[35]

Correa, who is the first leftist to win the presidency since Ecuador returned to democracy in 1979, refers to himself as a man of the "lower middle class."[36] Growing up in modest circumstances in the coastal city of Guayaquil, Correa was able to pursue his studies thanks to grants and eventually went on to get his doctorate in economics in Illinois.[37] When Correa took power, the 43-year-old economist traveled to the town of Zumbahua, located 90 kilometers south of Quito in the Andean tundra and populated by the Quichua, Ecuador's largest Indian group. As a volunteer with the Salesian fathers, a Catholic religious order founded in the nineteenth century, he taught religion and mathematics there during the 1980s.

What difference can Correa's election make for this chronically turbulent, unstable, and poverty-stricken nation? While Correa's task is not easy, the young leader intends to follow a similar political trajectory to Venezuela and Bolivia. Determined to overhaul the political system, he called for a national referendum on the need for a new constitutional assembly. The new body would have the power to dissolve the legislature and restructure the judiciary.[38] The move was necessary, Correa claimed, to limit the power of the traditional parties responsible for the country's problems. For example, he has claimed that some of the debt that accrued under previous governments was the result of corruption.[39] The president's confrontational stance put him on a collision course with the unicameral National Assembly and the opposition. Correa has long argued that Ecuador's political system is designed to benefit parties and not the people. His electoral victory underscored voters' disgust with the corruption and greed of the political elite. The president has attacked Congress as a "sewer" of corruption but has run no legislative candidates himself. In calling for the constitutional assembly, Correa hoped to win control over the new body. His moves echoed the first years of the Chávez administration, which had also created a new constituent assembly. Lawmakers were hardly amused by Correa's plan. "If Correa wants war, he'll get war," Congressman Luis Fernando Torres exclaimed.[40]

Like his counterparts Morales and Chávez, Correa also seems intent on reversing Ecuador's economic orientation. Through his studies as a graduate student, he became an avid follower of left-wing economist and Nobel Prize winner Joseph Stiglitz. A virtual political unknown when he was invited by the government of Alfredo Palacio to become the minister of economy in 2005, Correa used his position to criticize the United States and to get to know Chávez, Kirchner, and Lula. During the presidential campaign, he demonstrated a closer political affinity with those leaders than with the United States by declaring that George Bush was "dim-witted." Correa said that to compare Bush to the devil, as Chávez had done, was an offense to the devil.[41] After his election, the new president declared Washington's free market policies a failure and said that the "long neo-liberal night" had come to an end. Correa has called for an "economic revolution" that would renegotiate the foreign debt.[42] One of his favorite targets is the banking elite. He has set up a committee to investigate allegations that crimes committed by bankers between 1998 and 2002 led to a banking crisis and bailout. The crisis resulted in the "dollarization" of the economy, or adoption of the U.S. dollar as the country's unit of currency, and the bailout cost the dirt-poor country $8 billion.[43] In a departure from the right-wing governments that preceded him, Correa has called for a radical about-face in economic policy. First of all, he says, Ecuador should set up an international tribunal to decide what debt should be repaid.[44] The country should spend the money that would have gone to repay or service the rest for more progressive purposes such as health and education.[45] Correa has declared a state of emergency in Ecuador's health sector, and over the next four years the government intends to double investment in social projects by cutting debt-service payments by a third.[46]

Ecuador's new resource nationalism suggests that the country is moving closer to Venezuela. Correa in fact has never hidden his views about energy policy. As minister of economy, Correa modified a law guiding oil investment in the country, and in Caracas he signed a deal to refine oil in Venezuela, which put him afoul of his boss. U.S. oil companies have historically loomed large in Ecuador's politics, but Correa is intent on restoring a prominent place for the state oil company, Petroecuador. He has also appointed nationalist officials intent on bringing foreign oil companies under control of the state and holding them to account; the president also seeks energy integration with Venezuela. Correa has sought to renegotiate contracts with the oil companies so as to secure greater revenue and thereby make a dent in Ecuador's grinding poverty.[47]

What does Venezuela, the first country to elect a leftist leader during the region's recent series of elections, have in common with Brazil, Argentina, Chile, Bolivia, and Ecuador? That's a question I set out to answer during a two-month trip through South America. During my travels, I spoke with academics, experts, activists, and government officials to assess the current political situation within the region. This book encapsulates their analysis concerning such vital questions as the military, resource nationalism, the rejection of neo-liberal doctrines, and the relationship of social movements to national governments.

The work also addresses two other key points well worth considering in the present political context: cultural nationalism and the media. For years, countries throughout the region have had warm cultural ties to the United States. This still holds true, but many nations are now seeking to redefine themselves. While this has been most pronounced in Venezuela, other countries too have become more culturally nationalist in the past few years, particularly in the Andes. In yet another sign that South America is determined to set its own independent course, many countries have moved to assert greater control over the media. In a region whose media have traditionally been controlled by powerful interests friendly to the United States, governments have frequently lacked power in the information war. In this book, I provide a discussion of this thorny issue by considering recent developments across the region.

The many themes taken up in this book form a vital backdrop for understanding the geopolitics of the region and South America's wider role in the world. With so many like-minded regimes in power, how might countries start to foster greater ties? Could there be a viable future for South American economic and political integration? Though some economic and political differences remain, Mercosur, a South American trade bloc, could be the linchpin for greater unity. Could Mercosur move beyond mere trade issues and actually help to coordinate joint political initiatives? Might South America speak as one voice on the world stage? Such a development would deal a severe blow to U.S. power.

CHAPTER 1
ASSERTING ENERGY SOVEREIGNTY

One of the most spectacular industrial fires in the history of the Venezuelan oil industry occurred at the village of La Rosa situated on the lake of Lake Maracaibo, in June 1925.[1] According to an eyewitness, a well ran wild for a couple of days on the lake. Then, "there was trouble in shutting it [the well] in and during the next few hours some 5,000 barrels leaked through the blow-out preventer and formed a film of oil on the water." What happened next at the R–28 well was ominous: "on top of all this oil this big . . .gusher, R–28 came in and flooded the lake."[2] The blow-out lasted 48 hours, and left Lake Maracaibo contaminated with approximately 120,000 barrels. According to a glossy magazine published by the oil companies, the spill spread across Lake Maracaibo, leaving a film three inches thick.[3] By 1:30 the next morning, the oil had spread to the drilling wells belonging to two American companies, Gulf and Lago Petroleum Corporation.[4]

The situation was now extremely dangerous. When a bit of burning oil dripped from one of the oil companies' boilers into the lake, the spill exploded into a raging fire.[5] According to one eyewitness, "by some means the fire from the boilers used on the Gulf's Superior–8 set the oil on fire and almost instantly an area of twenty-five or thirty acres was ablaze."[6] Another eyewitness wrote that the well flared up into a torch as high as a skyscraper. Above the plume of flame, clouds of smoke billowed up to the sky.[7] The column of flame rose more than 300 feet into the air and could be seen 100 miles away.[8] Observers reported that local inhabitants were terrified, running out of their houses and seeking shelter for fear of their lives.[9] In addition to industrial damage to company property, there was also environmental damage in the surrounding area. One journal remarked that the fire burnt many fish alive within the lake itself.[10]

Though the fire was eventually extinguished, Venezuelans remember the environmental disaster at Lake Maracaibo and the arrogance of the oil companies, who ignored the welfare of the workers. Indeed, the companies exposed Venezuelan workers to industrial accidents and refused to pay sufficient compensation to injured laborers. Such abuses were not lost on the Venezuelan press, which denounced the companies. Newspapers also accused the companies of misrepresenting their costs and as a result reducing royalties payable to the dictatorial Gómez state.

Today, Venezuela, currently the world's fifth largest crude exporter, seeks to wrest much control of the oil industry from foreign corporations and to use oil proceeds as a means of promoting social development. While the petroleum companies enjoyed a substantial degree of independence during the heady days of the Maracaibo boom, the state has now become increasingly more assertive. The symbol of this combativeness is Bernard Mommer, a key figure in the Chávez administration who has pushed for greater resource nationalism. A former student radical, Mommer is part of a 1960s generation of activists that had been widely repressed in South America. Now, however, that generation has come of age, and come to the fore. Like many of his peers in the left-leaning regimes throughout the region, Mommer has achieved a degree of real power and influence, currently serving as vice minister of hydrocarbons.[11] Mommer, who maintains a diplomatic low profile, has remarked, "I am an expert, not a politician."[12]

In his capacity as vice minister, Mommer has lobbied the National Assembly for greater state control over the oil industry and has led sensitive discussions with U.S. oil companies about nationalization of their assets. In his dealings with the companies, Mommer has adopted a tough posture. For example, he has said that Venezuela has the right to take control of its natural resources, and any company that doesn't accept the government's terms should leave the country. What's more, Mommer has rejected the companies' right to resort to international arbitration in their claims. The Venezuelan legal system, he has said, is sufficient to handle any disputes. "We say 'no' to colonialist agreements," he has remarked.[13]

Mommer was born in the south of France in 1943. His father, a German Marxist and anti-fascist, was arrested by the Nazis in Germany. As a young man, Mommer studied mathematics in Germany, where he developed an interest in student radicalism and anti-Vietnam war activities. Graduating from school in 1968, he realized that he had a passion for political economy.

"My act of destiny," Mommer adds, "was when I started reading Adam Smith. I read whatever he wrote about capitalism and natural resources." A few years after reading Smith he went to Venezuela. "I just wanted to go somewhere," he remarks glibly.

As it turns out Mommer had met some Venezuelans and they had told him how "life was easy" in Venezuela. He arrived during a period of democratic but highly corrupt government. Under civilian rule, oil wealth had given rise to a bloated bureaucracy but had failed to eradicate poverty in the countryside. The young mathematician started to meet figures on the left, including the guerrilla fighter Alí Rodríguez. Mommer became an advisor to the Party of the Venezuelan Revolution, the political wing of the principal guerrilla group in the country, which later attracted such figures as Chávez himself. Mommer's meeting with Rodríguez proved fateful, and the German's ties to the insurgent would endure over the years. Meanwhile, he became a voracious reader, consuming "anything he could get a hold of" about oil, later writing a doctoral thesis on the political economy of petroleum.

When Venezuela nationalized oil fields in 1976, Mommer argued that the guerrillas should put down their weapons and devise other ways to take control over oil resources. In 1989, he went to work with PdVSA, but resigned five years later claiming that the company was hiding its earnings and was not generating revenue for social development.

In the wake of economic turmoil in Venezuela in the 1980s and 90s, Mommer grew increasingly concerned about government efforts to open up the oil sector to private participation. Through confidential meetings, he was able to discuss oil policy matters with Rafael Caldera, a leading conservative politician who was elected president in 1994. Mommer went to the presidential palace, Miraflores, three times to try to dissuade Caldera from pursuing oil *apertura*, or greater opening of the oil industry. When he realized he wasn't having any success in influencing the government, he gave up. "After that," Mommer says, leaning across the table, "I went to Oxford because I realized there was nothing else I could do."

Mommer spent six years living in England and working at the Oxford Energy Institute. Though he was now far away from developments in Venezuela, he avidly maintained his ties with key political figures such as Alí Rodríguez. By now, Rodríguez had left behind his life as a guerrilla fighter and was challenging oil *apertura* in the Venezuelan Congress. Rodríguez visited and conferred with Mommer twice in Oxford. The meetings proved fruitful, and the German became an advisor to the former guerrilla. While in Oxford, Mommer also had the chance to meet with Hugo Chávez, who was campaigning for the presidency at the time of his very first trip to England, in 1998.

At the time, privileged executives at PdVSA were asserting greater control over the company and its right to set oil policy. Chávez, who had championed a nationalist oil policy during his campaign, headed straight to the Latin American Centre after getting off the plane in England. According to my source, Chávez came off as very comfortable in England, demonstrating an uncanny ability to adapt and socialize in new and foreign surroundings.

"For me," Mommer says, "the Chávez meeting came as a surprise. I knew Venezuela was collapsing, but I didn't know who would pick up the pieces."

Mommer wasn't sure what Chávez would do about oil if he were elected. He relates that he was much more focused on working with Rodríguez, whom he had known since 1970. After Chávez was elected in 1998, Rodríguez became the Secretary General of OPEC and went to Vienna, where the organization's headquarters is located, to take up his post. Mommer accompanied his friend to Austria, serving as the former guerrilla's assistant and returning to Venezuela to take up his responsibilities as vice minister of hydrocarbons in 2005. Since his first meeting with Chávez, Mommer hadn't had much further contact with the Venezuelan politician.

He explains that Chávez had come a long way since his visit to Oxford. It had taken the government five years to get control over PdVSA, and it had not been easy. Following the coup of 2002, PdVSA executives and the opposition launched a combined oil lockout, sabotage, and work stoppage in order to get Chávez to resign. Though Chávez was ultimately able to defeat the effort, the lockout cost the nation $14 billion in the end.[14] In the wake of the economic disaster, the Chávez government was in no mood for compromise. It fired 18,000 PdVSA employees, most of them managers, administrators, and professionals.[15]

Having secured control over oil resources, Chávez now sought to use the company for his own ends. One of the intriguing things about PdVSA today is that it is not just a company but also a symbolic and social instrument. In line with the progressive vision of Rodríguez and Mommer, PdVSA has moved to massively fund Chávez's initiatives. Glossy magazines run features about the company's many ambitious plans. For example, Chávez recently launched the so-called "oil and gas Social Districts," essentially territorial units where the company promises to allocate over $6 billion a year to encourage social development programs.

The idea is to distribute oil wealth throughout the country, a move designed to facilitate demographic "de-concentration" and a lessening of massive rural-to-urban migration. What is innovative about the so-called Oil Sowing Plan is that communities design their own development projects and PdVSA provides the funding, lending credence to Chávez's claim that he is creating an authentic "participatory democracy." According to the company, there is no precedent anywhere in the world for a program like this one. In the words of Rafael Ramírez, PdVSA's president, "The PdVSA that neglected the people, and indifferently watched the misery and poverty in the communities surrounding the company premises, is over. Now the oil industry takes concrete actions to deepen the revolutionary distribution of the revenues among the people."[16] In 2005, PdVSA paid out $6.9 billion to social programs such as Misión Ribas (adult education), Misión Sucre (university scholarships), Misión Vuelvan Caras (economic cooperatives), Misión Guaicaipuro (indigenous land titling), Misión Barrio Adentro (community health), Misión Mercal (subsidized food markets), and Misión Milagro (eye operations).[17] Initiated in August 2004 Misión Milagro has enjoyed the support of Cuban President Fidel Castro. Designed to provide "the universal right to health under the principles of equality, solidarity, accessibility and justice," Misión Milagro, which is free, aims to perform surgery on 300,000 Venezuelans and 300,000 Cubans.[18]

Buoyed by his victory over PdVSA, Chávez asserted control over American oil companies. Reportedly, U.S. oil executives were hardly thrilled by Chávez's Hydrocarbons Law of 2001, which raised royalty taxes on the oil companies.[19] Under the law, the state was also allowed to form "mixed companies" with national and international capital. In 2005, PdVSA president and oil minister Rafael Ramírez announced that the 32 operating agreements that Venezuela signed in the 1990s would be replaced by mixed companies in which PdVSA held a stake of at least 51 percent.[20] Chávez turned up the heat on the oil industry by adding a clause to the companies' contracts allowing his government to raise taxes on crude oil extracted in the country.

Mommer says that when the government proposed the mixed companies in 2001, some corporations were helpful while others were not. But oil executives generally tended to be diplomatic. No company manager would ever dare call him up and denounce Chávez as some kind of dangerous communist—such a move would have jeopardized sensitive negotiations. In the end, the companies accepted the government's terms. In early 2006, the government converted all 32 operating agreements signed in the 1990s to joint-venture agreements.[21]

On the other hand, Mommer adds, the Orinoco Oil Belt, known in Venezuela as the "Faja," is potentially problematic. The area was home to multi-billion dollar oil projects held by American companies such as ConocoPhillips, Chevron, and Exxon Mobil. The companies had been lured to the Faja by low royalty rates and virtually no taxes. But now, with the spike in oil prices, Chávez claimed the companies were earning record profits. He was personally determined to claim a bigger piece of the pie for Venezuela, hoping to use the revenues to fund ambitious social programs to benefit the poor.[22]

It is likely that Venezuelan exports to the United States will continue. This is due to the nature of Venezuelan heavy oil. Along the U.S. Gulf coast, a short tanker trip away from Venezuela, specific infrastructure had been set up to process this oil. The heavy crude, Mommer said, was "investment specific," and so exports to the United States would likely continue "unless there was a big confrontation. But if it comes down to economics, no way." China might build refineries capable of processing Venezuelan heavy crude, but this would take at least five or six years.[23]

Greg Wilpert is editor of the Web site venezuelanalysis.com, specializing in news and analysis from Venezuela, written in English. I wait for Wilpert outside at Gran Café, a well-known spot near the metro station. The café is located in a kind of pedestrian walkway, cordoned off from chaotic and bustling street traffic and informal vendors. A heavyset, affable man who looks to be my rough contemporary in his late 30s, Wilpert explains that while teaching sociology at the New School in Manhattan, he met his future wife, a Venezuelan. He later went to teach at Venezuela's Central University on a grant from the Fulbright committee.

In the Orinoco, PdVSA had about a 40 percent stake in oil ventures, but sought to raise its participation to 60 percent or more in accordance with the provisions of the 2001 Hydrocarbons Law. The problem in the Oil Belt, Wilpert says, and the reason the government might not give such a good deal in compensation, was that the companies had invested huge sums of money, and it could prove difficult for the government to come up with the cash.[24] Two months after my interview with Wilpert, Chávez announced the government's intention to "nationalize" the four oil projects in the Faja.[25] Though the Orinoco projects were now estimated to be worth $30 billion, Venezuela said it was inclined to pay $17 billion with partial payment in petroleum; according to experts, the government might also provide some tax forgiveness. All companies except for ConocoPhillips signed agreements with the government, though the American firm said it would eventually cooperate. Some companies, however, expressed reservations about the deal. David O'Reilly, chief executive of Chevron, remarked that his company's future "will very much be dependent on how we're treated in the current negotiation. That process is going to have a direct impact on our appetite going forward."

State television showed workers in hard hats cheering the decision and waving the Venezuelan flag over a refinery and four drilling fields in the Faja. Chávez himself traveled to the refinery on May Day for a ceremony with oil workers dressed in red, the official color of his Bolivarian revolution.

While it's highly improbable that Venezuela will shut off oil exports to the United States any time soon, Chávez seeks to diminish his country's dependence on its northern neighbor. In 2000, Chávez and Castro signed an agreement under which Venezuela agreed to provide Cuba with 53,000 barrels of oil per day at preferential rates. In return, Castro promised to supply Venezuela with 20,000 Cuban medical professionals and educators. Four years later, Chávez expanded the plan by providing the island nation with 90,000 barrels a day, while Cuba raised the number of medical officials and teachers to 40,000. Oil ties deepened to such an extent that PdVSA even opened a branch office in Cuba. What's more, Chávez provides technological support for developing oil and gas production on the island.

The Venezuelan leader also formed a joint venture with Castro to revamp the Cienfuegos oil refinery in Cuba. Under the agreement, the two countries agreed to pump $1 billion into the scheme; PdVSA would hold a 49 percent share. The Cienfuegos refinery was built with help from the Soviets, but work on the almost-completed facility was halted in 1991 when the USSR collapsed. Finally, Venezuela also began to jointly explore for oil in Cuban waters. The venture, the first of its kind, brought PdVSA together with CUPET, Cuba's energy company. Venezuela and Cuba hope to discover light crude; the project covers almost 4,000 square miles.[26]

For Castro, Chávez's arrival on the world stage came as a political godsend. With the downfall of the Soviet Union in 1991, Cuba lost its largest trading partner and its economy suffered as a result. Though Castro restructured the economy to encourage more foreign investment, the Cuban standard of living still lagged behind Cold War-era levels, and a sizable percentage of the population lived in near-poverty. But Chávez's daily oil imports allowed Castro in May 2005 to double the minimum wage for 1.6 million workers, raise pensions for the elderly, and deliver cooking appliances to the poor. Venezuela also opened a state bank in Cuba and provided the island nation with $412 million worth of heavily subsidized goods.[27] Meanwhile, trade between Cuba and Venezuela in non-oil exports has skyrocketed in recent years.

In coming to the aid of a friend, Chávez helped to undercut the U.S. trade embargo. Though the Castro-Chávez oil alliance is understandable in geopolitical terms, it was certainly spurred on by the ideological and personal affinity between the two Latin leaders. While he was in prison after his failed 1992 attempt against then-President Carlos Andrés Pérez, Chávez read a number of books about Fidel. Over the years, the two developed a close personal rapport.

Chávez has used oil not just as a political instrument to cement ties to Cuba, but also to solidify his alliances across South America. Clearly, Chávez seeks to integrate South America's energy sector so as to be less dependent on the United States. By selling oil to countries at preferential rates or by bartering it for other goods, Chávez secures the goodwill and gratitude of his political counterparts. The Venezuelan leader has signed agreements with Argentina to develop joint oil and exploration projects, for example. Meanwhile, Brazil's state-owned oil company Petrobras or Petróleo Brasileiro has invested heavily in oil exploration and production in Venezuela. Both PdVSA and Petrobras are building an oil refinery in northeastern Brazil. And in Bolivia, Chávez has agreed to supply preferentially priced diesel and invest highly in the oil and gas sector, in exchange for Bolivian goods and services. Because of high world oil prices, Chávez has been able to extend assistance programs throughout South America, for example by providing millions in aid to Uruguay and Bolivia.[28]

American oil companies are not well regarded in Ecuador.

In 1967, Texaco found oil near the Ecuador-Colombia border. The first well was named Lago Agrio No. 1, or Sour Lake, in honor of the small Texas town that produced Texaco's first gusher. In the late 1960s, the region, known in Ecuador as the Oriente (the East), was a frontier area inhabited by Indians and missionaries, but Texaco rapidly transformed it with pipelines, roads, and oil wells. The once thick forest around Sour Lake became pockmarked by dirt roads, subsistence farms, open, unlined pits for storing liquid drilling wastes, and oil pumping stations where yellow flames burned off gas around the clock.

The company, which operated in the Ecuadoran Amazon between 1972 and 1992, dumped waste directly into the freshwater streams instead of using the safer disposal methods common in the United States at the time. For company officials, it was simply too expensive to try to curb pollution.

During its twenty years of operation in Ecuador, Texaco pumped 1.5 billion barrels of oil out of the country, most of it bound for California. By the time the company left, environmentalists estimated that it had dumped more than 19 billion gallons of waste and spilled 16.8 gallons of crude oil, which is one-and-a-half times the amount spilled by the oil tanker Exxon Valdez in Alaska in 1989 which caused a global outcry.[29]

The waste from Texaco wells became the focus of a lawsuit filed in the United States in 1993 on behalf of 30,000 local residents. Plaintiffs alleged that Texaco destroyed land, sickened residents, and contributed to the demise of Indian tribes. After much legal wrangling, a U.S. appeals court ruled in 2003 that Ecuador was the proper forum for the plantiffs' lawsuit. When Texaco commenced its well-drilling, the process produced "drilling muds." The muds, which can contain water, oil, heavy metals, and chemicals, were dumped into unlined pits. The highly dangerous waste product can also contain toxic levels of benzene, a known carcinogen, and lead, which may impede mental development in children.

Government officials claimed to be unaware of Texaco's environmental crimes at the time. The company told the government it was using state of the art technology. "We just didn't know," said retired General René Vargas, who headed the nation's Energy Ministry in the early 1970s and is a witness to the plaintiffs' suit. "If they had done in the U.S. what they did here, they would have been made prisoners. They knew it was a crime."[30]

Whether or not the government's pleas of ignorance are true, however, it is clear that the Ecuadoran state exercised less oversight than it should have. Pedro Espín, a former Texaco employee and president of state-run Petroecuador, remarked that "Texaco did what the authorities asked, the minimum required. Back then, nobody talked about the environment." In the 1970s, the Ecuadoran government, composed of a military junta, squabbled with Texaco over taxes, royalties, and production levels. The company, however, exercised its political muscle and economic resources to strike back. The U.S. Embassy provided Texaco with access to top officials during trade missions, and its executives dined with presidents and ministers. In an effort to curry favor, Texaco handed out contracts to current and former Ecuadoran military officials. When the company could not get its way, Texaco occasionally withheld payments to the government for the oil it was shipping out.

Today, Texaco's roads slice through the jungle. Settlers used those roads to slash and burn their way into the jungle. As a result of misguided development, 2.4 million acres of jungle have disappeared. Pipelines, meanwhile, snake through towns and schoolyards. Needless to say, Texaco did not pay the Indian tribes who inhabit the Amazon for use of their land. At least one tribe, the Tetetes, who lived near Lago

Agrio, simply disappeared. It is believed that they intermarried with settlers and abandoned all vestiges of their language and culture. Terrified,
another tribe, the Huaorani, moved deeper into the jungle. The Cofán,
helpless to ward off development, saw their territory cut into pieces by
roads and wells. Tribal shamans were confounded by unknown diseases
that proved resistant to traditional cures. The settlers fared little better,
and found themselves living in poverty amid environmental pollution
and oil infrastructure.

Texaco's history provides the backdrop to Ecuador's current energy
dilemma. Today, oil is vital to the Ecuadoran economy. The small Andean nation is one of South America's largest oil exporters, and oil accounts for 40 percent of export earnings.[31] After Venezuela, Ecuador is
the second largest South American exporter of oil to the United States.
But friction between U.S. companies and local residents has continued
over the years.

Efrén Icaza, an environmental activist based in Quito, has firsthand
knowledge of oil development in the Amazon. I catch up with him at a
café on Avenida Amazonas. We sit outside, where we are periodically in-
terrupted by a small Indian child begging for money. Icaza got interested in social issues through his father, a long-time member of the
Ecuadoran Communist Party and an employee at Texaco in the Oriente.

"As a boy," Icaza says, "I got to know the Oriente very well, the oil
fields and working conditions. I think you never would have found those
kinds of labor conditions in the U.S." Icaza recounts how his father used
to work 16-hour shifts. Together they'd drive 60 or 70 miles per hour
along miserable, oil covered roads to get from one oil well to another.
Not surprisingly, there were lots of accidents, and out of concern for his
colleagues, Icaza's father became the general secretary of the Texaco oil
workers union in the 1980s. With oil workers often spending up to 35
days in the jungle at one time, many working families disintegrated.
Meanwhile, foreign oilmen made much more money than any Ecuadoran. After his stint at Texaco, Icaza's father emigrated to the United
States along with many members of his family.[32]

Local communities and U.S. oil companies continued to come into
conflict. Fifteen years before my most recent visit, I'd come to Quito to
investigate the plight of the Huaorani. I'd been working as a reporter
for WBAI radio in New York and had heard a lot about social and political ferment in Ecuador involving the country's indigenous peoples. In

an article for an Ecuadoran newspaper, *Hoy*, I documented the relations between Maxus Energy Corp, a U.S.-based company, and the Huaorani. Maxus was operating in Block 16, a concession which lay within the Yasuní National Park, an area of extraordinary biodiversity. Ecuadoran and U.S. environmentalists were up in arms about Maxus's operations, which included a road into the Amazon and a pipeline. I remember speaking with Boris Abad, a Maxus engineer in charge of environmental affairs, about the company's operations. Abad claimed that relations between the company and the Indians were quite good, and a company doctor touted Maxus's health programs.

But not all Indians were pleased with oil development. In October 1992, in fact, the Huaorani had come to company headquarters in Quito to protest Maxus's highway construction. Moreover, when I went to visit the Indians in Toñampari, a village in the Amazon, I detected a fair amount of ambivalence toward the oil industry. In order to get to Toñampari, I had to take a bus to the Oriente, and from there hop on a propeller plane run by American missionaries. I stayed in a rudimentary house outside of the village, 30 minutes walking distance along a humid jungle trail. In interviews with the Indians, I got the impression that the older generation, who had physically battled Texaco long ago, was more opposed to oil exploration than some of the youths who had worked for the companies. At one point I took a boat up the Curaray River to Canawaeno, a nearby village. There, I met Tepa Wainwa, an elderly Hauorani woman who told me that there was little support in her village of 120 people for the Maxus highway.[33]

I left Ecuador in late 1993, but the unrest against U.S. oil companies continued. In early 2006, the state oil company, Petroecuador, was forced to suspend oil exports when protesters, unhappy about years of environmental damage, demanded the departure of U.S.-based Oxy and took over a pumping station vital to the functioning of a company pipeline. Protesters led by local politicians from the Amazon province of Napo demanded that the government provide funds for infrastructure projects in local communities.[34] Experts agree that the situation has continued to worsen in the Amazon. Some oil fields have been blockaded by angry local residents who are upset about the lack of economic development in the area. There have even been violent confrontations.

William Waters is knowledgeable about the oil zone in the Amazon, having worked on development sociology both in the highlands and in settler communities within the Oriente. His appearance is amusing: he sports a white beard and Yankees baseball cap, with wisps of white hair poking out from underneath. It's an incongruous site in the middle of Quito. During our interview, Waters explains that the oil situation in the Amazon might be one of the most significant challenges facing the newly elected Correa regime. The government, he said, would have to find a way to redirect economic resources to the region so as to avoid the kind of unrest that had plagued the region in the past. "If you've been to the Amazon," Waters says, "you'll see that despite some small improvements in paving roads, it is like going to another world. All the resources go out and very little goes in. The worst places to be in Ecuador as a resident are Coca, and anywhere up to Lago Agrio. This is exactly the area that has been extracting oil since 1972."[35] As a matter of fact, years ago I had been to Coca: a miserable oil-boom town, its main street was full of mud and oil that carried a horrid stench.

The task of reversing this sorry state of affairs and bringing more equitable economic development to the neediest falls in part to Alberto Acosta, the nation's minister of energy and mines. As a veteran of the oil industry, he has a historical perspective on Texaco and U.S. oil companies. Interestingly, Acosta is an economist but also an environmentalist.

The ministry is located on a busy commercial street, Avenida Orellana. Acosta's office affords a panoramic view of the city. An Ecuadoran flag, which features the same red, yellow, and blue colors as the Venezuelan flag, hangs behind Acosta's desk. I had heard that Correa was working his ministers to the bone, so I am not too surprised to see that Acosta himself seems distracted by all manner of business. I am taken aback, however, to hear jazz music playing in the background. Perhaps Acosta uses it to relax from his stressful job. A tall, thin, light-complexioned man with silver hair, Acosta is clearly a passionate government official.

"I believe politics should interest all human beings," Acosta says. "Everyone, in one form or another, should be involved in politics." Acosta excitedly goes over to his desk where he fishes out a rather ragged, miniature copy of some writings by Bertolt Brecht. "I'm going to read you something which I've brought along with me for a long time," Acosta declares. I'd expected to encounter some kind of dry and dull technocrat, but Acosta is not conforming to my stereotype at all. A dynamic, inspired man, he quickly starts to read Brecht aloud. The passage is a savage denunciation of "illiterates" who are proud of the fact that they don't participate in politics. Such characters are fools, according to Brecht, because they don't realize that the cost of living, including beans, fish, flour, shoes, and medicine all have something to do with political decisions. "I believe you have to have values," Acosta proclaims proudly, "and those values can be processed through political engagement."

Though Acosta was much more outspoken than Mommer, in many ways the two are emblematic of the new generation in power in South America. He explains that he has been interested in oil for many years. In the late 1960s, he had the unique opportunity to accompany Ecuadoran president Jose María Velasco Ibarra to the Amazon. There, Acosta witnessed the country's first oil exploration. The historic event made a big impact on the young man, and later his father, who wanted Acosta to become an oil auditor, insisted that his son study petroleum related matters. Acosta went on to pursue a business administration degree in Germany and later studied energy economics. Since 1974 he'd been working in Petroecuador and in the energy sector as a consultant.

Acosta's association with Correa makes political sense, as the two see eye to eye on environmental questions. Just prior to my arrival in Quito, Correa had threatened to cancel the contracts of foreign oil companies that damaged the environment. Acosta, for his part, is determined to halt environmental abuse, but also to get a fair share of oil revenue for the state. In the beginning, he says, the government had taken a sizable share of Texaco's oil profits. Things changed later, however, as the state and Petroecuador became less involved with Texaco and the government received a smaller share of the company's revenues. Acosta's story is familiar, as it reminds me of developments in Venezuela under PdVSA.

"We got to a point," Acosta says, "when private companies, from the U.S. and elsewhere, interfered with the policies of different ministries. Before, the oil companies would communicate with the president in an arrogant manner, almost an order, indicating what needed to be done."

Acosta lays out how things will be different under the Correa administration. Ecuador, he says, is no longer in the "difficult and complicated" era of oilmen running the show. From now on, the authorities won't accept "orders" from anyone. The ministry will continue to open the door to international companies, but only on the condition that they relate to the authorities on a different basis. According to Acosta, the oil companies had reacted to Correa's assumption of power "with curiosity, and I imagine worry."

"You imagine, or you've spoken with them personally?" I ask.

Acosta says he's met with company representatives personally, making clear the government's intention to develop an oil policy characterized by equal participation and mutual respect. But things haven't gone altogether smoothly: Ecuador's takeover of assets belonging to Occidental or Oxy, a U.S. energy company, prompted the company to launch an arbitration claim against the government. Prior to Correa's assumption of power, Petroecuador took over the company's assets, allegedly because Occidental had violated its contract by transferring some of its assets to another company. After the government terminated Oxy's contract, oil output in the company's concession area, known as Block 15, declined.[36]

In the United States, the press has referred to the Oxy controversy as an "expropriation." Everyone in Ecuador, however, believes that the company was asked to leave because it had not lived up to its contractual agreement. Technically, then, the case of Oxy isn't an expropriation or nationalization. "Occidental never lost the land," Waters explains. "They had their contract canceled. Did they lose investment? Yes. It's like being kicked out of your apartment on a technicality—for example, 'you weren't allowed to have a dog.'"

The controversy has had drastic economic consequences. Incensed by Ecuador's handling of the Oxy affair, the United States broke off discussions on a free trade agreement that had been going on for four years. As a matter of fact, the two parties had finally agreed on key terms when talks were abruptly severed. Waters remarks that, in his view, the government would not opt for "nationalization" but instead would simply choose to renegotiate the terms of the deals with the oil companies. There would "be a new way to share the goodies"; from the companies' point of view it "wouldn't be as sweet a deal as before," but they would still have an interest in operating in Ecuador. Oxy had brought the case before the World Bank's International Center for Investment Disputes, claiming $1 billion in compensation.[37] The company cited violations of the U.S.-Ecuador bilateral investment protection treaty, and also argued that Petroecuador had unlawfully terminated Oxy's contract.[38]

At first, the Oxy matter seemed like it would have a negative impact on U.S.-Ecuadoran relations. Instead of taking out the Big Stick, however, U.S. diplomats continued to speak softly, behaving prudently toward Acosta. "The U.S. ambassador," he says, pointing to a sofa at my side, "sat in that exact spot a week ago." During Acosta's meeting with the U.S. diplomat, the two discussed the Oxy problem. The ambassador agreed that the dispute should be submitted to arbitration but emphasized the need to maintain stable Ecuadoran-U.S. relations. The two wound up talking about jazz, one of Acosta's favorite subjects, and in the end the United States decided not to break ties over the Oxy affair but to take a wait-and-see attitude toward the Correa regime.

Speaking to Acosta, I get the impression that Correa is in a much better position than the embattled Chávez was in the first few years of his administration in Venezuela. Correa has a warm rapport with Petroecuador personnel. The company is much smaller than the huge PdVSA, a Venezuelan icon, and there is little risk of the kind of confrontation that led to the 2002–03 oil coup and lock-out in Venezuela. Petroecuador controls a large share of crude production, but the oil sector in Ecuador is open to private participation. According to reports, Correa plans to renegotiate existing oil production contracts in an effort to increase the government's take, while Petroecuador is trying to improve its image, which suffered immensely as a result of years of under-investment and poor environmental standards, particularly in the Amazon.[39] For example, oil spills from Petroecuador killed large numbers of freshwater pink dolphins within the Cuyabeno Wildlife Production Reserve, 934 square miles of Amazon lakes and rain forest near Lago Agio. Construction of oil service roads, meanwhile, gave 1,000 settler families access to half the reserve, further endangering the ecological balance.[40] Under Correa, the company would like to shed its disreputable past. Petroecuador plans to increase its investment profile, spending nearly a billion dollars on exploration and production.[41]

Given the similar oil policies of Correa and Chávez, could we see greater energy integration between Ecuador and Venezuela? In Caracas, Mommer had pointed out that Venezuela was seeking "to develop a common front of all countries which possess natural resources and whose sovereign rights are not protected." PdVSA, he added, could be a minority partner in Ecuadoran energy projects. Furthermore, Chávez has proposed uniting South America's state oil companies in a joint venture, known as Petrosur.

What would such oil diplomacy between South American countries portend for private U.S. companies? If Ecuador joins Petrosur, the situation there will certainly be more difficult for American companies, which have been in the process of irreversible decline since the 1970s. What's more, it is possible that Venezuela will become involved in the unfolding and chaotic situation in the Oriente. Recently, Petroecuador took over oil wells belonging to Oxy's Block–15 oil concession and also the Edén Yuturi and Limoncocha fields. PdVSA stands to benefit: the Ecuadoran government requested that the Venezuelans refine 75 percent of the 100,000 barrels per day extracted from Block–15. According to the Venezuelan newspaper *El Universal,* Ecuador is considering Venezuela as a possible partner in the fields formerly operated by Oxy.

As oil partners, Chávez and Correa are temperamentally suited to one another. Correa's connection to Venezuela started when he worked for the Alfredo Palacios administration, which came to power in Ecuador in 2005. As economy minister, Correa sent a team of his officials to Caracas to discuss the possibility of issuing bonds to Venezuela to cover Ecuador's debt-financing requirements. Prior to his election, Correa was also an advocate of closer energy integration between the two countries. On the campaign trail in 2006, he went to Venezuela and spent time with Chávez at his family home in the state of Barinas. Later, he remarked that he was proud to call Chávez a friend, and professed not to understand why the relationship could be considered a problem. "I am honored by the friendship," he said. "If I am a friend of Chávez, 'What a mistake!' If I were a friend of George Bush, they would have elected me man of the year."[42] In his rhetoric, too, Correa echoes the inflammatory Chávez, lambasting political opponents and the "lying oligarchy."[43]

Given the budding relationship between the two presidents, the outlook is positive for future energy integration. According to Acosta, PdVSA, as well as Enarsa and Petrobras—state-owned energy companies from Argentina and Brazil, respectively—might become involved in ongoing oil exploration in Ecuador. Additionally, Ecuador is interested in joining with PdVSA, Petrobras, and Enarsa to form a Latin American oil company. "How would the United States react to such a development?" I ask. Acosta shrugs off any hint of confrontation and tells me that energy integration would inevitably lead to political integration among left-leaning regimes throughout the region.

But might the question of the environment derail the integration efforts? Correa has said that his government will investigate companies who pollute the Amazon.[44] Analysts have interpreted the move as a veiled threat to Brazil's state-run Petrobras,[45] which operates Block 31, a concession area located in ecologically diverse Yasuní Park. In April 2006, prior to Correa's election, Ecuador's environment minister expressed her displeasure with Petrobras's environmental management plan.[46] Acosta acknowledges that Petrobras's not-so-sterling environmental record in Ecuador has led to tensions with the government in the past. There have been "certain calls, certain visits" of Petrobras company officials to Acosta's office.[47]

So far, though, concerns about environmental pollution don't seem to be causing much geopolitical disturbance, at least not between Ecuador and Venezuela. Local activists such as Icaza frankly admire Chávez. During our conversation, I bring up the issue of environmental destruction in the westernmost Venezuelan state of Zulia, where indigenous peoples stand to be affected by coal development.[48] Icaza is aware of environmental problems in Venezuela and Chávez's imperfect record on the issue. "If PdVSA comes in to areas where Oxy used to operate," I ask, "could we see the rise of protests again?" My contact says that if PdVSA failed to heed the needs of local communities, there could indeed be more confrontations over oil development. He insists, however, on the necessity of moving forward with energy integration so as to better the living standards for all South Americans. In any case, Icaza adds, even if there were protests, they wouldn't be decisive enough to halt the process of hemispheric integration taking place.

Bolivians tend to be wary of foreign oil companies. During the 1930s Chaco War with Paraguay, which many historians describe as a proxy battle between U.S. Standard Oil and Dutch-British Shell Oil over land thought to hold valuable petroleum deposits, Bolivia lost tens of thousands of soldiers and a wide swath of territory. Today, energy still looms large in the nation's politics: Bolivia has the second-largest proven natural gas reserves in South America after Venezuela.

During his first term as president (1993–1997), Gonzalo Sánchez de Lozada, known as "Goni," appealed to Houston executives to invest in the country's economic expansion. At the time, the oil and gas industry was one of several state-owned monopolies that the government was seeking to open to private investment. Encouraged by Goni, large energy companies such as the notorious Enron formed joint ventures to do business in the country. Goni, U.S.-educated and known as "El Gringo" for his American accent, privatized Bolivia's most strategic industries, including the oil and gas sector. Dubbing his plan "capitalization," Goni divided up the assets of the state energy company YPFB (Yacimientos Petrolíferos Fiscales Bolivianos) to form three public-private consortiums. Majority control of these firms—complete with over $11 billion in reserves and infrastructure—was given, free of charge, to foreign corporations like British Petroleum and Enron in exchange for nothing more than a promise of future investment. A new oil and gas law, a condition for an IMF loan, transferred an additional $108 billion of reserves to private control and cut oil and gas royalties on those reserves by nearly two thirds.[49]

In 2001, Argentine-Spanish Repsol-YPF led a consortium to develop the Pacific LNG project, which would have exported Bolivian gas to California via an export port in Chile. The plan was politically contentious for a number of reasons. In the first place, the deal stoked resentment because Chile has been Bolivia's historic enemy. In school, Bolivian children are still taught about how their country must regain its access to the ocean, as Chile seized Bolivia's last remaining access to the sea in 1879. However, polls showed that even if the gas were exported to California via another port outside of Chile, Bolivians would still oppose the deal. Though the IMF claimed the sale would be a boon to cash-strapped Bolivia, ordinary citizens suspected that the benefits would wind up in the pockets of corrupt politicians. What's more, critics charged that the terms of the contract with LNG were not to Bolivia's economic advantage. Not surprisingly, when he sought to go ahead and export gas to the United States via Chile, Goni met fierce resistance in Bolivia, a country characterized by grinding poverty (in 2005 the country had a per capita gross domestic product of $1,019).[50] Bolivians were in no mood to sell off the country's most lucrative assets.

It wasn't long before the country erupted in protest. Rather than have their government sell the gas to foreign investors, a coalition of unions, coca growers, and others sought to have the gas industrialized by the state to provide much needed employment and income. For days, the country was wracked by road blockades, strikes, and protests, resulting in dozens of deaths. During the so-called "Gas War," 10,000 people marched in the city of Cochabamba to express their discontent, including Evo Morales, who warned, "If the government decides to export gas through Chile . . . its hours are numbered."[51]

Things became particularly ugly when protesters staged a road blockade north of La Paz. Among those stranded by the blockade were 70 tourists from the United States, Germany, and England. David Greenlee, the U.S. Ambassador to Bolivia, recommended that the government send in the security forces to extradite people from the blockaded area. But when the forces arrived at a nearby town, they began to fire indiscriminately on *campesino* farmers and to shoot up homes and schools at random. A gun battle ensued, with *campesinos* firing back. Seven died from bullet wounds, including two soldiers, a sixty-year-old man, a student, a professor, and a mother and her daughter. Greenlee reportedly commented later that, despite the bloodshed, the intervention of the security forces had been justified.[52]

The repression led to more blockades in La Paz, further complicating Goni's political future. In the end, the president was forced to resign, and Vice President Carlos Mesa assumed power in late 2003. But when Mesa went against the popular mood and resisted implementing a referendum that called for re-nationalization of oil and gas operators, protests erupted and he too was forced to resign.

Given the highly "combustible" nature of gas politics in Bolivia, it was never going to be easy for Morales to satisfy activists. But following his election in February 2006, Morales, egged on by Chávez in Venezuela, embarked on a campaign of resource nationalism. His policy included the re-nationalization of hydrocarbon resources and renegotiation of export contracts. The country's recent earnings from natural gas exports have contributed mightily to economic growth.

How would the energy companies, including Brazil's Petrobras, Argentina's Repsol, and other foreign companies such as Total and BP, respond to Morales's more combative stand? Given other South American countries' involvement in the gas sector, would the government's stance endanger hemispheric integration?

Carlos Arze, the executive director of the Center for Labor and Agricultural Development, is an authority on the gas question. He explains that since 2000 there has been a strong political reaction against the previous policy of privatization. Over the past several years, the issue of hydrocarbons in particular has taken on acute political resonance in Bolivia. Under the current energy contracts with foreign companies, Bolivia has seen windfall profits.[53]

About a year before my arrival in La Paz, the government announced the "nationalization" of Bolivia's oil and gas sector and an increase in taxes and royalties. Government revenues from gas climbed 57 percent in one year, up to $2.03 billion in 2006, largely because of higher international energy prices.

On the other hand, the Morales government has been ground down as a result of political haggling. Though the regime negotiated new production contracts with individual companies, the agreements had still not been implemented by the time of my arrival because of disagreements between Morales and Congress.

Arze says that further confrontation over natural resources is unlikely, as the companies are in a very advantageous position and have Morales "over the frying pan," as they say in Bolivia. According to analysts, investment has been brought to a standstill since nationalization, with energy companies spending just enough to keep output at current levels. If investments don't pick up, much of Bolivia's gas reserves will stay underground.[54] In rare cases, the companies might invest in gas exploration, but at this point they are much more interested in selling off as much gas as possible from existing fields. The reason for this is that, under the terms of the current contract, the government refuses to recognize the cost of exploration if the companies come up dry.

"The government will have to cede more ground if it wants investment to stabilize in the gas sector," Arze explains.

Despite these problems, Bolivia recently signed on to Chávez's Petrosur scheme, raising the possibility of greater hemispheric energy integration and collaboration amongst state energy companies.

"Is Petrosur a viable project?" I ask Arze.

That would depend, he continues, on neighboring countries, and specifically on the Brazilian market and economic conditions there. Following nationalization, Morales forced Brazil to accept a hike in gas prices for importing Bolivian gas. That kind of economic nationalism has not gone over well in Brazil, which has responded by boosting its own gas output in an effort to avoid dependency on Bolivia. It remains difficult to see a way beyond the impasse.

Petrobras and the Morales government have also been at logger-heads over Bolivia's only two refineries, which Petrobras purchased in 1999. While Morales wanted a revived YPFB to take over the refineries, Petrobras has insisted on being compensated at market value, threatening to go to international arbitration if its demands were not met, much as Oxy had done in Ecuador.

I leave Arze's office with the impression that the Morales government is weak and will never risk confrontation. But shortly after my departure from La Paz, the government started to flex its muscles and to disprove the conventional wisdom. With relations becoming increasingly acrimonious between Brazil and Bolivia, Petrobras finally relented and agreed to sell its two refineries for $112 million, little more than half its original demand. Analysts attributed the decision to Brazil's dependence on Bolivian gas.[55] Could tension between Petrobras and Morales undermine energy integration in South America? Unlike Argentina, which long imported gas from Bolivia, Brazil hadn't developed the idea of integration with Bolivia to nearly the same extent. It was only recently, in 1999, that Brazil first started to buy gas from Bolivia.

However, *Petroleum Review* reports that Brazilian President Lula, like Morales a former union leader, "has favored a more conciliatory line with Bolivia than Petrobras would have liked."[56] It may be that ideological affinity between Morales and Lula has served to smooth things over. Indeed, both leaders demonstrated their combative spirit while coming up through the labor ranks, and both have been imprisoned for their ideals. Morales's political career began as an activist in the coca growers' union. In 1995, in the midst of unrest in the coca region of Chapare, the police picked up Morales on charges of endangering public security. Morales described his 21-day detention in jail as a "kidnapping," since the government was not able to come up with any specific charges against him. The detention, he said, was nothing more than an effort by the police to subdue the coca growers.[57] Finally, the government was forced to relent and released the popular leader. Similarly, during his days as a labor activist Lula served several brief terms in jail.

With the Brazilian imbroglio seemingly fading as a major impediment, could energy integration be back on track? I recall how, in Caracas, Mommer had highlighted the practical difficulties in achieving closer Venezuelan-Bolivian energy integration. In fact, he had completely ruled out the possibility that Venezuela would go into Bolivia to run the entire gas industry. Such a venture, he said, would require a lot of technical know-how, as well as countless lawyers and experts. It had taken Chávez five years just to get control over PdVSA, and Bolivia still had a long way to go if it wanted to change the prevalent mentality as well as administrative structure in the state energy company YPFB.

Experts agree that while PdVSA could play a role in reconstructing YPFB and contributing to energy exploration, the political risks would be significant. Fundamentally, PdVSA is not just a company but a symbol, a Venezuelan national icon. The Bolivian right wing, which is very politically active, could try to sound the alarm about Venezuela's enhanced economic role in the country. Morales's opponents fear that he might use the new constitution to tighten his grip on power, much as Chávez did in Venezuela. Bolivia's main opposition party, the Social Democrats, is led by former President Jorge Quiroga. During a rally at an upscale shopping mall, Quiroga warned some 200 followers that "freedom" was at stake in an upcoming vote for a 255-seat Constitutional Assembly. Quiroga has warned of Morales's ties with Chávez and Castro, remarking that "they're going to take your home away."[58]

Despite the political risk, Morales seems to be plowing ahead. Since he took office, PdVSA has offered to provide its expertise to Bolivia. In 2006, Bolivia and Venezuela announced a new venture between PdVSA and YPFB. Under the agreement, called Petroandina, PdVSA would fund gas exploration, drilling, production, sales, marketing, and training. YPFB, meanwhile, would operate the activities. In an act of solidarity, PdVSA would only take 10 percent of the profits, leaving the rest to strengthen the Bolivian hydrocarbons sector.[59]

Victor Bronstein is a professor in the University of Buenos Aires and an expert on Argentine energy policy. A happy-go-lucky man, he regales me with tales of Jews who had become rough cowboys, or *gauchos*, in Argentina. He goes on to explain how Argentina created its own state oil company, YPF, or Yacimientos Petrolíferos Fiscales, early on in the twentieth century. However, YPF was privatized in the 1990s and bought up by Repsol, a Spanish company.

At that time, Bronstein says, "people didn't realize what was going on," as they were distracted by economic distress and hyperinflation. While labor didn't outwardly support privatization, he says, it essentially let the government do what it wanted.

Nevertheless, the Kirchner government has taken steps to encourage greater government involvement in the energy sector, specifically through Enarsa, a new state company.

"How significant is Enarsa?" I ask Bronstein.

"Not at all," he says. "This restaurant," he says, pointing to some tables around us, "probably has more patrons sitting here than Enarsa has employees."

The company, he adds, doesn't have much capital: only about $10 million, a paltry sum for an oil company. To Bronstein's knowledge, there are no plans afoot to make Enarsa any larger.

Cristian Folgar is the undersecretary of fuel in Buenos Aires; I catch up with him at his office near the Plaza de Mayo.

"Enarsa is a small company," Folgar concedes, "which hasn't even been around for two years. However, it's beginning to pick up business and we expect the company to grow." At the current time, he explains, Enarsa's primary business consists of buying gas from Bolivia and selling it in Argentina.

The essential political and economic question, then, is the fate of YPF and not Enarsa. Folgar says that re-nationalizing YPF is "off the table," but that the idea of the government buying shares in the company is a possibility.[60] There are some officials within the Kirchner government who want to proceed with re-nationalization, and they have some political clout. Meanwhile, though Venezuela hasn't said so openly, the Chávez regime would clearly like to see the Argentines exert greater control over YPF as Chávez seeks to create a Latin American oil company. While it's unclear whether Venezuela will be successful in this effort, Chávez's profile is certainly pretty high in Argentina—remarkably so, given how small a role Venezuela played in Argentine politics just ten years ago. Recently, Chávez announced plans to buy up to $1 billion in Argentine bonds and perhaps help finance a $400 million plan to send natural gas to Argentina.[61] Additionally, PdVSA is talking with Enarsa, but also with Repsol, about developing joint undertakings in Argentina. Meanwhile, Repsol has significant investments in Venezuela and is interested in oil exploration in the Faja. Venezuela has even sent its PdVSA ships to be repaired in Argentina and imports cattle and agricultural machinery from its new political ally. Argentine exports to Venezuela have quadrupled since 2002, reaching $800 million in 2006.[62] Fabián Arráez, a diplomat serving in the Venezuelan Embassy in Argentina, claims that relations between the two countries are superb; as evidence, he points to the approximately 90 agreements between Venezuela and Argentina on a whole range of issues.[63]

Certainly, then, Chávez carries some weight when it comes to the handling of energy resources in Argentina. On the other hand, any move on the part of the Kirchner regime to re-nationalize YPF would inevitably be seen as a provocation by the Bank of Spain. Argentina is on good terms with Spain, and so would be unlikely to push for outright confrontation. At present, Jorge Luis Rodríguez Zapatero of the Socialist Workers' Party heads the Spanish government. A critic of U.S. foreign policy, Zapatero withdrew Spanish troops from Iraq two months after being elected.

"I think the Kirchner government is going to go to an intermediate point," Bronstein tells me, "where they buy up some shares in the company, without controlling the majority share."[64]

Energy may pull Argentina closer to other South American nations. In recent years, the use of gas in Argentina has exploded. The reason for the dramatic rise in demand, according to *Petroleum Review*, is that low prices have discouraged investors from searching for more oil or gas in Argentina itself. What's more, no new hydroelectric stations have been constructed for the same reason. Indeed, analysts write that "as a result of the increase in demand, Argentina's own reserves of gas have fallen to the point that it is no longer able to supply neighboring Chile, previously entirely dependent on gas from its neighbor." This deficiency has forced Argentina to import gas from Bolivia via an aging pipeline.

Could Morales' economic nationalism jeopardize energy integration with Argentina? Experts minimize that possibility. Argentina has been purchasing Bolivian gas since the mid-1970s, and has recently lowered its own internal gas production and begun to buy more Bolivian gas. Indeed, energy integration as a whole seems to be on track, though more often than not under the auspices of private companies. Enarsa doesn't have any investment in Bolivia, though there are private Argentine companies operating in the Andean nation. Meanwhile, Argentina has gas pipelines linking it with Chile, Uruguay, and Brazil, all under private ownership.

Experts see Chávez's Petrosur, or Petroamérica, much more as a political entity for coordinating energy policies rather than a concrete company. According to Folgar, energy integration has been "highly important and crucial" in furthering wider political and economic integration in South America. In the specific case of Venezuela, energy integration has been "fundamental" in enhancing ties. "Today," Folgar proclaims, "Venezuelan and Argentine businessmen view each other as potential partners in many areas, which was not the case before. Energy integration was in this case the trigger for developing greater ties." Folgar, meanwhile, has met with PdVSA, which has an office in Argentina.

"Today, for example, the president of PdVSA Argentina was here asking for information about Argentine gas," he says. "This month, I spent 10 days in Caracas. I have made 15 trips to Caracas in total."

What's more, now that Venezuela forms part of Mercosur, and Bolivia might join as well, the trade bloc has great energy potential. Formed in 1991, Mercosur groups Argentina, Brazil, Paraguay, and Uruguay into a common market. More recently, Venezuela joined the bloc. Chile and Bolivia were admitted as associate members in 1996. Venezuela, Brazil, and Argentina produce crude, and Bolivia, Argentina and Venezuela produce gas. Meanwhile, both Argentina and Brazil have turned into important exporters of bio-fuels. While Paraguay and Uruguay don't possess the same hydrocarbon resources, they are important in terms of hydroelectric power. Clearly, within Mercosur energy will act to solidify tighter economic ties. The real question, however, is what Mercosur truly represents and whether closer trading ties may in turn spur the creation of meaningful progressive economic integration. It is to this vital question that I turn in the following pages.

CHAPTER 2

INTEGRATION FOR SURVIVAL

From my time living in South America during the 1990s, I recall how many governments in the region were closely allied to Washington and its drive towards "neo-liberalism," an economic philosophy stressing fiscal austerity, privatization, deregulation, and cuts in social spending. It's startling to consider how far the political landscape has drifted since that time. Not only did neo-liberalism intensify poverty, social tensions, and inequality, but it also sparked political instability and the rise of left-leaning regimes throughout South America.

With Venezuela leading the charge, Washington's neo-liberal policies have been rolled back, and large financial institutions like the International Monetary Fund have lost much of their influence and credibility. According to Emir Sader of CLACSO, a think tank in Argentina, South America is now going through a crucial moment in its history: as U.S. power has weakened, a "crisis of hegemony" has taken root. Crucial political fault lines have emerged, dividing the economic allegiances of separate countries. Colombia and Peru might sign free trade agreements with the United States if the Democrats in Congress agree to pass the trade legislation. The United States has done its best to break hemispheric solidarity by hammering out separate trade agreements with Mexico, Central America, and Chile. On the other side of the continuum are countries such as Venezuela, Cuba, and Bolivia, which have prioritized regional integration. Occupying a middle ground are Brazil, Argentina, and Uruguay, which have maintained the neo-liberal model but have also moved towards regional integration. Within this unfolding political milieu, Ecuador is something of a wild card, and it's too early to tell where the incoming Correa administration will direct the country.

"It's unclear where it's all headed," says Sader. "But the continent has three or four more years left with these regimes in power. That's why it's possible to deepen the process of regional integration, not to the point of being irreversible, but relative irreversibility to the point that a new neo-liberal government might have problems changing course."

In a sense, Venezuela and Cuba have already carried out trade integration: Venezuela sells oil to Cuba at below-market prices, and the island nation sends doctors to Venezuela.[1] Quite by chance, while touring poor barrios surrounding Caracas with a U.S. peace group called Witness for Peace, I fall into conversation with a strapping 45-year-old man with a moustache. I learn that he is a Cuban doctor, and is working in a local Barrio Adentro clinic. I am surprised to have bumped into the doctor and pleased to have the unique opportunity to hear his story.

The man invites us into the health clinic, a modest, oddly shaped hexagonal building. The Cuban explains that the building is a primary care health facility: if people need further care, they are sent elsewhere. Inside there are posters of Fidel and Chávez embracing. As we crowd inside, the doctor tells us he will speak but on the condition of anonymity, as he was not authorized to give interviews. He also requests that we refrain from taking photos. Despite this cautious beginning, the man opens up and even grows excited in talking to us. "I enjoy *Huckleberry Finn!*" exclaims the Cuban, apparently in an effort to put us at our ease and demonstrate that he is not anti-American.

When he first arrived in Venezuela he was taken aback by the tall buildings and modern highways. The second shock was the acute drug-addiction problem in Venezuela, quite a vivid contrast to his native Cuba. He confided that though he was glad to help out in Venezuela, the health system here was vastly inferior to Cuba's. He looked at his presence here as a mere band-aid.

He had been working in the area for about a year, but had a wife and child in Cuba. Psychologically, it was quite difficult for him to be away from his family. Nevertheless, he had gotten on well with

Venezuelans and played baseball with local residents. Despite the rough conditions in the city, he was glad to be in Caracas. The climate was mild, and preferable to the risks—illness and wild animals—faced by those stationed in the Amazon.

Speaking to a Cuban doctor in the middle of this Caracas barrio is a jarring experience. I am struck by the man's commitment and willingness to spend so much time away from home. Indeed, the Cubans have assumed grave risks in coming to Venezuela and attending to the poorest sectors of the population. In 2006, Raquel Pérez Ramírez, a 53-year-old Cuban doctor, was killed by criminals in Caracas. Ramírez had been working in Venezuela as part of the Barrio Adentro program for three years. According to Chávez, Ramírez's case is not isolated, as many other Cuban doctors have also been robbed and killed in the country. In addition to Ramírez and my *Huckleberry Finn*-adoring companion, thousands of others have come to Venezuela to attend to the neediest. In just a few short years Venezuela and Cuba have been able to solidify ties and circumvent the market by engaging in exchanges: in this case, medical staff for oil.

Even as he carries out alternative economic arrangements, Chávez has campaigned against large financial institutions influenced by the United States. The president has paid off all Venezuela's debt to the World Bank and the International Monetary Fund and claimed that he wants these large financial institutions to "disappear soon."[2] When asked if he is seeking to replace the World Bank and International Monetary Fund with his own, oil-flush "Bank of Hugo," Chávez explained that he would like to create an International Humanitarian Bank as "an alternative way to conduct financial exchange." Chávez, according to the *Wall Street Journal*, has become his own "tropical IMF."[3] Indeed, bolstered by windfall oil profits, he is now offering more direct state funding to Latin America and the Caribbean than the United States. Just in the first eight months of 2007, Venezuela spent $8.8 billion in aid throughout the region. In terms of scale, the funding is unprecedented for a Latin American country.[4]

Though Chávez has not overturned capitalism, he has done much to challenge the more extreme, neo-liberal model of development. The Venezuelan leader has spoken about a vaguely defined "socialism for the twenty first century," which is neither Communist nor capitalist, but a mix of the two.[5] Government officials seek to impose greater regulation on private capital, though they stress that they are not against it as long as it "dignifies the human condition."[6] Spurred on by high oil prices, Chávez has defied conventional neo-liberal logic by massively increasing social spending, which went from $20 billion in 1999 to $59 billion in 2006. What's more, the government has encouraged the growth of worker-owned economic cooperatives, and social programs have contributed to a drastic reduction in poverty. According to government statistics, the percentage of Venezuelans living in poverty shrank from 42.8 percent to 30.4 percent under Chávez. Researchers at the Catholic University outside Caracas estimate the present rate at about 45 percent, below what they measured in 1999.[7]

Alarming the rich, Chávez also announced plans for a "luxury tax" on second homes, art collections, and expensive cars, aimed at redistributing wealth to the poor. Some fear he may go even farther and seize such assets. "In the short term," remarked Rigoberto Lanz, a senior advisor to the Ministry of Science and Technology, "Venezuela will not be an attractive market for foreign investment, because this search to define an economic model, twenty-first-century socialism if you will, is a bit complicated." He explained that officials are still working on that model. "They're trying to develop something to fit Venezuela, and that's not done in one day."[8]

Having taken such a novel approach to the domestic economy, what are Chávez's plans on the international front? Edgardo Lander, a sociologist who sports a flowing white beard, is an expert on Venezuela's new economic orientation. In 2006, he was involved in organizing the World Social Forum in Caracas, a kind of hemispheric summit of social movements and progressive figures. Presiding over the summit, Chávez called on social movements to "draw up strategies of power in an offensive to build a better world."[9] The six-day event in Caracas, which drew 50,000 local participants and 12,000 foreigners, encompassed workshops and seminars on a wide range of topics including politics, the environment, human rights, indigenous rights, culture, gender, imperialism, and the anti-war movement. Many of the participants who came from abroad traveled to Venezuela specifically to get a first-hand view of Chávez's social programs. Lander worked on the Venezuelan government's own FTAA negotiating committee. The FTAA or Free Trade Area of the Americas is the principal vehicle for free trade in the Americas, widely pushed by the Bush administration for years. The FTAA sought to facilitate the movement of goods and services from Alaska to Tierra del Fuego, uniting a region with a collective GDP of more than $10 trillion. The FTAA began in 1994 at the Summit of the Americas in Miami, where heads of state of 34 countries throughout the hemisphere agreed to create the free trade area.

"For the first two or three years of the new Chávez administration," Lander says, "the government confronted all kinds of immediate challenges and there was little awareness of issues related to the FTAA." Surprisingly, for a time the Chávez regime did not replace the earlier trade negotiators from the previous government, even as the president railed against the FTAA. "It was a fascinating experience working on trade issues," Lander remarks. He then offers an intriguing, inside view of the Venezuelan globalizing elite.

"You had these people who had a certain world view that was fundamentally different from the regime. These people are trained in U.S. universities or get their degree in economics. They all share a sort of neo-liberal outlook on life. They travel a lot, get together frequently, and stay in fancy hotels. They have a tremendous personal investment in the continuation of neo-liberal policies."

The problem was that no one really knew what the FTAA negotiations were about; they were absolutely secret. Lander says people even referred to the discussions as "Dracula," because they could only continue under cover of darkness. The minister of trade later requested that the negotiators submit progress reports, explaining the course of negotiations in vital areas such as intellectual property rights and agriculture. After three months the negotiators only handed in half the reports. In any case, Lander reports, "something like 99 percent of the information was absolutely useless."

The negotiators kept the notes to themselves and tried to sabotage the process as best they could. Fundamentally, the negotiators had become arrogant and not beholden to anyone. At long last, the authorities became exasperated and sacked the negotiators. The government found new people to appoint, but it wasn't easy at first. "We gave crash courses in trade negotiations to young economists, sociologists, and lawyers who were politically committed but who had no experience," Lander says. Meanwhile, the Venezuelan government invited veteran trade negotiators from Mexico and Argentina to offer their input and expertise.

By 2002 the Venezuelan government was starting to assume a more combative stance toward U.S.-imposed free trade. However, the Chávez government was totally isolated during the negotiations. "It was just amazing," Lander says. "You had a few Venezuelan representatives sitting at a big table, surrounded by representatives from 33 other governments. Except for Cuba we were radically isolated. There was not one thing that Venezuela said that got support from anyone."

Chávez, however, has gone from being "radically isolated" to leading the charge against U.S.-imposed free trade. By 2003, FTAA talks started to sputter. Much to the chagrin of the White House, the FTAA failed to come into being by its January 2005 deadline. Speaking in Porto Alegre, Brazil, at an earlier meeting of the World Social Forum, Chávez rejoiced in the U.S. defeat. "The FTAA is death," Chávez said. "U.S. imperialism did not have the strength to impose the neocolonial model of the FTAA."[10] Despite growing opposition to the FTAA throughout South America, the United States hoped to use a summit meeting of hemispheric leaders in Mar del Plata, Argentina, to restart talks. Instead, Chávez succeeded in upstaging Bush, proclaiming "I believe we came here to bury the FTAA. I brought my shovel to join in the burial."[11] By the end of the summit, in a public relations coup for Chávez, negotiators had failed to reach consensus on hemisphere-wide free trade integration.

Chávez has a sympathetic ear in Ecuador, where the FTAA faced repudiation by activists. In 2002, Quito was the scene of fierce protests. In advance of a meeting between ministers and representatives from 34 nations to debate the FTAA, demonstrators descended on the Ecuadoran capital from across Latin America. When several groups of protesters tried to gain access to a hotel where 900 business leaders from across the Americas were holding talks related to the FTAA, the police fired tear gas at the crowds. The protesters, including Indians and students, carried signs reading "No to the FTAA, no to imperialism."[12]

Though certainly dramatic, the anti-FTAA protests were hardly novel in Ecuador, where activists have long fought against neo-liberal reforms. When I was in Ecuador writing about U.S. energy companies in the Amazon during the early 1990s, popular forces were gearing up for a big battle with the government over fiscal austerity measures. Demonstrators overran downtown Quito, protesting the government's plan to privatize social services.

That decision galvanized support for labor, which was locked in a battle with the Sixto Durán administration. When the regime introduced a broad package to reduce the deficit, devalue the currency, increase fuel and electricity prices, privatize state-run enterprises, and freeze public sector hiring to be followed by dismissals, protests erupted around the country.

I covered the story for Pacifica Radio in the United States. I still vividly recall an interview I conducted with a labor leader about the situation. Stepping out of his office, I saw rioters set up barricades. Burning debris lay in the street. With the exception of some progressive minded folk in the United States, however, I doubt many Americans were aware of the situation in Ecuador.

After I left the country in 1993, successive right-wing governments continued to push neo-liberal reforms on an increasingly restive populace. One particularly controversial move had to do with the "dollarization" of the economy. The government adopted the measure in 2000, after suffering hyperinflation and a financial collapse that saw one million people migrate.

On my previous trips to Ecuador, in 1990 and 1992–93, the country's currency was still the *sucre*. But coming back to the country in 2007, I am taken aback by the currency switch and wonder what kind of psychological effect the adoption of the dollar might have had on the Ecuadoran people. Currently, one may use U.S. nickels, dimes and quarters, but also Ecuadoran coins.

The big push for dollarization came in 1999, under the regime of Jamil Mahuad. A banker of Lebanese descent, Mahuad is a Harvard-educated lawyer. Formerly mayor of Quito, Mahuad confronted a difficult economic milieu: the El Niño weather phenomenon had inflicted over $2 billion in damages, the price of Ecuadoran oil had fallen sharply, and the inflation rate stood at 43 percent, the highest in Latin America. Meanwhile, as the *sucre*'s value against the dollar decreased by more than 40 percent,[13] people scrambled and fought to obtain greenbacks at local Quito banks. In the wake of the currency's fall, foreign exchange operators suspended the sale of dollars, while some economists argued that the only way to stabilize Ecuador's foreign exchange market was through dollarization. The problem with dollarization, however, was that the economy of Ecuador, a small country, was weak and vulnerable. Mahuad himself said that he would consider dollarization, but only if Ecuador could secure IMF assistance.[14] Not surprisingly, the large financial institution did not hesitate to oblige, offering to send a mission to Quito to help Mahuad dollarize, a course the president ultimately did take.

Mahuad's decision drew both praise and criticism. Predictably, business circles welcomed the plan, as dollarization stood to reassure banks, international lending institutions, and Ecuador's other creditors. But protesters claimed that dollarization would be a disaster for millions of Ecuadorans living in poverty and would reduce their real purchasing power even further.

Throughout the country, unions, farmers, and business groups called for Mahuad's resignation and argued that the crisis called for a moratorium on the country's foreign debt payments and structural reforms rather than desperate measures. Dollarization, they claimed, would only benefit large businesses, exporters, and others dealing in dollars. As the protests accelerated, Mahuad was forced from power when the police and military refused to enforce order and demonstrators ushered a three-person junta into power. Years after Mahuad's ousting, however, Ecuadoran governments continued to pursue market-oriented solutions to the country's financial morass. The Alfredo Palacios regime, for example, hoped to sign a free trade agreement with the United States. Many in Ecuador have long assumed that the nation's economy needs to be driven by exports. The domestic economy is not very important, and Ecuador is not a country of consumers.

"You can buy very nice flowers here," says sociologist and American expatriate William Waters, "but you either take them to the cemetery or put them on your table. What you get are the leftovers from export—they're not long, straight, or big enough. They're sold here for a tenth of what you'd pay in Brooklyn."

Trade talks were politically and economically sensitive, however, as Ecuadoran domestic producers stood to be adversely affected by a free trade agreement. According to Agriculture Minister Pablo Rizzo, Ecuador sought to bring up the issue of agriculture during talks as the government was concerned about protecting sensitive products such as rice.[15]

As the two parties neared the final round of negotiations, the conversation turned towards the issue of rice. California was an efficient rice producer and could flood the Ecuadoran market. This would make rice a little cheaper, but would have wiped out 14,000 to 15,000 jobs. Within 10 to 15 years, domestic production would have been annihilated.[16]

Judging from my experience walking around Quito, many don't care for free trade deals. At one point, I find myself in Artigas Square. Under a statue, someone had scrawled graffiti reading, "NO TO THE FREE TRADE AGREEMENT." Indeed, just one year before my arrival in Quito, indigenous leaders vowed to keep up protests against the proposed free trade agreement with the United States. Thousands of indigenous peoples blocked major roads, demanding a referendum on the pact. According to protesters, the deal would benefit only the wealthy and harm indigenous culture.[17] Defiant, President Palacios refused to bow to the demonstrators, accusing them of trying to bring down his government.[18]

While exporters "didn't care much" about the prospect of undermining domestic industries, according to Waters, the government negotiators, who were well-known as holding left-of-center or progressive views, were sensitive to such political considerations. They sought to negotiate a good deal for Ecuador without "throwing in the towel" on items such as rice.

Though much was at stake economically for Ecuador, the story was quite different for the United States. From the point of view of American trade negotiators, the agreement was not really about trade but was instead meant to serve as a political instrument. "If the U.S. stopped importing goods from Ecuador, I don't think the American government or the American people would even notice, with the possible exception of bananas," says Waters. "The price of bananas might go up somewhat." In the end, the United States did not break off negotiations over trade but over the Oxy affair, when the Ecuadoran government cancelled the energy company's contract.

In the wake of the breakdown in negotiations over the free trade agreement, where is the political wind shifting now under Correa? Experts believe that Correa is not anti-United States. "He's spent some of the best years of his life in the U.S. and has many friends there," says Waters. Perhaps Correa's academic pursuits while at university offer a clue into the new president's world view. Werner Baer, an economics professor at University of Illinois and Correa's dissertation advisor, remarked "I would be surprised if he [Correa] followed the lead of Chávez and Morales." According to Baer, Correa believes in the market economy and property rights and shouldn't be characterized as a dangerous leftist. "I assume that he will be more like President Lula—market-friendly policies with a concern for more social equity."

As a student Correa was very concerned about the issue of income distribution. Indeed, one of his dissertation essays took up the subject of neo-liberalism and its impact on Latin American growth and income distribution. According to Baer, "He [Correa] has always been concerned by the uneven distribution of income and his efforts will be to ameliorate the situation of the poor." What's more, Correa was critical of Ecuador's moves towards dollarization.

Later, as minister of finance in the Palacios administration, Correa urged Congress to modify a fund, created in 2002 at the urging of the International Monetary Fund, to collect and distribute part of Ecuador's oil revenue. Almost 40 percent of Ecuador's export earnings and one-third of its income are derived from oil. However, more than half of its 13 million inhabitants live in poverty. Correa saw that the fund established in 2002 was glaringly unjust: it provided 70 percent of its resources to service Ecuador's foreign debt to international lenders, including the World Bank. The remaining 30 percent was set aside to stabilize oil revenues (20 percent) and to improve health and education (10 percent).

As a result of Correa's lobbying, Congress reformed the oil revenue fund, increasing the amount allocated for health and education to 30 percent and lowering that for debt repayment to 50 percent. Though hardly radical—the largest portion of the fund continued to go to Ecuador's creditors—the move was unacceptable to the World Bank, which responded to Ecuador's action by canceling the previously approved loan.[19] Correa's boss Alfredo Palacios was reportedly none-too-pleased by Correa's rhetoric lambasting the World Bank for its policies in Ecuador.[20] Correa also sought to sell Ecuadoran debt to Chávez, a move viewed by financial observers as anathema to the IMF, an institution the young economist was wont to criticize.[21]

As president, however, Correa might not be able to emulate Chávez. Though Correa uses Chávez's own phrase, "twenty-first-century socialism," to refer to his plans to redistribute wealth to the poor, he has little choice but to cut deals with business and opposition groups. Correa has doled out cash to fund social programs, but his pockets are not nearly as deep as Chávez's. Nevertheless, Correa seems intent on asserting as much independence as possible while ruling turbulent and unstable Ecuador, and as president he has proposed an economic model very different from those implemented by previous administrations in Ecuador—a move that might not be to the liking of the United States.

When Correa assumed power, a huge proportion—38 percent—of government revenue went to service the external debt.[22] He sent the country's bond markets tumbling by declaring that he would seek to restructure Ecuador's foreign debt, reducing it by 75 percent. Correa said he would use the savings on debt service to increase social spending. He has bucked neo-liberal trends by doubling a monthly payment to poor families to $30 a month. Additionally, he allocated $100 million to housing subsidies for the destitute, and "microcredits," grants of $350, have been "dished out with abandon." The government spends some $3 billion a year on public subsidies for energy and fuel.[23]

Meanwhile, Correa's relationship with international financial institutions has been stormy. For example, he threatened to expel the World Bank's representative in Ecuador if, in Correa's words, the government was "pressured" by the organization. He also announced that he would no longer negotiate with the IMF. In an escalating tactic, Correa declared that Ecuador reserved the right to bring charges against the World Bank for damages caused by the cancellation of its earlier loan. In the summer of 2007, Correa launched a "debt audit commission" composed of local and international experts. Correa has sought feedback from indigenous movements and environmentalists to investigate the country's debt burden with foreign creditors on a loan-by-loan basis. The government has asked the experts not simply to audit loans, but to delve into legal questions, financial terms and conditions, and the social and/or environmental impacts of the individual loans.

Though Correa has not moved to replace the dollar as the country's currency, he said he would not sign a free trade agreement with the United States, because such an agreement would be "tremendously harmful" to Ecuador. The problem, Correa explained, was that Ecuador didn't have its own currency and couldn't control its value. Peru and Colombia, countries seeking to sign their own free trade agreements with the United States, can reduce their currency's value and correct imbalances in the event of problems in the external sector. Ecuador, however, wouldn't be able to do that; the consequences could be "incalculable."[24]

Meanwhile, Correa has alarmed foreign investors and the moneyed classes with his rhetoric and policies. He has not assuaged international capital, either, by seeking to participate in Chávez's ALBA or Bolivarian Alternative for the Americas, an initiative designed to encourage greater trade, solidarity and exchange between nations standing outside of the usual market-based strictures. Ironically, it may be that the United States, by cutting off free trade negotiations, will encourage Ecuador to strengthen ties to Venezuela and to solidify South American integration. Though Ecuadoran exporters lost out when negotiations fell through, now the path might be clear for new types of economic arrangements. Pointing down the street from where we are talking, Waters draws my attention to a business two doors down selling sweaters and sweatshirts. "You have another group of people in Ecuador who produce goods for the national market," he explains.

The textile industry, based on local businesses like the one next door, have a long history in Ecuador going back some five hundred years. Today, one might buy a hand-knit sweater, a real Panama hat, alpaca rugs, or ready-to-hang hammocks in the town of Otavalo, a few hours north of Quito on the Pan American Highway. Part of the Indians' business success comes from their entrepreneurial spirit. The Otavalans were first conquered by the Inca, and then the Spanish. For centuries, Indian farmers endured forced labor in the *obrajes,* or textile workshops, set up by the Spanish conquerors. In fact, a large share of the textiles used by Spanish settlers throughout South America came from Otavalo. Based on small factories, the textile industry today might sell to 10–12 million people in Ecuador, as well as to consumers in neighboring countries.

"I was just at a trade fair," Waters says. "It involved an entire community called Atuntaqui, located north of the town of Otavalo. When I first went to Atuntaqui, it was just a few buildings. There are now more than 500 businesses, including workshops and small factories. Most of the businesses are in textiles, cottons or synthetics."

Waters expresses some astonishment in recounting his trip to the town, which was entirely taken over by the trade fair. Local producers were selling their products locally, but also exporting to Colombia, Venezuela, and Peru. "I don't know how much they're exporting," he exclaims, "but it's an alternative. I don't think these people are interested in trading to the United States."

Now that trade negotiations have fallen through between the United States and Ecuador, the path could be clear for increased South American economic integration. At present, Ecuadoran participation in the Brazilian economy is minimal. While Ecuador imports many goods, it exports practically nothing. But now, the country could be having the same kind of discussion with Brazil that it formerly had with the United States. By adding up Brazil, Argentina, Chile, and Uruguay, one winds up with a market as large as the United States.

To what extent is Chávez's ALBA really politically and economically important, and will Mercosur overshadow any radical agenda? Mercosur will surely be crucial to any growing economic integration. In the short-term it looks as if the huge trading bloc will be consolidated, and there is even a sufficient push to create a common currency. In light of these developments, joint financial and monetary policies, and even the creation of a central bank, might be possible. Assuming that the United States is not able to divide Mercosur by concluding separate trade deals with individual countries, the bloc will be free to consolidate and extend economic integration. But Mercosur, a mere free trade bloc between South American countries, hardly represents a viable break with the neo-liberal model.

Bolivia has recently put in a bid to join Mercosur as a full member, but the Andean nation doesn't have a clear position about transforming the organization from the inside. Indeed, even if it wanted to, Bolivia, a weak nation, might not be able to take a significant leadership role within Mercosur. Somewhat torn in terms of its economic allegiances, Bolivia currently holds the presidency of the Andean Community and is intent on restoring the bloc's unity and credibility.

There is a debate going on, however, over whether the Andean Community, a trade bloc formed in 1969 and grouping the nations of Bolivia, Colombia, Ecuador, Peru, and Chile, should ultimately dissolve and unite with Mercosur. Such a decision might "subordinate" the Andean countries to the more important economies of Argentina, Brazil, and Venezuela.[25] Other experts are unsure whether Bolivia's participation in Mercosur might interfere with ALBA, or whether the two might be compatible. Perhaps, a tug of war between the strong market model (as represented by Mercosur) as opposed to the strong state model (as represented by ALBA) is inevitable.

Jason Tockman is a graduate student at Simon Fraser University in Canada who has been studying ALBA and its impact on Bolivian society. In his early thirties, Tockman lived a colorful life in South America—including a stint working at Chávez's office of International Relations—before entering academia. In search of more adventure, he decided to specialize in Bolivia, "a much more optimal place because things are still being figured out here." "South American integration and moving away from U.S. influence, as well as the rejection of the neo-liberal model," Tockman says, "is one of the most exciting things happening in the world right now."

In particular, Tockman is enthusiastic about the growing integration between Cuba, Venezuela, and Bolivia. Up to now, this integration has taken more of a social form, and much of the economic component had yet to be "fleshed out." Nevertheless, ALBA's impact has been profound in Bolivia: already, Cuban doctors had arrived in the country and were carrying out eye operations and contributing to a literacy campaign.

The turn toward ALBA represents a shift from Bolivia's economic orientation during the 1990s. Under the leadership of Goni, who worked in tandem with international lending institutions like the World Bank and IMF, Bolivia downsized government in a move to encourage unfettered free markets. Morales on the other hand has extended ties to Cuba, a country that continues to resist neo-liberal economic doctrines. According to the *Irish Times*, in May 2007 there were 766 Cuban health workers in Bolivia, and another 300 doctors were scheduled to arrive later in the year. In 2006, Cuban specialists carried out 56,144 eye operations. Indeed, the Cuban and Venezuelan governments have announced that they are offering free eye surgery to anyone living in the western hemisphere. Morales himself remarked in his state of the nation speech in January 2007 that Cuban doctors had attended more than 3 million Bolivians, more than a third of the population. The Cubans saved 4,179 lives and sent 564 tons of medical supplies.[26] March 2007 marked the third anniversary of ALBA and the first anniversary of the so-called "Peoples Trade Treaties," which group Venezuela, Bolivia, and Cuba as complementary members.

Inside the entrance of the Cuban embassy in La Paz is the obligatory photo of Che Guevara. I am taken straightaway to a comfortable living room, accompanied by the ambassador, Rafael Dausá, and his wife, who takes careful notes on my questions during the interview. Born in 1959, the year Fidel Castro was just assuming power in Cuba, Dausá has an impressive diplomatic résumé. Following a stint at the Cuban interest section in Washington, D.C., he went on to serve as Cuba's ambassador to the United Nations from 1998 to 2001. He had only recently arrived in Bolivia, in April 2006. From the moment he arrived, he says, he started to fall in love with the country because of its ecological and cultural diversity.

"I've dealt with *compañero* Evo a lot," Dausá explains. "He's a very honest and transparent person, who has come up from modest origins. He's an example of a true Latin American revolutionary."

I think back on the lobby portrait of Che Guevara, someone who sought to stir up revolution in Bolivia 40 years ago. Originally, Guevara hoped to use Bolivia as a training base and staging ground for guerrilla operations in Argentina, Peru, and possibly Brazil; his vision was a continent-wide revolution. Guevara chose the Bolivian Amazon as his base because, though it was remote from roads, it straddled the Peruvian and Brazilian borders. Guevara seems to have misjudged Bolivian politics, however. Though he was a legend by the time he traveled to Bolivia in 1967, Guevara was not a Bolivian, and older Bolivian Communists withheld vital support. At the time, the Communist Party was the most organized political force on the left and was strong in Bolivia's cities and mining communities. Without help from the party, Che's hopes to foment revolution in Bolivia were doomed. Che's arms-supply link with Peru across Lake Titicaca, for example, never materialized. Neither did he establish vital links with Indian miners in the mountains.

But perhaps Che's biggest blunder was choosing to conduct his operations from a rugged range of hills located between the city of Santa Cruz and the oil town of Camiri, an area penetrated by important U.S. interests such as Gulf Oil and American Protestant fundamentalist missionaries. Any move to foment revolution in an area where American oil companies had interests was bound to attract the attention of the CIA.

Guevara moved through villages belonging to the Guaraní Indians, who had been evangelized by the U.S.-based Protestant Summer Institute of Linguistics. The Indians offered little support, and to make matters worse, deserters revealed to the authorities the location of Che's training camp. At the time, the military government of Brazil pledged to help the Bolivian government defeat Che. Argentina even offered to intervene with troops.

As it turned out, that help was unnecessary. The CIA moved its operatives into Santa Cruz and sent C–130 transport planes from the Panama Canal Zone. They unloaded napalm, weapons, radios, and medical supplies. Meanwhile, U.S. Green Berets trained 600 Bolivian rangers, who successfully tracked Guevara. Falling into an ambush, Che and his men retreated into a narrow forested canyon. Wounded in the leg, Che was taken alive by Bolivian rangers and brought to a nearby school house, where he was executed. Proud of their victory, the Bolivian armed forces strapped Che's body to the runner of a helicopter, later landing at a nearby airport.[27]

In light of the confrontational past between Cuba and Bolivia, it's startling to consider how far political relations have advanced between the two nations in recent years. Indeed, Morales has often been described in the Western media as a reincarnation of Che Guevara. *The Independent* saw Morales walking "in the footsteps of Che Guevara," while a *Los Angeles Times* editorial was entitled, "Where 'Che' Left Off."[28] While such characterizations are surely sensationalistic, Morales himself once remarked, "When it comes to Che Guevara, our only difference is the armed struggle—I don't accept armed struggle. Maybe it was the way in the '50s and '60s, but we want a democratic revolution."[29]

"I would say that relations between Cuba and Bolivia right now are excellent," declares Dausá. I ask the Cuban diplomat whether Bolivians might feel any resentment over outside interference in their internal affairs. He shrugs off the suggestion, remarking that neither Venezuela nor Cuba had interfered in Bolivia's internal politics. This was pure propaganda, he says, manufactured by the Bolivian opposition in order to discredit the Morales regime.

Whatever noise the Bolivian right has been able to make has apparently had little effect. The Cuban embassy has just added a commercial and economic attaché, who will work on broadening commercial ties.

For Dausá, ALBA represents the future of Latin America, because it underscores a new type of relationship based not on market profit but on economic complementarity. He claims that ALBA has had a positive social impact in Bolivia, and starts to rattle off statistics: in 2006, the Cuban government helped to construct 20 new hospitals; in 2007, the Cubans would help to construct 23 more.

It's not every day that I get to talk with Cuban diplomats about growing radicalization in South America, and I want to know about the nature of the relationship between Fidel and Morales. "What I can tell you," says Dausá, "is that *comandante* Fidel Castro knows what's going on in Bolivia in detail. There's a great friendship between Fidel Castro and *compañero* Morales." In 2006, Dausá continues, Morales had traveled four times to Cuba.

"Could there be economic radicalization in Bolivia and have there been discussions about communism?" I ask.

"Bolivia is not going to copy nor should it copy the Cuban experience," Dausá says. "But I think in time Bolivia will undertake a revolutionary process."[30]

Up to now, ALBA has served a political purpose but has had little effect on the overall volume of trade. However, according to the *Irish Times*, Cuba's and Venezuela's efforts to help other nations in health and education have fast eclipsed U.S. assistance in the region.[31] Furthermore, Venezuela has moved into the banking sector in other South American countries. Recently, the Venezuelan state-run economic and development bank, BANDES, opened offices in Ecuador and Uruguay. According to BANDES President Rafael Isea, the bank will put up $20 million to finance social projects in the Andean nation.[32] BANDES also has a branch in Bolivia, and the bank has dispensed millions there for educational programs.

In addition, Bank of the South, an institution flush with oil money and promoted by Chávez, could eclipse the IMF within the region. Presently, the main headquarters of the bank is located in Caracas, while Bolivia and Argentina have been chosen to be the bank's sub-headquarters. Recently, however, Bank of the South has been caught up in political infighting between Venezuela and Brazil over startup funds, headquarters bases, membership, size, and mission. Another question is whether financing should come from each country's foreign currency reserves and how transparent the lending policies might be. Lula isn't the only politician with doubts: even Correa has said that it might be better to establish a regional monetary fund, in line with Brazil's suggestion, as opposed to Bank of the South.[33] What's more, Bank of the South will have to define its mission more precisely, as there are already a multitude of regional funds available, including the Brazilian Development Bank and the Andean Development Corporation. Currently, the doors of the bank remain closed. Assuming that structural problems get ironed out, however, Bank of the South could eventually have some clout in the region.

"U.S. influence through international financial institutions like the IMF has collapsed," Tockman pronounces emphatically.

After spending ten days in Bolivia, landing in Chile is a shocking experience. The airport is incredibly modern, and the highway leading into Santiago is state of the art. The city itself is a remarkable contrast to La Paz, which is ramshackle and run down. I don't see any sign of poverty during my trip downtown except for some shacks along the highway. Downtown Santiago, full of banks, is reminiscent of London's financial district. In contrast to Bolivia, Chile has not embraced Chávez's new approach to economic development. Indeed, the country's free trade agreement with the United States, signed just a few years ago, eliminated tariffs on 90 percent of U.S. exports to Chile and 95 percent of Chile's exports to the United States.[34]

By signing the agreement, Chile was continuing in a long tradition of market-oriented policies. Under Pinochet, a group of economists known as the Chicago Boys (because many of them had studied at University of Chicago) came to power. They had few reservations about working for a military dictatorship, and their university training taught them to put their faith in market forces and lift all restrictions which might impede them. Milton Friedman, a free market fundamentalist and U.S. economist who had close ties to the Chicago Boys, once remarked during a trip to Chile that the country's problems would be resolved by "shock treatment that will amputate the diseased limb (the state sector), and open the economy to the cold but invigorating winds of world competition." The "shock treatment" turned out to be a massive cut in state expenditures, privatization of state companies, and a devaluation of the Chilean peso.[35]

To this day, the free-market approach is alive and well in Chile. Manuel Cabieses is the director of a left-wing newspaper, *Punto Final*, and an astute veteran observer of Chilean political affairs. In the front reception area of his office, an elderly woman takes calls. Cabieses's office is modest and sparse. On his desk is an outdated typewriter. Cabieses, who sports a moustache and combed-back white hair, looks to be in his seventies.

According to the long-time journalist, there has been fairly robust political support for the free-trade model. Since the end of the Pinochet era, more than 90 percent of Chileans have expressed support for the model by voting for either the center-left Concertación or the right, both of which have promoted free market policies. Given widespread acceptance of the free trade model, there is little chance that Chile will ever back out of its trading pact with the United States. Even certain sectors within organized labor look favorably on free trade.

"They believe what the media has told them," Cabieses remarks dismissively, "that the prosperity, this dynamic export economy, will filter down from the top towards the bottom."

To be fair, Cabieses acknowledges, many have benefited from the export model. There has been a great modernization and growth in telecommunications, roads, airports, ports, and all sectors linked to export. Out in the countryside, a half hour out of Santiago, agro-export farms are booming.[36]

Interestingly, however, some businessmen have become disillusioned with Bachelet who, they claim, is not complying fully with free market initiatives. Jaime Bazán is the director of the Chilean-American Chamber of Commerce. An unassuming man, he declares the free trade agreement to be wholly positive for Chile. Bilateral trade between the United States and Chile, he says, has increased more than 140 percent since the agreement came into effect. Chile has become practically the most important exporter of salmon, wine, and fruit to the United States. Judging from what I've seen at the Park Slope Food Coop in Brooklyn, a market where I do my shopping, Bazán is certainly correct. Blueberries from Chile are a welcome treat in January or February.

Bazán offers more than just propaganda on behalf of Bachelet's government, however. "We are not very optimistic about what's happening in Chile," Bazán says. "After we signed the free trade agreement with the U.S. in 2004, we expected U.S. investment to increase. The truth is, it hasn't worked out that way."

"How do you explain that?" I ask.

I had expected Bazán to praise the pro-business Bachelet government, and I am a little taken aback by his comments.

He explains that Chilean investors had high hopes after the free trade agreement was signed, while society as a whole also had "high expectations." There was a certain hope that businessmen would invest in Chile in order to expand their operations in the wider region. But neighboring countries such as Argentina had not exactly embraced an investor-friendly economic policy. Though investors viewed Chile as attractive only a few short years ago, they were now getting skittish. Fundamentally, Chile had not advanced in the best manner to maintain a competitive edge. "While other countries are running," Bazán says, "Chile is walking."

For investors, the Bachelet government has failed to live up to the standards set by the Ricardo Lagos regime, which pursued more market oriented policies. While other countries such as New Zealand and Uruguay were carrying out necessary reforms and modernization to attract investors, Bachelet has not created the requisite incentives.

What's more, no sooner had Chile signed an agreement with the United States then it started to enter into trade agreements with a whole host of other countries such as China and Japan. Chile topped that off by starting feasibility studies with Thailand and Malaysia, concluding a Partial Scope Trade Agreement with India and commencing trade pact discussions with Australia and Vietnam. In March 2007 Chile opened its first trade office in Vietnam.

"In a certain sense," Bazán says, "the agreement with the U.S. has been left aside. In my view Chile is losing an important opportunity." Chile was one of the first Latin American countries to sign an agreement with the United States. But now, Central American countries have signed CAFTA, and Peru and Colombia would likely follow with their own accords. "We're not going to be the only ones any more," Bazán notes ruefully. "So the possibility of Chile consolidating a position in the U.S. has been lost."[37]

Even more serious, Chile has gone from being the darling of the United States to being a somewhat suspect country. According to a report issued by the U.S. trade representative, Chile's failure to protect intellectual property has complicated its trade relationship with the United States. The report concludes that Chile fell short on "patent and test data protection in the pharmaceutical sector and copyright piracy of movies, music and software."[38] In an effort to preserve its international reputation for upholding intellectual property rights, the Bachelet government has introduced a whole host of new measures. But according to analysts, the moves, which might help stem digital piracy, will do little to satisfy the multinational pharmaceutical corporations. Indeed, the drug makers have taken issue with crucial aspects of Chile's Industrial Property Law, which has not been modified.[39]

Businessmen lament Chile's serious intellectual-property problem with the United States. The Bachelet government, they believe, is concerned about the high cost of pharmaceuticals and the political fallout at home. As a result, the government is unwilling to implement certain reforms called for under the free trade agreement. "This problem," says Bazán "has put us on the intellectual property priority watch list in the U.S. This doesn't mean anything in terms of sanctions or actions. But it's a warning."

The ambivalence of the Bachelet government may have something to do with disillusionment over the net benefits of the free trade model. Indeed, it may be that the country's economic development has reached its zenith. Though the economy had been growing at a rate of 6–7 percent, in 2006 it dropped to 4 percent and is hardly expected to improve much in 2007.

"The dynamism of the neo-liberal export model," Cabieses says, sipping his coffee, "seems to have reached a plateau because Chile lacks necessary infrastructure. Fundamentally, the export model is based on mining, especially copper. The rest is fruit and wood. But there's no capacity to promote greater development, and we lack diversified technology to compete."

As a result of these shortcomings, the number of permanently unemployed remains high—some 500,000 people. Meanwhile, though the export model has reduced poverty, extreme wealth concentrated in the hands of a minority has grown. While investors have reaped fabulous profits as stock prices have soared over the past few years, salaries and pensions have suffered.

It may be that the free trade model will sow the seeds of future unrest. Many now view the traditional political parties as illegitimate, and the contradictions between wealth and poverty are growing ever sharper. A social and political alternative has not yet arisen to challenge the free trade model, but it might be only a matter of time before things start to shift in Chilean politics.

"The same political conditions are being generated here that we observed before the rise of Hugo Chávez in Venezuela, or Ecuador on a permanent basis, or Bolivia," Cabieses proclaims. "These conditions will generate a difficult political and social milieu in future."[40]

Barring some kind of radical social explosion in Chile, the country seems to be on a very different trajectory from Bolivia and Venezuela, for example. But what of the intermediate group of countries, those that have sought regional integration but have not challenged the neo-liberal paradigm? Within this group, Brazil is clearly the most influential and economically important: with roughly half of South America's population and half the continent's total GDP, Brazil is a regional powerhouse. Without Brazilian support, any move towards regional integration would lack real teeth.

But, it is going to be difficult to get Brazil to adopt an alternative economic course. For years, the country has pursued market-friendly policies. After the military took power in 1964, the government was charmed by foreign bankers and made the opening up of Brazil to foreign capital one of the central pillars of its new economic philosophy. Spurred on by cheap labor flooding from the rural hinterland to Brazil's mega-cities, Brazil went through the so-called "Economic Miracle" characterized by high growth rates. But workers were repressed in the cities, job security was abolished, wages fell precipitously, and income inequality grew.[41]

Later civilian administrations have not fundamentally altered the country's pro-market orientation, and it is highly unlikely that Lula will change course either. Back in the late 1980s, Lula criticized Brazil's servicing of the foreign debt. Were he to become president, he pledged, he would halt interest payments and conduct an audit on the origin of the debt, most of which was contracted under military rule during the 1970s and 1980s. In order to reach a long-term solution, Lula declared, Brazil should negotiate, either alone or in collaboration with other indebted South American countries.

"It is not possible that a nation like Brazil has to discuss the foreign debt with some banker," Lula thundered. "We think the debt is a political question which has to be discussed government to government."[42]

Lula's strident rhetoric is a far cry from the reality of his administration today. Paulo Fontes is a historian and research fellow at Princeton University and an expert on Brazilian politics and Brazilian-U.S. relations. "Let's be honest," he says, leaning over a pile of books. "Lula's first term was very conservative in economic terms. It was clear that the government on the whole was very careful not to openly confront international market forces." More often than not, Brazil has played the role of "moderation" while Chávez has been the "bad boy."[43]

On the other hand, one must also consider important social programs such as Bolsa Familia. Under the plan, modest monthly stipends were provided to poor families who committed to send their children to school and have their health monitored regularly. According to reports, Bolsa Familia has benefited some 7.5 million families.[44]

Meanwhile, Brazil has played an important role in blocking the FTAA. Perhaps if the Iraq war had not absorbed so much domestic attention in the United States, the Bush administration would have been tougher towards Brazil over the FTAA.

A couple months after interviewing Fontes, I am in São Paulo, a city characterized by extremes of poverty and wealth. If Lula is ever to be taken seriously as a politician of the left, he will have to lessen the polarization of wealth in São Paulo. Corporate headquarters are prominent in the downtown area, which is ringed by neighborhoods of condominiums and walled mansions. A shopping mall called Daslu is not open to pedestrians, and access is granted only to the right kind of car driving through one of several checkpoints.[45] However, São Paulo has seen in recent years the rise of so-called "new poverty": educated whites thrown out of work by freer trade, privatization, and economic change. Most are not hungry, but they are angry. That's to say nothing of the "old" poor, who failed to benefit under years of neo-liberal economic policies. Currently, one of every six people in the city lives in a dirt-poor *favela* without basic services. The *favelas*, neighborhoods constructed by rural poor fleeing the countryside for a better future, have been plagued in recent years by bands of drug smugglers. Organized crime gangs recently attacked public buildings and police headquarters, killing police officers and incinerating their vehicles. The attacks were organized by a well-known capo using a cellular phone from his prison cell in São Paulo.[46]

Historically, Lula's core constituency in the city has been labor. What do the unions think of the president's economic orientation? That's a question I set out to answer by going to see Tarcisio Secoli, a prominent labor official. To get to Secoli's office, I must go to the "ABC" region, an industrial area of the city. I take the metro to Jabaquara, the last stop. From there, I get on a bus to Ferrazópolis. The ride takes me through neighborhoods of improvised housing, as well as ugly areas full of factories. The industrial landscape seems to go on forever. Finally, after 45 minutes, I get off at the last bus stop. A woman remarks that the metal workers' union is located not far away. Sure enough, I see the union's gigantic painted sign on the side of a building about a block from the bus stop.

In the entranceway of the union is a portrait of Che Guevara similar to the one in Dausá's office in La Paz. I trudge up the stairway of a large five-story building. My contact is busy talking with his co-workers, and while I wait I glance around at the offices on this floor, which include a credit fund for the workers. Secoli wears a simple white T-shirt and takes me into a side room which is noisy from construction outside.

In Lula's first term, Secoli admits, the government's economic policies were very conservative. However, Bolsa Familia had mitigated some of these conservative tendencies and gone against the usual recommendations of the International Monetary Fund. In this sense, the Lula government had taken a different tack from the earlier Cardoso regime.

"When I came in here I saw a poster of Che Guevara, the principal enemy of the U.S. for many years. Do you want Lula to adopt a more confrontational policy towards the U.S.?" I ask, hoping to provoke Secoli. It would be unrealistic to adopt a confrontational stance, Secoli says. Argentina depended a lot on U.S. trade and Brazil even more so. In his second term, Lula would be unlikely to radicalize by, say, instituting socialism. "I think Lula's government is a transitional period, from neoliberalism towards something else," Secoli remarks.

Later on, as I am leaving Ferrazópolis and taking the long bus ride back to Jabaquara, I reflect on Secoli's phrase "transitional period." To be honest, I feel a little dubious that the Lula government represents any fundamental kind of shift towards a more progressive era in Brazil, given that Lula has done his utmost to dilute the progressive social agenda throughout South America. Behind the façade of unity within Mercosur, serious political fissures remain between Venezuela and Brazil. Publicly, Chávez and Lula maintain friendly relations. However, even as Chávez busily travels around South America conducting oil deals, attacking U.S.-style capitalism and proclaiming socialism for the twenty-first century, Lula continues to maintain close ties to the United States and seeks to promote Brazil's sugar cane-based ethanol within the region. Riordan Roett, a professor at Johns Hopkins University, remarked "It's quite a spectacular show of aggressive diplomacy going on. At the end of the day, it's all about who will have more influence in the region, who will the smaller countries look to."[47]

It's not an idle question. While Chávez would clearly like to advance ALBA and progressive economic arrangements within Mercosur nations, Lula has another vision. Recently, the Brazilian president has been touting the so-called "Santiago Consensus," a kind of revived version of the neo-liberal "Washington Consensus" but with a social conscience. Under Lula's plan, regional integration would be predicated on high economic growth but also close attention to education, the environment, R & D investment, and efficient taxes and infrastructure. In calling for his more moderate development model, Lula clearly has the ear of Chile's Bachelet.

With the United States distracted in Iraq, there could be a political battle to see which country, Brazil or Venezuela, might wield the most influence within Mercosur. Behind the rosy exterior of summit meetings, Roett notes, the two countries are growing "increasingly wary of each other." According to Roett, Kirchner has cozied up to Chávez as a way of countering Brazil's big footprint in the Southern Cone. Meanwhile, Chávez seeks Kirchner's help to overcome Brazil's concerns about Venezuela joining Mercosur. "For Kirchner," Roett says, "it's a way to poke the eye of Brazil. The Brazilians have always seen Mercosur and the Southern Cone as their area. Kirchner is playing a precarious game with Chávez."[48]

Chávez has clearly been successful in cultivating ties to Argentina. But without the support of Brazil, by far the most economically important country in the region, it will be hard for the Venezuelan leader to encourage the spread of any kind of alternative economic model. For the moment, the future of South American economic integration remains cloudy.

CHAPTER 3

OVERCOMING A BRUTAL PAST

When most people in the Unites States think of South America, they typically think of a region plagued by repressive, right-wing military rule. But South America today has shaken off its military past, and its governments are making great strides to bring their armed forces under civilian control.

What's more, within the military in South America today there is a certain degree of sympathy for left-leaning regimes. The United States, which once relied on compliant armed forces to wield great influence over South America, has suffered a political setback. Where is the military headed in the region, and what are the geopolitical stakes?

Gonzalo Sánchez Paz teaches international relations at George Washington University, in Washington, D.C. "Most Latin American countries supported the Rome Treaty for the International Criminal Court," he tells me, the blustery winter wind whipping outside of the Starbucks café. "The United States completely rejected this new organization. The U.S. asked many countries to grant concessions on this treaty."[1]

Indeed, though President Bill Clinton signed the Rome Treaty in the last days of his presidency, incoming George Bush, citing fears that Americans would be unfairly prosecuted for political reasons, renounced the signature. He initiated bilateral immunity treaties with dozens of countries, preventing them from handing U.S. citizens over to the new court. When Latin American countries signed on to the Rome Treaty, the United States cut military training to some nations in retaliation. As military relations suffered a setback, Venezuela, Uruguay, and Argentina stopped sending military personnel to the School of the Americas, recently renamed Western Hemisphere Institute for Security Cooperation or WHINSEC, located in Fort Benning, Georgia. Human rights activists have accused the school of training Latin American officers working for regimes that committed human rights abuses.

The leftward tide in South America is also making it difficult for the Bush administration to secure permanent military bases in the region. Currently, the only U.S. base in South America is located in Manta, Ecuador. But the base, used for drug over flights of Colombian air space, faces an uncertain future as Correa will most likely refuse to extend the American lease beyond 2009.

If the United States is booted out of Ecuador, it might encounter problems in seeking to relocate the Manta base elsewhere. Currently, the United States is talking with the Colombian government about the possibility of establishing a military base there. However, Colombia is not a good option, as American troops would be exposed to a high risk of attack from the left-wing rebels fighting against the U.S.-backed government.

Meanwhile, neither Peru nor Brazil—and certainly not Venezuela—has shown any interest in hosting the U.S. military on its soil. Underscoring its own isolation in the region, the United States has had to turn to smaller, weaker countries such as Paraguay. In 2005, U.S. and Paraguayan officials denied claims that the Americans were seeking to establish a base at Mariscal Estigarribia, near the Bolivian border. According to the U.S. government, Paraguay merely approved several small-scale American exercises in its territory. In May 2005 Paraguay upset its neighbors by hosting 400 United States troops for 13 joint military exercises. The arrival of troops stoked concerns in Paraguay that the United States was secretly trying to establish a permanent base similar to Manta in the country, or perhaps wanted to establish a staging ground from which to intervene in Bolivia.[2] The tri-border region is home to the Guaraní Aquifer, one of the world's largest reserves of water. Bolivia's natural gas reserves are located near the Estigarribia air base. White House officials have used rhetoric about terrorist threats and networks in the tri-border area (where Paraguay, Brazil, and Argentina meet) to bolster their case for military operations. However, according to noted journalist Benjamin Dangl, there is little evidence of terrorist activity in the region.[3]

At first, it looked as if the United States might be able to secure a vital ally in the region. However, relations recently took a decisive turn for the worse in December 2006, when the Paraguayan Senate and executive branch, in response to pressure from neighboring countries, voted to end U.S. troops' immunity to prosecution under the terms of the Rome Treaty. Paraguay, it seems, saw the economic writing on the wall: the country would have been excluded from Mercosur if it had continued to grant immunity to U.S. forces. Incensed, the United States suspended economic aid to Paraguay in response. But the U.S. reprisals had little effect: the American troops that arrived in Paraguay in 2005 have apparently left, and the latest U.S. proposal to send troops back to the country has gained little support from the Paraguayan Congress or President Nicanor Duarte.

Even as the United States loses military influence, South American militaries are in the middle of an identity crisis and in some cases have taken on new roles in society. In Venezuela, Chávez has beaten back the older, right-wing officers who took part in the 2002 coup. In the wake of the coup, Chávez announced the purchase of 100,000 AK–47 assault rifles and several helicopters from Russia, in addition to light attack and training Super Tucano planes from Brazil. Chávez claimed the purchases were necessary to defend its borders from Colombian insurgents. The moves put further strain on Venezuelan-U.S. relations, which were already in tatters.

In 2005 the Venezuelan president, who has repeatedly accused Washington of trying to overthrow his government, announced plans to increase the reserves from 50,000 to 2 million. Recruits say they want to be ready to repel any U.S. attack.[4] As justification for the buildup, Chávez can point to the unannounced presence of U.S. military vessels near Venezuelan waters off the island of Curaçao. Venezuelan Navy commander Armando Laguna said the presence of U.S. military ships near Venezuela is part of the ships' "routine maneuvers."

However, Laguna assured that the United States did not announce the presence to the Venezuelan "as they traditionally have been doing it."[5]

Despite Laguna's declaration, the reports gave way to a wave of paranoia within Venezuela and rumors of an imminent U.S. invasion. Rumors of a new coup, calls to buy food, to "prepare to fight," and questions about Chávez's whereabouts circulated widely via cell phone text messages and e-mail throughout the country. Prominent Chávez officials pounced on the reports and declared that the U.S. presence formed part of a plan to intimidate and provoke Venezuela.

Reservists are drawn largely from the poor and are paid decent wages by Venezuelan standards. Many women have joined the reserves and see their involvement in the armed forces as an opportunity to advance their rights. Critics of the plan say that Chávez is imitating a Cuban military model. Domingo Irwin is a military historian who teaches at the Pedagogical Institute in Caracas. He explains that he initially became interested in the military through his family. One of his uncles was in the armed forces, and when he finished high school he thought about going into the ranks. However, his father, who had lived through the dreadful Pérez Jiménez dictatorship in the 1940s and 1950s, tried to dissuade his son. "My father," Irwin remarks memorably, "thought that going into the military was the equivalent of intellectual annihilation." After Chávez's aborted 1992 coup, he explains, he started to feel concerned about the rise of the military and its political implications for society. Like other Chávez critics, Irwin says that creating the reserves is a thinly veiled attempt by Chávez to extend his control and create a parallel military force responsible only to him.[6]

Irwin expresses concern about the military's growing presence in public life. "The military has always had a presence in the state sector," he says, "but it was discreet and strategic. But since 1999 the military presence has been massive, public and notorious." He is particularly fearful of William Izarra, a retired Air Force officer and lieutenant colonel. Izarra, who was involved in a November 1992 coup attempt against the unpopular Carlos Andrés Pérez regime, later went on to become a political operative in the Chávez administration in the style of Karl Rove. As chief strategist for Maisanta Command, the president's campaign organization in 2004, he contended that his boss's victory would usher in a more radical phase in Venezuelan politics. [7] During a later stint as deputy minister for foreign affairs of the Asia-Pacific and

Middle East, Izarra sought to further Venezuelan ties to such "rogue" nations as North Korea. Nowadays, Izarra has turned into a spokesperson for the Bolivarian Revolution and has been touring abroad and at home. Armed with a laptop computer, Izarra conducts PowerPoint presentations with photos of Che Guevara, the red, blue, and yellow Venezuelan flag, Bolívar, Jesus Christ, and Chávez himself wearing a presidential sash.[8] Izarra's political vehicle, the Center of Ideological Training, spreads the notion of Chávez's "Twenty-first-Century Socialism," a system, according to Izarra, based on humanism, direct participation of the people, and the common good. Izarra's workshops have spawned so-called "ideological centers" and cadres that spread the word of the Bolivarian Revolution. According to Izarra, the workshops have reached more than 60,000 people.[9]

Talk of ideological centers and cadres is exactly what makes Irwin nervous. Elements linked to Izarra, he says, are interested in imposing Cuban-style communism in Venezuela. "How many people does Izarra control?" I ask. Irwin says he doesn't know, but he remains firmly against liberal-minded foreign writers who present a naïve view of developments in Venezuela. I become very intrigued by his discussion of the leftward tilt within the Venezuelan military. To what extent does this represent a growing trend within South American militaries as a whole?

While Chávez has done much to rein in the right wing military faction in Venezuela and bring the armed forces more into line with his political agenda, the situation in Ecuador is much more unsettled. At the lowest levels, the Ecuadoran armed forces are comprised of the "popular classes": *cholos* (people of mixed indigenous and European roots), Indians, and blacks. In recent years, the armed forces have played a prominent role in the country's volatile political life. In fact, over the last decade the military has publicly withdrawn its support for three different presidents during street protests, thus contributing to their ouster.

The Ecuadoran security forces have also been involved in their share of human rights abuses, though not on the level of the atrocities committed by militaries in the Southern Cone. Ecuador's human rights situation became worrisome by the 1980s when, under the conservative government of León Febres Cordero, torture and killing by the military as well as disappearances and arbitrary arrests multiplied. A few years later, non-governmental groups accused Ecuadoran President Sixto Durán, another conservative, of failing to improve the country's human rights record. The country saw the rise of death squads to eliminate criminals and increased use of torture by the security forces.

Correa's challenge is to assert civilian control over the armed forces, not an easy task in such a volatile and unstable country. After assuming power Correa entrusted the military with the construction and upkeep of Ecuadoran roads. "The political will of this government," Correa remarked at a military ceremony, "is that in this era of peace the armed forces should decidedly work on behalf of social and economic development." Army commander Guillermo Vásconez hailed Correa's remarks, saying that the armed forces were pledged to uphold progress and development.[10]

Alberto Molina, a retired colonel in the Ecuadoran army, seems very eager to speak with me. A newspaper columnist and outspoken individual, Molina got interested in the military through family connections. "Here in Ecuador," he confides, "every family normally has one priest and one person in the military." As a young man, he fell under the spell of his uncle, a left-wing officer in the military. When he became a captain, Molina's relative retired and started to pen articles for a left-wing magazine. "I always used to go on vacation," Molina tells me, "and talk to my uncle about social problems. I think he was a motivating force for me entering the military."

During our conversation, Molina remarks that there were stable relations between the incoming Correa administration and the military. As a result, Molina didn't see much risk of a military coup. While Molina may have been right to write off the possibility of a coup, I still can't help wondering whether the military man is playing down real tensions. A couple months prior to my arrival in Ecuador, reports surfaced that the military high command was uncomfortable with Correa's proposals to name a civilian as minister of defense.[11]

Later, the president followed through on his promises by naming Guadalupe Larriva as Ecuador's first ever woman defense minister. She was also the first person to head the armed forces without ever having served in the military. "Ecuador will really become a democracy when all the institutions of the state are clearly subject to civilian society," Correa remarked. "That is why it is very important to break the tradition of putting an ex-officer in charge of the Defense Ministry and put in a civilian, and if possible a woman."[12]

Correa's tapping of Larriva was significant in that it seemed to echo the efforts of other emerging South American regimes to rein in the military and to turn the page on the region's brutal and repressive past. Hilary Burke, a reporter with Reuters, remarked that South America had a tradition of "macho, charismatic strongmen." However, she added, "women are increasingly giving orders on matters of defense." Larriva's appointment, in fact, was not unique in the region. Since 2002, five South American countries have named women to head their defense ministries. "These appointments," writes Burke, "underscore women's progress in recent years in the region, while also reflecting greater political control over the armed forces and the changed role of the military."[13]

Larriva, who never concealed her admiration for Chávez and the Bolivarian Revolution, was born in the southern Ecuadoran city of Cuenca. Larriva became a teacher at a local school and went on to teach courses in geography in university. She has described herself as someone born out of grassroots social organizations, and her personal story validates the claim. A dedicated activist, she served as the president of the National Union of Educators in her native province of Azuay. She went on to become president of the Socialist Party, which formed part of Correa's Alianza País (AP) party.

A few days before she assumed her position, Larriva remarked that the armed forces should have greater concern for social issues and should support environmental and health awareness programs and agriculture in the countryside. A fierce critic of the U.S.-funded drug war in neighboring Colombia, she opposed the aerial spraying of coca crops in that country on environmental and health grounds. She promised to strengthen presidential control over the military and make the promotions system more transparent. She said she expected more "curiosity" than animosity from Ecuador's military brass "over whether a woman can lead in this role."[14]

Tragically, Larriva was never able to see her progressive vision for the military fulfilled. In January 2007, just nine days after Correa assumed power, Larriva was killed in a helicopter crash. The tragedy occurred near the U.S. military base at Manta, on the coast, when her helicopter collided with another helicopter in midair. Larriva's seventeen-year-old daughter, Claudia Ávila, died in the crash as well. According to Inter Press Service, the incident "awakened suspicions among government representatives and political and social organizations that do not rule out the possibility of foul play."[15] The helicopters were in good condition, had received fine maintenance, and were piloted by a well-trained crew.

Gustavo Larrea, the interior minister, remarked that it was highly unusual for two helicopters to be traveling together at night and pressed for an inquiry. The Socialist Party, which Larriva had headed herself, expressed doubts about the circumstances surrounding the crash and also pushed for a probe. Social organizations suggested that the incident was not an accident, and pointed to apparent opposition from senior military officials who opposed the appointment of a civilian and Socialist to head the Ministry of Defense. Víctor Granda, a Socialist leader, remarked, "We find it strange that an accident like this could occur so close to a large, heavily monitored base that is so well-equipped, not only by the Ecuadoran air force, but also by the U.S. Air Force."[16]

Given the climate of suspicion, Correa set up an independent commission to look into the circumstances of the crash. Meanwhile, in a sign that he would not back down and would continue to press for civilian control over the military, he appointed university professor Lorena Escudero to replace Larriva. He also sacked armed forces chief Padro Machado, citing security errors that led to Larriva's helicopter crash.[17]

With such a murky and dramatic opening for civil-military relations under the Correa administration, I wonder what the future may hold. Bertha García is a political scientist at Quito's Catholic University and an expert on military issues. While I wait in García's office, the secretary hands me a copy of *El Comercio*, a major Ecuadoran daily. Opening up the paper, I am intrigued to read an interview with a well-known U.S. activist, Medea Benjamin. The interview, which is accompanied by Benjamin's photo, concerns the U.S. air base at Manta.

As I am pondering what prompted the paper to speak to Benjamin in the first place, Dr. García arrives. A small woman who has difficulty walking and carries a pair of crutches, she quickly impresses me with her incredibly in-depth knowledge of the inner workings of the Ecuadoran military. I have the impression from talking to her that civil-military relations in Ecuador are still in flux under the new Correa administration. For the moment, Correa was treading quite lightly in his dealings with the military. While García wouldn't discard the possibility of a military coup, Chávez was now a factor in South American politics and there was some sympathy for the Venezuelan leader within the ranks. But it was still unclear whether Correa would encourage tight civic-military links as had been the case under Chávez in Venezuela.[18]

With civic-military relations still getting sorted out in Ecuador, I turn the discussion to Ecuadoran-U.S. military relations and the Manta base. One key source of friction between the Correa regime and the United States is the American military presence at Manta, a city on the coast 160 miles southwest of Quito. The Manta facility is a large installation, comprising a naval base, an air base, an airport, and the FOL (Forward Operation Location). Technically the base is not controlled by the United States but belongs to the Ecuadoran air force. The public mood has turned against the base, which the United States uses for drug over flights of Colombian airspace. The base, which is the U.S. military's lone outpost in South America, houses some 220 U.S. military personnel. American planes, chiefly A–3 AWACS and P–3 Orions, play an important role in keeping cocaine and heroin from reaching the United States and reportedly are responsible for about 60 percent of drug interdiction in the eastern Pacific.[19] In 2006, the Manta base flew 850 missions.[20]

According to the Associated Press, many Ecuadorans believe that the United States is trying to draw their nation more deeply into the long-running Colombian conflict, which has started to spill over the border. Indeed, leftist rebels often cross over into Ecuador, and "tens of thousands of Colombian refugees crowd into lawless border towns plagued by drug traffickers and child prostitution." U.S. officials deny that planes taking off from Manta spy on Colombia's leftist rebels, claiming that the flights are solely destined to intercept drug flights and eavesdrop on radio communication.[21]

Such pronouncements, however, don't square with statements put out by the likes of Javier Delucca, himself a U.S. commander at Manta. In August 2006 he said that Manta was very important within Plan Colombia, a U.S.-backed Colombian military campaign against left-wing guerrillas. Delucca later recanted, saying that he was mistaken and that the principal mission was against drug trafficking.[22]

The air base at Manta was leased to the U.S. military for 10 years in 1999, and Correa had made it clear even before he was elected that he did not plan to extend the lease once it expired in 2009. Guadalupe

Larriva reiterated Correa's position, adding "With respect to the possibility of reprisals by the United States, well, I hope they don't occur."[23]

Some in Ecuador are unhappy about the base, García tells me, because it seemed to be focused more on counter-insurgency than on halting drug smuggling. "The armed forces haven't questioned the Manta base," she says. The real opposition to the base came not from within the ranks but from civil society: intellectuals, workers, Indians, and environmentalists.

As it happens, I am quickly able to verify García's statements. Walking around campus, I see something going on within one of the university buildings. Inside, I observe a large exhibit with photos of U.S. military bases worldwide. When I inquire, someone tells me that, just coincidentally, there's an international conference being held against U.S. military bases.

Excited that I may get an opportunity to speak to activists at long last, I tour the exhibit. On the wall, I see a poster reading, "No More U.S. Outrage, Cut Down and Abolish the U.S. Bases, Japanese Delegation, Japan Peace Committee." The poster features images of a U.S. air craft carrier, fighter jets, and a photo of Mount Fuji, where the U.S. military had carried out live shell practice. Walking further, I see another poster reading, "Hawaii Stands Against U.S. Bases, Free Hawaii."

At a table, a woman is registering people to go on a bus trip to the coast to protest the base at Manta. For a moment I consider going on the tour, but then realize that it would conflict with my busy interview schedule.

I head into a large auditorium where representatives from peace groups around the world have gathered. Everyone has earphones for simultaneous translation, and people are listening intently to a panel discussion. An American woman stands up, speaks into the microphone, and asks the panel how the anti-U.S. military base network ought to be organized. She looks somehow familiar, and then I recognize her: it's Medea Benjamin, the same woman who had been interviewed in that morning's edition of *El Comercio*.

Later in the hallway, I meet Gualdemar Jiménez, the president of Peace and Justice Service, Ecuador. He agrees to discuss the Manta issue with me and we head into a quiet alcove off to the side to tape an interview. Jiménez tells me that he'd personally done a lot of political organizing in Manta against the U.S. airbase. In total, his peace group had been organizing around the issue for four years and had studied the negative effects of the Manta base on the local population. "Manta used to be a purely fishing town," he explains. "Now the fishermen don't have access to certain parts of the ocean, which are closed off for security reasons."[24]

According to reports, the Manta base not only carries out surveillance flights of northern Ecuador and southern Colombia, but also monitors boats suspected of carrying drugs.[25] During the 1990s, most drug smuggling from the region was by air, but this later shifted to the high seas once the so-called "air bridge" was closed down.[26] On the sea, U.S. marines had intercepted Ecuadoran boats, even sinking some vessels. "The marines are not the Ecuadoran coast guard," Jiménez declares indignantly.

He goes on to tick off a number of other problems associated with the U.S. airbase. For example, the base had gradually expanded over time. This expansion had displaced *campesino* farmers from their traditional lands. In addition, there had been environmental damage: within the local area, hillsides had been destroyed in an effort to acquire the necessary raw materials to mix asphalt and repave the runway.

According to reports, the Manta air base contributes some $7 million to the local economy annually.[27] But activists are critical of the lack of real economic development in the area. They claim that there have been very few beneficiaries from the Manta base. Meanwhile the marines didn't do any shopping in Ecuadoran markets, nor did they utilize local transportation. "The only thing they contribute to is local discos and prostitution," Jiménez explains bitterly. He insists that Ecuador, a peaceful nation, should not play any role in the Colombian conflict or allow its territory to be used as a staging ground. The protests against the base had increased, and local residents were mobilizing in the province of Manabí, on the coast.

Activists are not the only ones who question the Manta base. Journalists are frequently frustrated when they are unable to get information about crucial details regarding the activities of the facility. Mónica Almeida is chief editor at the Ecuadoran daily *El Universo* and the wife of Marc St-Upéry [see next chapter]. "I went to Manta to visit the base just after the U.S. got there," she says. In the beginning journalists used to make a lot of visits to the base but later it became more difficult to gain access, and one had to jump through a lot of hoops." While the U.S. Embassy could help journalists gain access to the Manta base, one had to request permission from the Ecuadoran air force or the Ministry of Defense.

As a journalist, Almeida quickly grew frustrated with U.S. authorities who failed to supply her with information concerning the Manta base. It took the U.S. Embassy a month to tell her the amount of drugs seized as a result of radar reconnaissance flights. (According to the Manta commander, in 2006 the U.S. military seized or intercepted 275 tons of illegal drugs, mostly cocaine, through the Colombia overflights.[28]) "I'm not saying they're necessarily hiding the information, but there's no transparent mechanism in place to inform people of their activities," she remarks.[29]

With tensions reaching the breaking point, and Correa likely to suspend the base's lease, I am curious to learn more about the political mood within the ranks. For answers, I query Molina for his insider perspective. "What does the Ecuadoran military think about the School of the Americas?" I ask Molina, bringing up the controversial U.S.-funded school that had been involved in training Latin American militaries in torture.

"I studied there," Molina remarks, much to my surprise.

He attended the school twice, first as a cadet in 1968 for two months. At the time, he enrolled in a jungle survival course; many of the instructors were Vietnam veterans. He returned later as a captain in 1981 and studied at the school for three or four months. In general, he says, U.S.-Ecuadoran military ties had been quite good. "Did you get trained in torture?" I ask, feeling that I don't have much to lose by being direct.

Molina says no, chuckling at my question. But, he confides that he was aware of the controversial nature of the school and questioned the underlying mission of anti-guerrilla warfare and protecting democracy against communism. "What was it like studying in the U.S., given the influence of your uncle?" I ask. "I viewed the Americans with a little bit of distrust," he confesses.

Sipping on a *naranjilla* milkshake in the café where we are conducting our interview, Molina asserts that there is "no need" for Ecuador to break off ties to the School of the Americas as Chávez had done so publicly on his TV show, *Aló, Presidente!* As long as the Ecuadoran military benefited from U.S. training, the relationship would continue. On the other hand, he now sensed a certain amount of distrust within the ranks of the Ecuadoran military toward the United States.

I

During the 1960s, Manuel Cabieses was a journalist at the Chilean Communist Party paper, later becoming a militant with the Revolutionary Leftist Movement (known by its Spanish acronym MIR). Two days after the Pinochet coup, he was detained in the street in downtown Santiago. "I was in a car," he explains. "We were all obliged to get out of the vehicle, and someone in the street recognized me. The dictatorship had issued advisories, warning that certain people should hand themselves over, including me." Cabieses was imprisoned for a little more than two years, in different prisons all over Chile. Finally, he was expelled from the country along with his family. He lived in Cuba for about four years. Astonishingly, he returned to Chile willingly. "I returned secretly with my woman, that *señora* outside who you saw in my office," he says. "We spent almost ten years living in secret here in Chile, working with the MIR."[30]

Though Cabieses doesn't share Bachelet's political orientation, like him she was also a victim of repression. In 1975, she was detained at Villa Grimaldi, a three-acre estate on the outskirts of Santiago. Though Villa Grimaldi served as a gathering place for many Chilean artists and intellectuals in the nineteenth and twentieth centuries, Pinochet's secret police or DINA took its suspects there for blindfolded interrogations.

The estate became an infamous detention center where thousands were tortured; hundreds taken there "disappeared," never to be seen or heard from again. Prisoners were forced to undergo endless interrogation, electric shock, and sleep and food deprivation. One survivor reported that he was subjected to every kind of cruelty, including hanging by his heels and near suffocation when his torturers placed a plastic bag over his head. The same victim reported witnessing three male guards sexually assault a woman with an iron rod.[31]

Bachelet and her mother recently revisited Villa Grimaldi, which now looks very different. When it abandoned the property, the DINA, hoping to conceal its crimes, destroyed almost all the buildings, including a tower where prisoners spent their dying last days. Today the site has become a memorial to Pinochet's victims and a park with a meeting space for theatrical performances and cultural events. Flower gardens now grace areas where horrible crimes against humanity were committed. Names of the dead are inscribed on a bronze wall.

Though some officers now reject the 1973 coup, others have concluded that there must have been good reasons for Pinochet to have intervened in the political process. On the other hand, the Chilean military has made progress in certain respects. Bachelet did not encounter resistance from commanding officers while working in her capacity as minister of defense. The armed forces did not make an issue of Bachelet's gender, nor have they ever questioned her authority as president.[32] Indeed, Bachelet had become so emboldened by her own success that she later appointed a woman to succeed her as minister of defense. But when Vivianne Blanlot, an economist, took up her new post, she ran into problems with Pinochet supporters. When she attended Pinochet's funeral in December 2006, for example, she was loudly booed. "Go away, go away!" chanted hundreds of Pinochet's mourners.

Blanlot stayed put, her expression implacable. "I was not the one who had to leave, but them," she remarked. "I'm the one who is in charge."[33] The very next day Blanlot audaciously shot back by stripping Pinochet's grandson of his army captaincy for defending Pinochet's repressive rule in his funeral eulogy.

With such fractures still prevalent within the military, I am curious to know what the armed forces think of the United States. Guillermo Holzmann is coordinator of the Security, Defense, and Strategy Area within the University of Chile's political science department. He lives in a comfortable Santiago apartment, and I am greeted by his gracious wife, who has laid out some appetizers on the terrace. My host explains that unlike many other academics, he's been able to enter the military milieu. Not only had he taught many military officials, but he had been invited into the barracks, where he'd conducted extensive conversations with them.

He says that though the Chilean military still has warm relations with the United States and collaborates with the Southern Command based in Miami, in many ways the armed forces have turned the page. Many officers blamed Pinochet for human rights violations during the dictatorship and viewed his policies as unacceptable. In recent years, many officers had gone on to get higher degrees and studied human rights and democracy. "They know more than civilians about democracy," Holzmann relates.

I'm interested to pursue the issue of lawsuits over the abuses of the Pinochet era, which were now gathering steam. According to *The Economist*, Chile's judges had grown bolder in the wake of Pinochet's legal troubles in Britain. [34] Overall the armed forces have accepted the lawsuits being launched against officers involved in human rights violations during the Pinochet era. As for further political unrest, there is little chance of another coup d'état, according to Holzmann.

Sitting on the train back to my hostel, I reflect on my interview with Holzmann and wonder what I'll find in Argentina. I eagerly await the opportunity to speak to more officials and experts across the border in an effort to ascertain whether the Southern Cone had, indeed, moved past the dark past of U.S.-supported military rule.

In terms of sheer brutality, Argentina made the repression in Pinochet's Chile look like mere child's play. But underscoring the new commitment to human rights and the principle of civilian control over the military in Argentina, President Kirchner appointed a woman, Nilda Garré, as minister of defense. She was Argentina's first woman to occupy the post. A lawyer, Garré was the leader of the Peronist youth of the 1970s, which sympathized with the Montonero guerrillas. Once the military took over, she became a political prisoner. Garré was married to Juan Manuel Abal Medina, a well known Montonero guerrilla who spent seven years in asylum in the Mexican embassy when the military dictatorship began in 1976.

Garré quickly demonstrated that she was in no mood to put up with any nonsense, declaring that former military officers could no longer use state secrecy laws as a pretext for refusing to testify about the abductions, torture, and disappearances that occurred under military rule. "The rules of secrecy cannot be transformed into an obstacle to truth and justice," she remarked, as she announced a presidential decree that would compel more officers to testify. [35]

How might the military react to such a combative attitude? Rut Diamint is an academic expert on military affairs who has also worked within the Ministry of Defense. A no-nonsense woman, she answers my questions patiently, if somewhat succinctly. A critic of the military dictatorship, she later worked as chief of cabinet in the Ministry of Defense. After she stopped working there she'd still had some contact with the military, but less than before. When I ask her what it was like working at the Ministry, Diamint smiles. "Why are you smiling?" I ask, trying to interpret her reaction.

"Because I believe we did not achieve civilian control over the military. In Argentina, the military still enjoys autonomy."[36]

Diamint's assessment is hardly surprising. Recent reports suggest that tensions between the civilian and military branches continue to run high. Recently, six retired military officers took part in a public ceremony attended by approximately 3,000 people to honor the victims of the guerrillas in the 1970s. Kirchner was not amused. He charged that the officers were endorsing "an apology of state terrorism."[37] The six officials were arrested for participating in a "political act."[38]

A scant five days later, the tensions escalated yet further when the president attended a military ceremony commemorating the army's 196th birthday. When he criticized key figures of the military regime, Kirchner was heckled by a group of officers. Bristling, he said, "As the President of Argentina, I have no fear, I don't fear you."[39] Kirchner then stalked off, later ordering strong sanctions against the officers.

Reacting strongly to the incidents, Garré said that it would be necessary to "expunge infectious cells (in the armed forces) of those that cling to anti-democratic fantasies that will not be tolerated."[40] Perhaps it's not surprising that she would use such unusually harsh language. According to *The New York Times*, Argentina's naval intelligence agency has spied on Kirchner as well as Garré herself. The Naval Mechanics School served as one of the most infamous torture centers under military rule.

Diamint's inside view corroborates much of this underlying tension. In 2003, when she was immersed in military circles, there was a large group within the ranks that was opposed to President Kirchner. Some in the military believed that officers who were being tried in court for past misdeeds had been victimized by their superiors and had been unfairly scapegoated. The majority of the military, she adds, was still quite anti-Communist and disliked Kirchner's policy of promoting former Montonero guerillas within the government. Other officers viewed Chávez as a "clown," and few supported the Venezuelan leader's civic-military model.

Nevertheless, as in Chile, there was also a desire for change within the ranks. With more lawsuits against human rights violators likely, some officers within the military are unsupportive of their colleagues already on trial. This next generation simply wants to end the entire matter and get on with the court cases.[41] Indeed, according to a recent report by the Associated Press, Argentine troops are now "headed back to class for a different sort of basic training—in human rights." Garré has insisted on the new initiative, which would send some 600 army, navy, and air force officers to three-month, civilian-taught courses on the role of the state in a democratic society and conflict resolution and justice.[42] Additionally, one small faction in the military is loyal to Kirchner, Diamint says, and "would even join in a popular militia with Chávez" if it was requested to do so. According to experts, opposition to Kirchner has decreased over time. This is due, Diamint says, in large part to economic recovery in the country which has contributed to political stability.

For an inside perspective on civil-military relations, I catch up with Andrea Chiappini, who is part of the new generation at the Argentine Ministry of Defense. An advisor to the deputy minister of defense, she works in a rather forbidding looking building near Kirchner's Casa Rosada. When I meet Chiappini, she seems out of place in her casual civilian clothes, looking more like the NGO staffer she used to be than the deputy defense minister she is now.

Chiappini says there is widespread agreement that civilian control over the armed forces represents the way forward. As for future military coups, she rules out the possibility entirely. "What is it like working here as a civilian?" I ask, genuinely curious. There's a long pause.

"In general I haven't experienced any problems," she says.

"What is it like to be a woman working here?" I say, perhaps a little boldly. Chiappini explains, much to my surprise, that the atmosphere is rather tolerant. She adds that the minister herself is a woman, which has had an impact on the male-dominated culture within the military.

"What was the impact of the Abu Ghraib scandal here?" I ask. "We're trying to encourage a different kind of education within our armed forces," she says, referring to the human rights training now common within the ranks.[43]

Not only has the Defense Ministry pressed for the courses, but Garré has also severed ties to the notorious School of the Americas or

WHINSEC. The school made headlines in 1996 when the Pentagon released training manuals used at the school advocating torture, extortion, and execution. In taking the momentous step to break with the school, Garré followed close on the heels of Hugo Chávez, who severed ties in January 2004.

I query Chiappini about the School of the Americas, and how the Argentine military viewed the institution. "I was at WHINSEC myself," she says, taking me totally by surprise. As hard as it was for me to imagine the Ecuadoran Molina at WHINSEC, it was even harder to picture Chiappini, a woman and a civilian, taking classes at the notorious school.

"I took a course there in 2004 in civic military operations," she exclaims good naturedly. "How did it go?" I ask, a little hesitantly. "It went very well," she replies, laughing. "I went alone, without other military personnel. I was the only woman, the only civilian, and the only Argentine in the course."

"How did that feel?" I ask, not quite knowing what to say. "It felt good because I came out first in my class!" she declares. "The director even offered to keep me on for a second course, because it was the first time that a woman had come out on top."

On the other hand, she tells me, it was useless to have the military go to the United States to learn about terrorism and drug smuggling and "all these new threats" because Argentina already had other government agencies to deal with these specific issues. What's more, there was a very clear legal framework to guide the military. Because of Argentina's past history, the armed forces are forbidden to carry out police work.

The drop-off in military collaboration between the United States and Argentina represents a significant departure for the two countries. Though the Carter administration held Argentina at arm's length and proclaimed its faith in human rights, President Reagan sought to improve ties with Argentina's rogue government. In fact, between 1981 and 1983 Reagan carried out a spirited defense of the military junta's human rights record. In the midst of widespread abductions and torture by the security forces, Reagan met with General Roberto Viola, the head of the junta, and said he was considering a request to Congress to repeal the embargo on military aid that had been in place since 1978. Later, Reagan sent a number of U.S. military leaders to Argentina to discuss closer cooperation between the two countries' armed forces. Reagan carried out a long certification battle in Congress to resume military sales, loans, and training programs to Argentina. In a victory for the president, the House Foreign Affairs Committee finally relented and approved a measure that ended the military ban. Intent on securing Argentina's support for counterinsurgency operations in Central America, Reagan also invited Viola's successor, General Leopoldo Galtieri, to Washington. Perhaps the alliance between Galtieri and Reagan would have continued had the junta not miscalculated in invading the Falklands Islands and provoking war with the United Kingdom. Forced to pick sides, Reagan supported Prime Minister Margaret Thatcher, thus confounding Galtieri's expectations.

Military ties continued, however, after the fall of the junta and return to civilian democracy. According to David Pion-Berlin, a political scientist at University of California, Riverside, "under President Menem, the country doggedly pursued a policy of convergence with Washington. Its objective was to shed its status as the erstwhile regional pariah while becoming a faithful servant of the new world order." During the Persian Gulf War, Argentina deployed two navy vessels and several hundred cadets to the region. "No other country in the Southern Cone, or in Latin America for that matter, has so willingly followed the U.S. lead on so many issues," writes Pion-Berlin. While there was no official "quid pro quo" for collaboration with the Pentagon, the United States designated Argentina a major non-NATO ally.[44] To this day, the United States continues to provide the Argentine armed forces with military equipment and hardware.

On the other hand, with war raging in the Middle East, Argentina's historic relationship with the United States has become somewhat more strained. In 2006, there wasn't a sole bilateral military meeting between the two countries for the first time in many years. Initially Argentina could not fix a date, but when the government proposed a time to meet, the United States responded that "the Pentagon was being restructured" and could not schedule a summit.[45]

With so much economic and political integration already occurring in South America, an intriguing question is whether there can be any meaningful military integration. In 2006, Chávez invited Kirchner and Morales to a military parade in Caracas, where he proudly announced "We must form a defensive military pact between the armies of the region with a common doctrine and organization."

In another speech, Chávez added: "We must form the armed forces of Mercosur, merging warfare capabilities of the continent." During a trip to Bolivia, where he was accompanied by Venezuela's army chief, Raúl Baduel (a military man who was loyal to his boss during the coup of April 2002, as I explain in great detail in *Hugo Chávez: Oil, Politics, and the Challenge to the U.S.*), Chávez declared that there was a need for a Latin American alliance akin to NATO "with our own doctrine, not one that's handed down by the gringos."

Most experts seem to regard Chávez's proposals as nothing more than hot air. In Caracas I ask Irwin about recent news reports that Chávez had sent Venezuelan troops to Bolivia. "Would it be possible for Chávez to do the same and send troops elsewhere?"

"Please, by God!" he exclaims. "Do you know how much logistics and cost are involved in maintaining just one battalion? It would be an unbelievable expense."

If Chávez ever did manage to deploy forces around South America, Irwin says they would be hardcore activists and not professional soldiers. As for Chávez's South American army, this was a pure "fantasy": there was no historical precedent for creating such a force. Indeed, the Chilean armed forces have an enormous amount of pride, have never lost a war, and might not want to form part of a larger force.

"Maybe you could form something like NATO," Irwin remarks. "But why did NATO work? The alliance functioned because Europe confronted an external enemy. What is our external enemy?"

If such a force were under Venezuelan leadership, this would inevitably run into conflict with Brazilian strategic interests. According to news reports, Mercosur officials have ruled out the idea of forming a common military alliance, and Brazilian army commanders have expressed opposition to Chávez's proposals.[46]

Not only has there been opposition to the Venezuelan leader's ideas within the Brazilian military, but the Brazilian left also has reservations about the former Venezuelan paratrooper. While Chávez's image amongst the Brazilian left—including academics, labor leaders, and some government official—has improved recently, he has historically not been held in particularly high regard. Part of the left perceives Chávez as a buffoon and distrusts him, and some people think he lacks a commitment to democracy, a sticking point for Brazilians who revile the country's period of military dictatorship and identify strongly with the notions of liberal democracy, free elections, and constitutionally limited executive power. When Chávez first appeared on the scene, he was distrusted because of his ties to the military and his role in the coup of 1992. "For my generation," says Brazilian academic Paulo Fontes, "the military was a bunch of brutes."

It's also unlikely that the Ecuadoran military will consider working with other South American nations, as the small Andean nation has had tense relations with its neighbors. For instance, Ecuador was opposed to a military initiative called Plan Colombia and would not carry out joint operations with the Colombian military. Ecuador has long complained about the harmful effects of aerial spraying on coca plantations in the border region and is eager to avoid being drawn into Colombia's conflict. Recently Ecuador beefed up its military forces on the Colombian border, threatening to shoot down any unauthorized planes making incursions into Ecuadoran airspace. The move came in response to reported sorties of Colombian military planes and a series of reported incursions by Colombian troops, supposedly in "hot pursuit" of guerrillas.[47] Meanwhile, though Ecuador is on better terms with Peru than it was in the 1990s when the two nations fought a nasty border war, there is little chance that their respective militaries will carry out joint exercises any time soon.[48]

Bolivia is currently the South American nation with the greatest ideological affinity with Chávez, and it's no surprise that Morales has sought greater military cooperation with Venezuela. According to reports, Bolivia's chief of staff, General Freddy Bersatti, backs the idea of "merging" the Venezuelan and Bolivian armed forces. Chávez has provided helicopters to Bolivia and says he will send weapons to replace equipment. The Venezuelan president has reportedly pledged to provide up to $22 million to build 20 military bases in Bolivia. U.S. officials' frequent complaints regarding Chávez's allegedly expansionist aims in the region have received little sympathy from Chile, Argentina, and Brazil, who remain unconcerned by reports of Venezuelan-Bolivian military ties. In late 2006, Venezuela's ambassador to Bolivia, Julio Montes, remarked that "if for some reason this pretty

Bolivian revolution were threatened, and they asked us for our blood and our lives, we would be here."[49]

Argentina has also set up a bilateral military commission to Venezuela, raising the possibility of future collaboration. Experts such as Diamint regard Venezuela's proposals as "pure rhetoric, just like everything with Chávez." There has been some technological exchange between the Venezuelan and Argentine military but no joint exercises. Nevertheless, Kirchner's tapping of Garré for his nation's top military post may have raised some eyebrows at the Pentagon. Before coming to the Ministry of Defense, Garré was the Argentine ambassador to Venezuela. In Caracas, she was a vocal Chávez supporter, and when she got the call from Kirchner offering her the new job, the Venezuelan president phoned to congratulate her.[50]

While Argentine-Venezuelan military integration is unlikely, there has been a good deal of cooperation between the Chilean and Argentine armed forces. Indeed, unlike the Andes where military tensions run high over the U.S.-fueled drug war, the Southern Cone has made great strides toward integration. Blanlot and Garré recently signed an agreement to form a combined military force for peacekeeping missions; the force will be ready for deployment by the end of 2008. Blanlot remarked that the pact was the result of hard work and that Argentina and Chile were moving closer to integration.[51]

Some observers have noted the remarkably changed military relations within the Mercosur nations. During the 1970s and 1980s, rivalries among the military dictatorships of the Southern Cone ran high. "But," notes one expert, "with the transition toward democratic government, first in Argentina in 1983, then Brazil in 1985, and finally Chile in 1990, relations changed." Argentina, in the midst of efforts to bring its armed forces under civilian control, is keen to avoid an arms race in the region. More so than any other country in the region, it has avidly pursued regional military cooperation, which would include joint strategies, doctrines, operations, and arms purchases. Having competed with Brazil for centuries for regional domination, Argentina has now buried the hatchet by agreeing to develop nuclear technology for peaceful uses only; Brazil has responded in kind. The two nations have agreed to make their nuclear energy policies compatible, exchange information, visit each other's sites, and create compliance and enforcement mechanisms. Within the climate of lessening tensions, armies from both countries have engaged in joint exercises. Under democratic governments, Chile and Argentina have likewise buried long-simmering border disputes and conducted joint military exercises.

While no one is expecting Chávez to succeed in creating a continent-wide army any time soon, the recent emergence of left-leaning regimes in the region raises an important question: What military role, if any, would South America like to play on the world stage?

That issue was recently thrown into stark relief when South American troops deployed to the chaotic island nation of Haiti. In early 2004, violent uprisings forced Haitian President Jean Bertrand Aristide from power, leading interim Prime Minister Gérard Latortue, who received Washington's backing, to form a transitional government.

Aristide claims he was kidnapped. In a telephone conversation with U.S. Representative Maxine Waters, he reportedly remarked that he had been threatened by U.S. diplomats. If the Haitian president did not leave Haiti, warned the diplomats, paramilitary leader Guy Philippe would storm the palace and Aristide would be killed.[52]

The United States led a Multilateral Interim Force, or MIF, into Haiti, ostensibly to restore stability. A few months later, the UN replaced MIF with MINUSTAH, a multi-national peace keeping force with substantial Brazilian, Uruguayan, Argentine, and Chilean troop participation. MINUSTAH was to secure stability by reforming the Haitian police, supporting the political process, and monitoring human rights.

The force was led by Brazil, which sent 1,200 troops, the most of any country. But the 9,000 soldiers of MINUSTAH have found it difficult to maintain peace and security in Haiti. The mission has been plagued with problems, including kidnapping and assassinations and the death of UN peacekeepers.

In May 2006 René Préval, originally an Aristide supporter, was inaugurated Haiti's new president. Attending the ceremony was Juan Gabriel Valdés, a Chilean and the head of the MINUSTAH mission. Nearby protesters shouted slogans in favor of Aristide, who was in exile in South Africa. "We voted for Préval so that Aristide would return again," shouted the demonstrators, who also demanded that Latortue be brought to trial to face assorted allegations.[53]

During the election Préval was protected by Argentine troops. In February 2006 Garré traveled to Haiti. Meeting with President-elect Préval, she reaffirmed that the blue helmets sent by Argentina would continue to form part of the UN mission. For his part, Préval thanked Argentina for the protection its forces had recently offered him.

Argentines agree that their country should participate in a general way in peacekeeping missions commanded by Latin American officers, and most accept Argentine involvement in the specific case of Haiti. However, experts say there isn't much interest in the issue. Left-wing groups, which represent "less than 2 percent of the vote," according to Diamint, have claimed that Argentina is carrying out dirty work for the United States.

In Brazil, however, MINUSTAH has come under more widespread criticism. "A major troop-contributing country," notes a UN report, "Brazil's involvement reflected its willingness to appear as a major regional power able to take care of Latin America's security."[54] In June 2005 Brazilian General Augusto Heleno Ribeiro, who headed the Brazilian forces on the island, said his forces had been the target of a "campaign." The general and his troops had been virulently attacked by the Haitian business sector and even interim Prime Minister Latortue for not doing enough to prevent violence and kidnappings.

Assailed on all sides, Ribeiro resigned his post, remarking "I wanted to stop and now is the time for me to be replaced, to give the opportunity to another Brazilian general to have the fantastic experience that I have had in Haiti."[55] That "fantastic" opportunity fell to General Urano Bacellar, who died in an apparent suicide in January 2006. Police experts and UN officials said that the evidence, including a head wound from Bacellar's own gun, did indeed suggest suicide. But Brazil's vice president and foreign minister expressed doubts about the suicide thesis. Some have wondered how an officer of such high rank, who had trained for war his entire life, could end his own life. On the night of his death, witnesses reported that Bacellar was neither tense nor depressed. The Bacellar incident led leftist lawmakers to reiterate their calls that troops be brought home, and even conservative newspapers criticized the nation's involvement in Haiti.[56]

Valter Pomar is secretary of international relations for Lula's Workers' Party or PT. A veteran of social struggle, Pomar has been involved in politics since the late 1970s. While working for the PT, he'd had the opportunity to travel to practically all South American countries.

"What does the PT think about the Brazilian military mission in Haiti?" I ask. Pomar explains that the party would like to substitute technical and humanitarian assistance for the military component as soon as possible. In fact, the party had passed a motion to this effect in April, 2006.

Talking to Pomar, I sense a certain amount of friction between the rank-and-file members of the PT and the Lula government. He complains that the PT was never consulted when the government decided to send troops to Haiti. Within the party, there were those who felt that Brazil's presence in Haiti was frankly imperialist, while others thought it would help to bring about peace. "I personally believe that we should not have sent troops to Haiti," Pomar explains. "The fundamental problem in Haiti is not military in nature, it is social and economic."

The longer the Brazilians stayed in Haiti, Pomar says, the greater the risk that the military force would start to take on an essentially police role, and this would go against the underlying premise of the peacekeeping mission, which was to assist with social and economic reconstruction. Even more serious, Pomar says, is the dubious nature of Brazilian interference from a legal standpoint. When the troops first arrived, there was no legitimate government in place to request their assistance. Given these problems, Pomar tells me that the PT would strive in future to convince the Lula government to withdraw Brazilian troops as soon as possible. While it's unclear what kind of role the Brazilian military may play on the international stage in future, influential figures such as Pomar are pushing to redefine the military's mission abroad and to rethink Brazil's wider place in world politics.

CHAPTER 4

LIGHTS! CAMERA! CHÁVEZ!

Near the Bellas Artes metro station in Caracas is an impressive set of murals, all showing the political history of Venezuela. On one panel, there's a painting of El Dorado, the mythical city of gold long sought after by the Spaniards. Another panel depicts the decadent owners of cocoa plantations in the colonial period. An image of slave owners dressed in fine clothes is juxtaposed with scenes of African slave revolt. The most striking panel of all depicts Juan Vicente Gómez, a brutal twentieth-century military dictator, who sits on top of a big barrel of oil.

It's the summer of 2006, and Caracas has been transformed by brightly colored murals painted on the side of the highway. One mural shows Chávez's profile. A quote underneath reads: "We are anti-imperialist because we show solidarity with the rest of the world." Further along the road, I see other murals of Simón Bolívar, the great hero in the struggle for independence from Spain and Chávez's role model. One particularly jarring mural depicts Uncle Sam wielding a dagger reading "CIA." There is no face underneath the hat, just a bare skull.

Some observers agree that the murals are extremely powerful but wonder whether they will actually have an impact on Venezuelan popular consciousness. "Is the murals' effect greater than the products of an international, globalized consumer society?" asks Steve Stein, rhetorically. "Am I more interested in anti-imperialism or Colgate toothpaste?"[1]

Caracas's new face-lift forms part of Chávez's new cultural policy, which seeks to do away with so-called "elitist" art so as to encourage a new sensibility amongst the people. One casualty of the new policy was Sofia Imber, director of the city's Museum of Contemporary Art. The institution was considered to be one of the best museums of its kind in Latin America. I recall touring the museum in 2000 and feeling impressed with the collection's holdings, which included paintings by Braque, Kandinsky, and de Kooning. Chávez considered it "elitist." In 2001 he fired Imber.

"The message was clear," writes the *Boston Globe*. "Chávez . . .would not tolerate the stature of the cultural elite." Chávez claimed his government aspired to "a culture that is at the service of the human revolution, of creation, of the liberation of the Venezuelan people."[2]

When art curator Miguel Miguel found himself in the museum after the shakeup, he thought he had made a mistake. The museum had set up a government-sponsored "mega-exhibit," in which amateur artists were invited to hang their work next to modern masterpieces. "In Venezuela, we used to be the envy of Latin America in terms of the quality of our museums," he lamented. "Today it's grand populism, a grand confusion, and mediocrity. . . . I thought I was at the wrong place."[3]

Not everyone mourns the new direction in cultural policy. Benito Irady, president of the state-run Foundation of Ethnomusicology and Folklore, remarked that the government should make culture accessible to all social strata.[4] Under the leadership of Francisco Sesto, minister of "Popular Power for Culture," the state has sought to promote traditional artisan crafts. Meanwhile, local community museums are flourishing. In the working-class neighborhood of Catia for example, women were invited to reflect on and write about their most painful experiences. At the Jacobo Borges Museum, the women displayed their testimony at an exhibit entitled "The Language of Mourning." The exhibit grew out of a literary workshop that was held at the museum.

Adriana Meneses, the museum's director, has held other workshops in the facility on everything from puppets to poetry to crafts. The idea is that the community generates material for the exhibitions, which spur other local residents to become involved.

On the surface, Venezuela seems to have become much more culturally independent and nationalist. However, on closer inspection, I sense a much more ambiguous and contradictory attitude. Venezuelans have strong cultural ties to the United States, and I am struck by the gigantic shopping malls in the capital of Caracas.

Centro Comercial Sambil, a shopping complex in the area of Chacao, even has U.S. fast food chains such as Pizza Hut, Wendy's, and KFC. The entrance to the Sambil mall is frequently so clogged with people that it is difficult to walk.

For Chávez and his followers, "Sambil society" has become a dirty word. But rejecting consumerist society is a hard sell in Venezuela, where even the poor spend their paltry income on Nike sneakers, and satellite TV antennas can be seen on top of makeshift cinderblock homes.[5] Indeed, Venezuela has always seemed more fixated on U.S. fast food than other South American countries I have visited. Though Venezuelans boast that they are now drinking more *guarapo* or sugar cane juice, I saw no evidence of this; most people I observed drank soda pop. There are two movie theaters screening the latest summer fare from Hollywood, including *The Da Vinci Code* and *Poseidon*.

Compared to other Latin American countries, Venezuela seems to have a more insatiable desire for the trappings of U.S. consumerism. On the crass private TV stations, which provide a bizarre daily contrast to Chávez's state TV, commercials advertise the latest U.S.-style consumer products.

Chávez constantly harps on the virtues of Venezuela's indigenous peoples and is proud of his own Indian features. However, the cosmetics adds on billboards throughout Caracas are dominated by European or white-looking women.

American pop music is everywhere, though Chávez is trying to reduce its presence. The president himself has never attended a classical music concert at the well-known Teresa Carreño Theater in Caracas, preferring the mournful love songs or "rat-a-tat" ballads of *llanera* music from the Western Plains of Venezuela.[6] The songs, which deal with fast horses and romantic sunsets, are often bawdy. The instruments are simple: *bandolas, cuatros* (small guitars), *maracas*, and harps. Under the Law of Social Responsibility, 50 percent of what deejays play must be Venezuelan music.[7] What's more, under a cultural law approved in 2004, at least 50 percent of all that music must be "folkloric." As a result of the new laws, *llanero* and *gaita* (lilting music from the city of Maracaibo) musicians have been doing a thriving business.[8]

But Chávez hasn't stopped with music. Hoping to spur Venezuelans to read more, the president has founded a state-run publishing house, El Perro y la Rana. Chávez himself has a taste for left-wing authors such as Michael Moore and Joseph Stiglitz. He appeared on television waving a book by Noam Chomsky, whose U.S. book sales soared as a result. (Sad to say, Chávez failed to do the same for my own book, despite my attempts, through various Venezuelan contacts, to have him tout it.)

Armed with cutting-edge technology and an expert design team, Chávez's new publishing company has produced millions of free or low-cost editions. The political opposition, not surprisingly, has attacked El Perro y La Rana, claiming that the government is only interested in publishing its own brand of left-wing books. Miguel Márquez, who heads the publishing house, denies the charge, remarking that the company "does not discriminate between political ideas which each writer professes, we base our decisions solely on the quality of the works."[9] It is certainly true that El Perro y La Rana publishes books on Marxism. El Perro y La Rana has also produced a book about the conceptual and legal aspects of Chávez's so-called Communal Councils, neighborhood-based councils that initiate local policies and oversee development projects. On the other hand, the publishing house publishes books on widely diverse subjects and not just politics: in the cultural sphere El Perro y La Rana produces books about theater, photography, literature, music and dance. The publisher's catalog even includes lighter fare including a book about the history of Cuban cocktails.[10]

Along with the new cultural policy, Chávez has also sought to build up Venezuelans' sense of history. Books on the South American independence leader Simón Bolívar are selling like hotcakes. Given the prominence that Chávez has attached to Bolívar in his public speeches, the skyrocketing sales are hardly surprising.

With the possible exception of Fidel Castro, Simón Bolívar is by far the most widely recognized Latin American historical figure. In military terms, Bolívar was a brilliant tactician and liberated half of South America from Spanish rule. But Bolívar was more than just a soldier and founder of new nations, or "Liberator" to use his preferred title. He was a thinker who analyzed the significance of what he was doing in historical perspective and in a wide international context. He drafted constitutions and decrees that he hoped would make the future more bearable. Bolívar opposed slavery, issued decrees for the establishment of schools (for boys as well as girls), deplored the misery of indigenous peoples, and ordered the conservation of forest resources.

In Venezuela, Bolívar is revered as a God-like figure to this day. Indeed, a popular religion based on the fertility goddess of María Lionza has appropriated Bolívar as one of its central ritual figures. The faith is based on indigenous, black, African, and Catholic roots, and priests hold ceremonies in which the spirit of the Liberator is channeled through a medium who coughs when Bolívar is present, since the general had tuberculosis. Meanwhile, religious altars of the faithful generally feature a portrait of Bolívar.

The country's currency, main squares, and universities bear the Liberator's name. His sayings are taught in schools, broadcast on the radio and emblazoned on government buildings. Chávez supporters or Chavistas have dubbed the areas they control "liberated zones of the Bolivarian Republic," and adorn offices and homes with portraits of the Liberator. Meanwhile, Chávez champions Bolívar's idea of a unified South America, and echoes the Liberator's words during his televised speeches. Chávez also likes to appear on television with a portrait of Bolívar near his head.[11]

In Caracas, a key historic landmark is Bolívar's native house. Located along downtown streets crowded with informal vendors, the house is often full of visiting school children. Mercedes García, the museum's director, says that Chávez's speeches have awakened an interest in the Liberator. The volume of people visiting the museum has been increasing, and at the time I visited, 3,500 individuals were showing up every week. In particular, there was great curiosity among the military, and soldiers from all over the county were paying visits to the museum.

A couple months later I am back in Caracas, this time not to tour the city murals but to learn about cultural policy under the Chávez regime. The authorities had recently created an "audiovisual school," which would train producers for a new cultural TV station, Ávila TV. The new channel, which would join Vive TV, Venezuela's other cultural station, commenced its work with 140 enrolled students and a budget of $5 million.[12]

The authorities had also created Villa del Cine, a film studio designed to counteract the influence of Hollywood. Inaugurated in June 2006 amid much fanfare, the $42 million project supervised by the

Ministry of Culture aims to produce 19 feature-length films a year, in addition to documentaries and television series.[13]

"They inoculate us with messages that have nothing to do with our traditions," the Venezuelan leader said during the inauguration ceremony.[14] Though some foreign films were "enjoyable," Chávez remarked that most Indians and Latin Americans in them were portrayed as people that were "savage and dangerous, who have to be eliminated."[15] "Hollywood sends a message to the world that tries to sustain the so-called American way of life and imperialism," Chávez said. "It is like a dictatorship."[16]

Through this "Bolivarian Cinecittà," Chávez seeks to spur production of films dealing with social empowerment, South American history, and Venezuelan values. Chávez himself has long favored such movies. *El Mercurio* reports that two of Chávez's favorite films include *El Caracazo* (*The Caracas Smash*), directed by Roman Chalbaud, which depicts popular protests and riots against the government of Carlos Andrés Pérez in 1989. The second, *Amaneció de Golpe* (*The Coup Awakened*), by Carlos Azpúrua, deals with Chávez's attempted military coup against the Pérez regime in 1992.[17]

In Altamira I head to CANTV and speak with Lorena Almarza, the director. To my surprise, she agrees to an interview the very next day. The studio is located about a half hour away from Caracas on the highway going towards the city of Guarenas, some 30 kilometers to the east.

According to a man checking in at hotel reception, I would "stand out like a sore thumb" if I took a public bus at Petare, widely considered to be a dodgy area of town. Instead, I opt to hire a driver to take me to Guarenas.

Villa del Cine is modern looking and impressive. Rush hour traffic has proved to be very mild, and we've arrived an hour early. My driver takes me into Guarenas, which is ramshackle and run down in comparison to the spanking new Villa del Cine with its fresh coat of white paint. The town itself is dotted with tall, gray, and unappealing housing blocs. It's also much hotter than Caracas.

Inside Villa del Cine, a young and energetic staff is busy working at the latest computers. The government has spent lavishly here, and the facility includes two film studios, audio and video equipment, warehouses and an administrative building with areas for post-production, animation, costumes, casting, and food service.

I sit in a waiting room, waiting to speak to Almarza. A woman arrives at long last: I take her to be the secretary, as she's no older than I am. But it's Almarza herself, who takes me down the corridor to her immaculate office.

Almarza studied social and political psychology and became particularly interested in culture as a means of encouraging development and community organization. Growing up in the western city of Barquisimeto, she familiarized herself with the writings of Antonio Gramsci and Paulo Freire. Meanwhile, she frequented local film clubs and became interested in cinema.

"Later I went to Caracas to study psychology in the Central University," she explains. "I started to work as an usher. After that I began to organize film festivals."

Once Chávez came to power, Almarza worked with the state-run Bolivarian schools, helping to bring movies to children and provide manuals explaining how students might interpret images and psychological profiles of different characters. When I ask Almarza to talk about her work at Villa del Cine, she explains with enthusiasm that she is proud to be part of an "experimental" state project.

Historically, the Venezuelan state had provided minimal resources towards cultural promotion, Almarza says.[18] But the Chávez authorities established a distributor, Amazonia Films, as an alternative to the commercial networks. Since its opening in 2006, Amazonia has acquired films from Latin America, Europe, and Asia. The following year, the authorities also started to provide support to independent film producers, with cost reductions of up to 35 percent.[19] Instead of merely providing minor funding towards incipient film production, the state was now creating incentives to increase film production but also to enable people to acquire their own equipment.

The new minister of culture, Francisco Sesto, began to encourage the creation of audiovisual cooperatives. These groups would bring proposals to the table, and Villa del Cine would decide if the government was interested in promoting the project. "It's all about the transformation of the state," Almarza says, "and how people might become participants in the development of film through their own art."

So far, Villa del Cine had shot in all 24 Venezuelan states; in 2005–06 the studio filmed 357 productions. Almarza had overseen the production of TV series documenting educational developments under

Chávez's Bolivarian Revolution. But Villa del Cine had also shot films about Indians and music, and the studio planned to commence work on some fictional films in 2007.

The authorities also hope to spur the creation of a network of community movie theaters. In 2006, 80 new theaters were created, and authorities are seeking to build yet more to show films produced at Villa del Cine.[20]

Almarza denies any interference from high-level authorities. She had never spoken to Chávez individually, though she and her colleagues at the Ministry of Culture had the opportunity to speak to him as a group. Despite the lack of overt interference, Chávez's influence on the studio's cinematic choices is clear. In 2006, Villa del Cine celebrated the two-hundredth anniversary of Francisco de Miranda's return voyage to Venezuela by producing a film about the exploits of the late-eighteenth-century hero, considered to be a forerunner of later independence figures in South America. The film, which opened in 35 of Venezuela's 400 movie theaters, did quite well at the box office and surpassed Hollywood blockbuster *Superman Returns* during the summer 2006 season.[21] Villa del Cine's movie led to controversy. The Venezuelan opposition claimed that the studio's vision of Miranda was ideological. Almarza was frankly puzzled by the reaction. She concedes the opposition could launch a boycott of the film, but "Whatever project Chávez supports, the opposition will attack it."

Miranda, who was born in Caracas to Spanish parents, spent the last days of his life as a prisoner. He died in a military fortress in Cádiz in 1816. Within the National Pantheon of Caracas, where Bolívar lies in state, there's an empty tomb awaiting Miranda's body. A group of Spanish scientists has tried to determine whether certain remains in the fortress indeed belong to Miranda. The scientists have extracted DNA from bones in the fortress and will compare the genetic material to Miranda's descendants in order to reach a final determination. Not surprisingly, Chávez has expressed personal interest in the investigation. Though obscure, Miranda is one of Chávez's favorite historical personalities. In the run-up to the December 2006 presidential election, Chávez hailed his followers by nicknaming them Miranda's electoral "battalions."[22]

Miranda is not the only historical figure that has concerned Villa del Cine. Almarza explains to me that her studio will also produce a TV series about Ezequiel Zamora, which will later be turned into a feature-length documentary film. Zamora was one of the principal protagonists of Venezuela's Federal War in the nineteenth century. He carries key symbolic significance for Chávez, who has named his land reform program after the peasant leader. More recently, Chávez named a sugar mill in his native town of Sabaneta after Zamora.

Before coming to power, Chávez led MBR 200, a conspiratorial movement within the military that sought to revive the memory of Zamora. According to *El Nacional*, a Venezuelan newspaper, one of Chávez's favorite books is *El Tiempo de Ezequiel Zamora* (*The Era of Ezequiel Zamora*), by Federico Brito Figueroa, a well known academic and communist. In his book, Figueroa sought to cast Zamora as a revolutionary and proto-socialist, a kind of precursor to the Communist Party's later land struggles in the countryside.[23] The government has reclaimed lands as part of Chávez's land reform program. For Almarza, Zamora is an emblematic figure who stands for liberty and land.

Currently, she explains, there are almost two hundred people working at Villa del Cine, and the studio contributes to the local economy in Guarenas by employing costume makers from the area. But Villa del Cine is already becoming much more than a local Venezuelan affair. Though the studio spurned Hollywood, Villa del Cine has attracted big stars, such as Danny Glover, co-star of the *Lethal Weapon* and *Dreamgirls* movies. An ardent defender of Chávez's Bolivarian Revolution ever since the Venezuelan leader was elected in 1998, Glover, 60, also supported the creation of Villa del Cine in 2006.

"We have a very fraternal relationship with Glover," Almarza says. "He came here to Villa del Cine in 2006. He's interested in developing some productions. As a matter of fact Glover helped to finance a film in Africa about African countries and debt. So, in addition to being an important figure in the Afro-American community, he supports Third World cinema."

In fact, Villa del Cine will funnel $18 million to Glover's new epic film, *Toussaint*,[24] about Francois Dominique Toussaint Louverture, one of the fathers of Haiti's independence from France in 1804. Haiti, a great symbol to enslaved Africans, was the first black nation to throw off imperial rule and become a republic. The film represents Glover's directorial debut; the star will also co-produce the movie.

One of the goals of the studio is to get film makers to look toward Venezuela instead of Los Angeles to handle post-production services.

Word of Villa del Cine had already intrigued well-known South American directors such as Miguel Littín, a Chilean. A documentary film maker, he fled to Spain during the Pinochet years. Littín had submitted a proposal to work with Villa del Cine on a film about concentration and torture camps set up under Pinochet. Chávez officials want to press further by developing film producing partnerships with other Mercosur nations.

At the mention of other South American directors, I query Almarza about how she sees Villa del Cine in terms of larger integration efforts taking hold. The issues touched on in the Zamora film are hardly unique to Venezuela, she says. There were tense fights for land throughout the Andean region involving the Indians in Bolivia and Ecuador.

"The indigenous struggle across the continent is something which unites us," she declares. Almarza's opinion echoes the point of view of the many South American governments that are currently placing more importance on indigenous cultures. For Almarza, it's all "a pressure cooker" that's become impossible to cover up with so many long repressed social movements coming to the fore.

Speaking to Almarza, I cannot help but feel moved by her eagerness and enthusiasm. But I wonder what Villa del Cine really amounts to in the larger scheme of things. According to Sarah Miller Llana of the *Christian Science Monitor*, almost all of what is shown in Venezuela comes from Hollywood—only about two Venezuelan-produced films are released a year.[25] On average, Hollywood releases 110 pictures a year in Venezuela, grossing about $60 million, or 86 percent of Venezuela's total box office.[26] The Venezuelan film industry is so small, remarks Llana, "that it isn't even monitored by major box-office research firms."[27]

Under a recent amendment to its 1993 Film Law, Chávez has sought to level the playing field. The new regulations included a distribution quota requiring that 20 percent of film releases be local. Despite the success of the Miranda film, however, the new film policy had not succeeded in giving the Americans a real run for their money. Though the number of local releases had risen from a pitiable two to three pictures annually to a dozen in 2006, few moviegoers patronized Venezuelan films. Even Chávez's favorite, *El Caracazo*, lured only 70,000 people.[28]

The idea is to diversify the big screen so that you might see Villa del Cine films in any shopping mall along with the usual Hollywood fare. Venezuela cannot compete economically with Hollywood, but Villa del Cine seeks to provide alternatives to globalized homogeneity. Film, Almarza says, is a useful tool in the "combat of ideas."

Film makers at Villa del Cine have ample reason to be pleased. Confronted with insufficient private and state funding, they used to be able to work only two to four months a year while laboring the rest of the time in advertising or other professions. "You cannot make a living through filmmaking in Venezuela, not even if you have a big hit," Swedish-Venezuelan filmmaker Solveig Hoogesteijn has remarked.[29] Villa del Cine is a Venezuelan film maker's dream come true: the complex sports a costume room and within a noisy warehouse, carpenters are busy at work constructing stage sets. Set on a rack are some colonial-style red coats made at the studio.

Outside I meet a documentary film maker who had recently helped to form a Latin American network of his peers. A self-proclaimed "sympathizer" with the Bolivarian process, he'd received a certain amount of support from Villa del Cine and as a result didn't have to spend much time on fund raising. While he was an optimist about politics in the Chávez era, he was also wary of expecting too much. "The danger, he explains, "is that there is a bureaucratic class in power, and despite its revolutionary pretensions, we still have the cultural structures in place from the earlier capitalist period." On the other hand, he was hopeful that Chávez's emphasis on greater citizen participation in politics could help to counteract the bureaucracy.

We walk upstairs into an editing room with state-of-the-art equipment. He explains that he is working on a documentary about the cultural history of oil in Venezuela. In conjunction with the film, he'd interviewed people in the town of Cabimas. I perk up at the mention of the oil-boom town, which I'd written about in my dissertation on the environmental history of oil.

The man shows me a rough cut of his new film on the computer. Amid stark images of oil pollution, a solemn voiceover intones, "The birds had died." Discordant notes played on a piano accompany more images, this time of oil blow-outs in Lake Maracaibo during the early twentieth century.

I'm amazed to see the newsreels of American oilmen, and wonder how this young director has managed to acquire the old footage. Interviewed by the director, natives of Cabimas relate how their ancestors were abused by the oil companies.

Before arriving at Villa del Cine, I didn't expect to see much high-caliber work being done. But my expectations are totally exceeded as I watch the oil documentary and speak with Villa del Cine staff.

In the parking lot I catch up with Ramón, my driver, who had fallen asleep in the car. As we are heading back through Caracas, I spot a curious, brightly colored sign reading "Center of Socialist Education." The facility forms part of Chávez's ambitious educational programs, including the newly created Bolivarian University. The new university is the largest in the country and aims to educate the underclass and promote social activism. It plans to train physicians to staff the country's free health clinics. Social workers will also get their diplomas here, and later work in literacy centers. The government hopes that journalists who get their schooling at Bolivarian University will help to provide an alternative to the anti-Chávez media. Since there are no entrance requirements anyone may enroll, even former criminals imprisoned for murder or foreign tourists looking to learn more about politics. By 2009, Chávez hopes that enrollment will reach 1 million, with students scattered over more than 190 satellite classrooms around the country.[30] The school, which was founded as an effort to counteract what Chávez calls Venezuela's other "elitist" universities, is completely free of charge.[31] For the disadvantaged, the Bolivarian University provides a stipend of $75 a month. Only a high school diploma is required for admittance, and there is no entrance exam.

The Bolivarian University is inculcating in students much of the nationalism that has characterized the Chávez regime in recent years. In one recent class on "Latin American and Venezuelan political thought," students provided a presentation to their peers on Venezuelan national identity.[32] One student remarked that the national psyche was in "danger" because of the influence of such consumer products as Nike, McDonald's, and Sony PlayStation—"American thought."[33]

The campus itself is a potent physical symbol of the charged politics in Venezuela. As visitors approach, they are greeted by block letters taped above the university entrance spelling out "Long Live Socialism." Within the campus parking lot, vendors sell Che Guevara T-shirts.

Nearby is a mural that reads, "Against Imperialist Aggression."[34] The school is housed mostly in former buildings belonging to PdVSA, a company Chávez wrested control over after the crippling oil strike of 2002–03. "Offices once reserved for executives who favored free-market economics," notes *The Washington Post*, "are now decorated with posters of the socialist icon Che Guevara."[35]

Unlike many U.S. universities, most walls are bare on campus, an attempt by university administrators to protect the institution against what they call the "mercantilization" of education. Not surprisingly, there are no "For Sale" boards, nor any traces of corporate sponsorship.

In the campus library, students may find a generous collection of books written by authors aligned with Chávez's socialist outlook, with a couple of titles from opposition leaders sprinkled in. The American author with the most titles under his name is Michael Moore, not surprising given Chávez's interest in the noted U.S. filmmaker. On the wall of the checkout counter, patrons can spot a poster depicting a mouse with fur painted with the U.S. stars and stripes. The mouse is caught dead in a trap.[36]

While professors at the Bolivarian University acknowledge a political slant, they say that critical thinking is encouraged. Yamileth Uzcátegui González, coordinator of Political and Government Studies, remarked that the Bolivarian University focused on "collective success," while other universities promoted personal advancement and wealth.[37] Central University, located two blocks from the Bolivarian University, is a bastion of the Chávez opposition.

The Bolivarian University also flies in guest lecturers, such as Professor Mike Cole, a lecturer at Bishop Grosseteste University College in the United Kingdom. Cole, the author of *Introduction to World Systems— Global Imperial Capitalism or International Socialist Equality: Issues, and Implications for Education*, debated issues in his book with students on campus. The book was translated into Spanish and given to 3,000 university students.[38]

On campus, students talk politics in an outdoor café. Voicing admiration for the U.S. founding fathers as well as other prominent figures such as Martin Luther King Jr. and Malcolm X, they also expressed puzzlement at the American government's lack of regard for the poor.

But unlike the American poor, whom many on campus perceive as politically powerless, students at the Bolivarian University are determined to take a greater role in society. In their first year, even as they attend class, students get involved in working on community projects. The whole program, explains Wilpert during our interview, is centered on helping the poor and developing the means to overcome poverty.

Not surprisingly, students have become politicized on campus. Many crowd on buses to attend political rallies in downtown Caracas in favor of Chávez.[39] When the Chávez government opted not to renew a license held by the private TV station Radio Caracas Televisión (RCTV), which played a leading role in instigating the April 2002 coup against Chávez, thousands of students from the Central University and other campuses protested the move. Undeterred, students from the Bolivarian University went on TV to debate their more conservative peers about the RCTV affair.

In summing up his experiences at the Bolivarian University, Professor Cole remarked that the feeling of revolution had permeated Venezuelan society. "The Government and the people," he declared, "believe that the revolution is happening. It's not just something that could happen in the future."[40]

To what degree might Chávez be able to export his educational model abroad? In July 2006, during a visit to The Gambia, Chávez said he would like to create a "University of the South," which would seek to facilitate integrated development and provide training for doctors, petroleum engineers, and agricultural technicians.

Chávez has also established important cultural exchanges with other countries throughout the hemisphere. In early 2006, Venezuela and Cuba agreed to set up a cultural fund under ALBA. Under the initiative, both countries will create an ALBA publishing house designed to showcase the work of prominent intellectuals, as well as an ALBA record label.

Other South American countries have expressed interest in signing cultural agreements with Venezuela. Francisco Sesto is particularly interested in setting up a network of "ALBA houses" in Buenos Aires, Quito, and La Paz. More than mere bookstores, exhibit halls, or movie theaters, the ALBA houses would spur dialogue among intellectuals in the region and facilitate integration of peoples throughout the hemisphere.

During a recent gathering, the ministers of culture from Cuba, Venezuela, Ecuador, and Bolivia met to discuss their future plans. Abel

Prieto, the Cuban minister, described the countries of the region as locked in a struggle to preserve their cultural diversity against the forces of globalization.

"The defense of our own multiple identities and traditions is a priority," Prieto said. "It was a necessity," he added, "to confront racism as well as all forms of colonization and exclusion."[41]

CHAPTER 5

COCA AND NATIONALISM

Having toured Venezuela and observed some of the more ambitious cultural initiatives launched by the Chávez regime, I am curious to see whether other South American countries have followed the Venezuelan president's lead. I reason that Ecuador, a country which has just elected a Chávez protégé, might be interested in mimicking some of Venezuela's programs.

Like his Venezuelan counterpart, President Correa has sought to capitalize on cultural symbols for maximum political effect. During his inauguration, the Ecuadoran dressed in a white shirt emblazoned with indigenous motifs from the Jama Coaque culture of the Ecuadoran coast, which lasted from the fourth century B.C. to the arrival of the Spanish in the sixteenth century A.D.

Correa has said that working with indigenous peoples as a young man was a personally enriching experience.[1] In Zumbahua, he realized that the indigenous problem had to do with poverty, and "if you are Indian you have a 90 percent chance of being poor."[2]

Correa was picking up on longstanding racial injustice, common not only to Ecuador but also to the whole Andes mountain range. For centuries, writes *The Times* of London, Indians have had to suffer exclusion at the hands of white elites within a system of "virtual apartheid." Within the region, they have been economically exploited, culturally ignored, and denied a voice in political decision making. During the colonial period, Indians were subjected to a caste system and were organized into a forced labor system called the *mita*, a Quichua word meaning "one's turn." The mita was gradually replaced by debt peonage. Coercion kept the Indians at their looms within the *obrajes*; in fact debt peonage was rigorously enforced by imprisonment. Weavers worked from dawn to dusk and were sometimes even chained to the looms themselves. What's more, Indians were also compelled to pay tribute to the authorities. Though tribute was eliminated during the more liberal era of Bolívar, it was later restored in the late 1820s. During the independence era, Indians did not enjoy juridical rights or jurisdictions to Indian communities common in the colonial era. They were also denied the right to corporate landholdings and/or hereditary chiefdoms. In the nineteenth century, the Indians staged uprisings against cultural domination, loss of land, deplorable labor conditions, high tribute payments, and sexual abuse of women. White authorities brutally suppressed the revolts. In the late twentieth century, Ecuador's ruling classes still held Indians in low regard and the word Indian was a term of contempt.[3]

Local residents confirm that Correa has been open-minded, culturally sensitive toward the Indians, and has demonstrated an ability to work with indigenous peoples. Correa is still remembered in Zumbahua, where Indians crowd around him in colorful suits and salute him. To this day, they refer to him affectionately as "*ñuca huaqui*" or "our brother" in Quichua, the language of Ecuador's highland Indians.

During his stay in Zumbahua, Correa learned the indigenous language, in which he still converses. Correa says that he wants to overturn centuries of entrenched racial discrimination against Ecuador's Indians. During his inauguration speech, he invoked the memory of slain U.S. civil rights leader Martin Luther King, Jr. As he closed his address, he remarked in Quichua, "A new day has arrived. This government belongs to all men and women. Let us not be frightened. God bless our land!"[4]

Marc St.-Upéry is a long-time French expatriate living in Ecuador. A writer who knows South America well, he is an expert on politics and race relations. He's also worked with the Indians in Patchakutik, supposedly a multi-cultural party but implicitly the political arm of the Indians.[5]

In 1996, Patchakutik won 10 percent of the seats in Congress; by 2000 it had garnered five of the country's 22 governorships and 36 of its 225 municipal governments. Two years later, it entered the government of Lucio Gutiérrez, and indigenous leaders were entrusted with the ministries of Foreign Relations and Agriculture.[6]

St.-Upéry lives in a pleasant house full of antiques and oil paintings. His book-strewn study looks out on a garden with a *tomate de arbol* tree. In the early 1990s, while working as an editor in Paris, he met an Ecuadoran journalist, Mónica Almeida. The two married and moved to Ecuador.

Like Chávez, Correa has proven adept at appropriating historical symbols for political ends. Currently, St.-Upéry says, there is a possibility of furthering ties between Ecuador and Venezuela because of "this whole mythology of Manuela Sáenz."

A native of Quito, Sáenz was Simón Bolívar's lover during the wars of independence. To this day, Ecuador and Venezuela still have the same flag colors. Sáenz belonged to the aristocracy and met the Liberator after the famed Battle of Pichincha. She accompanied Bolívar on his military campaigns, carrying out intelligence work, raising funds for independence forces, and cheering on the troops. Sáenz also demonstrated great valor on the battlefield, seeing action during the Battle of Ayacucho. In recognition for her efforts, Sáenz was raised to the rank of *coronela* or coronel.

Sáenz's love letters to Bolívar are preserved in a Quito museum, along with some of her garments and an oil painting showing her in her childhood. To this day, she carries great psychological and symbolic significance for Ecuadorans. Recently the Ecuadoran president, who accepted Chávez's gift of a replica of Simón Bolívar's sword during his inauguration, elevated Sáenz to the rank of *generala* 151 years after her death.

Like the Venezuelan leader, Correa has placed great emphasis on multiculturalism. Once he was elected he appointed Mónica Chuji, a Quichua Indian woman from the Amazon, to be his communications secretary. He also appointed Antonio Preciado, an Afro-Ecuadoran poet, native of the port city of Esmeraldas and former Ecuadoran ambassador to UNESCO, to head the Ministry of Culture. It was the first time that a black had been named to a cabinet post in the country's history. Preciado's poetry deals with the daily life of blacks on Ecuador's coast. But one must take the government's cultural nationalism with a grain of salt. Though the minister of culture is an Afro-Ecuadoran, Correa hasn't shown much interest in advancing any kind of solid cultural agenda.

Bit by bit, however, historic racism has been challenged. In recent years Indians have been remarkably militant; as a result the constitution was amended in 1998 to declare Ecuador a "pluricultural" and "multi-ethnic" society. Under the law, indigenous juridical systems and procedures were recognized and agencies were created to implement policies affecting indigenous peoples, such as bilingual education.

Still, the Indians have a long road ahead if they wish to reverse centuries of discrimination: among the petty bourgeoisie in the countryside, which is white and *mestizo*, racism remains strong. Things in Quito are not much better. Manuel Castro, communications director for the CONAIE, remarks tersely that living in the capital is "complicated." He is a former mayor of the municipality of Suscal but had been in the city almost three years. He adds that Ecuador is very racist; moreover, migrants like himself are not well regarded in Quito and are "minimized."

Even as the Indians make strides, they view the United States with a certain ambivalence. While some Indian "ideologues" working with leftist parties employ anti-U.S. rhetoric, many indigenous peoples deal with the Ford Foundation and other U.S. NGO's. Indeed, Indians feel more comfortable dealing with Americans or Canadians working for NGOs than with local businessmen. Intellectual Indians pride themselves on "ethnic authenticity": they don't live in the countryside anymore, but they're the ones who dress most like Indians. In Otavalo, a town north of Quito favored by tourists, there's a bourgeoisie which strongly identifies as Indian. The Otavalo Indians, however, also travel to New Jersey and Brooklyn in search of work.

As a foreigner, St.-Upéry says he feels a little strange around indigenous people. "Within Patchakutik, how did they see you as a white man?" I ask. He explains that the Indians' relationship with foreigners is "perverse." "On the one hand, if you're from Europe they think you know everything. On the other hand, one senses a great distrust."

Unlike Ecuador, Bolivia's Indians are in a better position from which to extend a culturally nationalist agenda. The rise of Morales and the

Aymara represents a political and historic landmark. In the thirteenth century, the Inca state extended its influence over the Aymara. Three hundred years later, the conquistadors and Francisco Pizarro put an end to the Inca, but the Aymara, as well as other indigenous peoples in the region, were subjected to marginalization, discrimination, and mistreatment.

As in the American South under Jim Crow, the municipal government of La Paz practiced certain established forms of discrimination in the beginning of the twentieth century. Indians had to sit in the back on public buses and trams and had virtually no chance of attaining important government positions. Moreover, the Indians had little access to education.

Morales himself has said that the Aymara, who are dominant in the westernmost Andean region of Bolivia, were exploited during the Spanish colonial period as well as the country's period of independence. Nevertheless, the Aymara had tenaciously guarded their traditions over time, and the Spaniards were unable to extinguish the Indians' so-called "idolatrous practices."

To this day, the Indians continue to practice their own Andean religion, which is linked to the agricultural calendar. Offerings to Pachamama, the Mother Earth, begin in August to scare away malevolent spirits of the dry season and to encourage a good harvest. Offerings consist of llama fetuses, sweets of various colors, coca leaf, and other herbs. The *yatiri*, or indigenous priest, burns the offerings in a bonfire while muttering prayers to the *achachilas*, gods that inhabit the mountains.

Morales's efforts to reclaim the culture of his Aymara compatriots have been explicit and clear. For example, prior to the election of representatives to the Constituent Assembly, Morales's party, MAS, stated that it wanted to redefine Bolivian history as that of the "indigenous-popular resistance to discrimination and poverty."[7]

Indigenous peoples, according to a MAS document entitled "Refundar Bolivia" ("Refounding Bolivia"), should have the right to self determination and their own traditional medicine. Moreover, Morales's party seeks to make Bolivia into a "plural" democracy, based on the "diversity of people." The party wants to make Quechua and Aymara into official languages alongside Spanish. Lastly, MAS intends to afford the *wiphala*, a multi-colored flag belonging to the indigenous movement, the same recognition as Bolivia's current red, yellow, and green flag.[8]

With Aymara nationalism on the rise, what are the consequences for race relations in Bolivia? My cab ride from the La Paz airport into the center of town only makes me more curious about the nation's identity politics. The driver, a *mestizo*, complains that under Evo Morales there had been inverse racism against non-Indians in the country.

While I doubt the situation is as extreme as my cab driver claims, the Indians certainly have advanced politically in recent years and are demographically strong in the city of El Alto. A bustling indigenous metropolis located at 4,000 meters above sea level, I glimpse the city the next day from my hotel window.

According to the 2001 census, more than 80 percent of El Alto's 900,000 inhabitants define themselves as Indian. Long excluded from power, the Indians have crowded into the area and are enjoying a kind of cultural reawakening. The younger generation, the sons and daughters of urban Indians, or *cholos*, as they were referred to disparagingly, have now developed their own hip hop culture.

Heading to the Calle Linares, I spot Indian women hawking some unusual items including llama fetuses, love potions wrapped in racy packaging, and what looks to be a dried armadillo. I think about striking up a conversation with them but change my mind. Here in La Paz, I feel very self conscious of my whiteness and reluctant to raise political questions.

In my guidebook, I read about an ancient archaeological site called Tihuanaco (or Tiawanaku). Located some 70 kilometers from La Paz in the *altiplano*, Tihuanaco was the capital city of a splendid civilization which lasted from 1580 B.C. to 1172 A.D. The Tihuanaco culture covered western Bolivia, northeast Argentina, and the coastal area of Chile. Today the 12,000 foot high plateaus surrounding Tihuanaco are home to the Aymara Indians. The ruins have such potent symbolic meaning to indigenous people here that Morales himself has participated in sacred Andean rituals at the site.

Early one morning, I set out with my Indian driver, Victor, for the ancient site. As we speed out of the city, I spot the steep, snow-topped peaks of the Andes. After passing through El Alto, we reach an arid and sparsely populated plain. Victor, who routinely brings tourists to Tihuanaco, knows his way around and leaves me at the entrance gate to the site.

I enter an exhibition hall, where I find a calendar explaining the different historical phases of the Tihuanaco culture. The residents here, I read, successfully harnessed the resources of the area through irrigation and agriculture. It is hard to imagine that anyone was able to carve out a living for themselves from this barren and forbidding landscape. It is a testament to the hardiness and endurance of the indigenous people that Tihuanaco was able to survive as long as it did.

I notice some sculpture with feline characteristics, some pottery remains, a mummy, and early examples of metal technology. What really catches my eye, however, is a macabre assortment of human skulls. They display odd physical deformations and are slightly oblong in shape. I am surprised to read that the Indians inflicted the ghoulish abnormalities upon themselves in an effort to create a sense of social differentiation within the community.

Walking outside, I can make out the bare outlines of the archaeological ruins. Within the sprawling site I discern the remains of a courtyard and temples. Victor had warned me of the strong sun, and I am careful to walk with my jacket draped over my head.

Waiting in the parking lot, I notice a sign for some kind of upcoming indigenous festival. Driving up, Victor explains that Tihuanaco is extremely important culturally for the Aymara and instills a sense of pride. I'm interested in pursuing this subject further with Victor in the car, but I feel exhausted by the heat and sun at the ruin site.

We pass a sign reading "llama lasagna," and Victor starts to talk animatedly about how he used to eat llama and how the meat is low in cholesterol. After a certain point however I don't hear anything he's saying, as I'm deep in sleep in the front seat.

Tihuanaco has now taken on keen political significance for Morales. In fact, before being formally sworn in as president, Morales sat on a throne during a ritual ceremony at Tihuanaco as if he were the reincarnation of an Inca.

The event was highly choreographed. Morales first walked barefoot up the Akapana pyramid, where he put on a bright red tunic decorated with traditional Aymara patterns. Priests then blessed Morales and offered him a baton adorned with gold and silver, symbolizing his new leadership. It was the first time that the *mallkus*, or indigenous authorities, had handed over a staff of command and ceremonial vestments to an elected Bolivian president. After putting on sandals, he descended the pyramid to speak to the crowd in front of the Kalasaya temple. Morales thanked Mother Earth for his victory, praised the native leader Tupac Katari, who tried to capture La Paz from the Spanish in the eighteenth century, and promised to do away with the last vestiges of Bolivia's colonial past. "With the unity of the people, we're going to end the colonial state and the neo-liberal model," he said. It was an emotional moment for the Bolivian people.[9]

Morales spoke mostly in Spanish but also offered greetings in the Aymara language he grew up speaking as a boy. Spectators dressed in dark red ponchos and fedoras waved the *wiphala*.[10] They had walked many miles to listen to their new leader, passing through thatched adobe huts and grazing sheep.[11]

Following his speech, Morales accepted gifts from visiting Indian delegations from other countries. Then, a big party was held, complete with a cake made of quinoa, an ancient grain common to the Andes. The cake was large enough to feed 40,000 people and was decorated with Morales's face as well as the sacred Andean peak of Illimani. Musicians played Andean music while Indians performed dances that were prohibited during three centuries of Spanish rule.[12]

Now that Morales has true power, the Indians are in the position to reclaim key cultural symbols such as the coca leaf. For the Indians, Mama Coca is the daughter of Pachamama, and throughout the Andes Indians share coca in agricultural rituals.

The coca museum is located in back of the San Francisco church within a small dark courtyard. Inside, a man offers me a handful of coca leaves to chew and a peculiar-looking black square. He explains that I should chew the black material, made out of the ashes of banana leaf, which would react with the compounds in the coca leaf.

I stick the leaves in my mouth along with the entire black square. Very quickly, however, I develop an alarming, burning sensation on my tongue. "You're only supposed to bite off a small chunk of the tablet!" exclaims the man at the desk, laughing.

I run to the bathroom and spit out most of the banana leaf. Trying to forget the burning in my mouth, I proceed to take in the exhibit which focuses on coca leaf's cultural, historical, religious, and medical significance. During the colonial period, the show explains, Indians chewed coca leaf in an effort to withstand the horrible working conditions within Bolivian mines.

Coca chewers, notes one expert, "typically begin by blowing on three carefully selected leaves held between four fingers, and follow a protocol of prayers and invitations as elaborate as a Japanese tea ceremony." During the colonial period, coca was revered as a great symbol of indigenous pride. During the uprising of Tupac Katari in 1781, rebels crammed coca leaves into the mouths of Spanish speakers and forced them to chew, thereby "humiliating those who saw in coca a symbol of native people's inferiority." To this day, Katari is revered. The manifesto of the pro-indigenous Katarista movement proclaims, "*Tupac Katari vive y vuelve, carajo!*" ("Tupac Katari is alive and returning, dammit!").[13]

Morales employs coca as a potent political symbol. When speaking before adoring crowds, he drapes a garland of coca leaves around his neck and wears a straw hat layered with more coca. Morales has even appointed Felipe Cáceres, a coca growers' union leader, as his point man in halting drug trafficking. Those types of moves play well at home, where the *cocalero* movement preaches Katarista ethnic pride as well as anti-globalization. On the floor of congress, representatives of the *cocaleros* frequently deliver speeches in native languages while chewing coca.

Currently under the Morales administration, coca in its natural state is sold through markets established and controlled by the government. The regulation forms part of a government plan to industrialize and export coca to other countries such as Argentina. Under the initiative, legally established companies, cooperatives, or organizations may opt to acquire coca, according to the quantity needed for consumption, from legal markets without any interference from retailers.

Though Bolivian officials claim not to possess information about the relative importance of coca in the Bolivian economy, clearly the leaf plays a vital role for many. The Adepcoca market in La Paz is the largest coca market in the country. A constant stream of poor Indians arrives here, day and night, seven days a week, to weigh and sell coca. Women dressed in traditional Aymara clothing haul 23-kilo *taquis*, or sacks of coca leaves, to waiting vans. All the buyers are registered and the coca they buy is supposed to be used for chewing or tea.[14] Morales recently inaugurated the first coca industrialization plant in the town of Chulumani. The plant will produce and package coca and *trimate* (herbal tea made out of anise, chamomile, and coca leaves). Perhaps not surprisingly, the project is being helped by Venezuela, which has donated $125,000 under the People's Trade Agreement signed by Cuba, Venezuela, and Bolivia.[15]

Bolivian cultural pride does not go over nearly as well in Washington. It's no secret that U.S. officials have been dismayed by Morales's policy which seeks to increase the amount of coca that can be legally grown and asks farmers to voluntarily tear up their plantings above half an acre. The policy, which promises to crack down on cocaine, abandons previous efforts of government-forced eradication of coca plants. Recently, the U.S. Office of National Drug Control Policy predicted that under Morales's "zero cocaine, not zero coca" policy, coca production would expand.[16] Indeed, the State Department, while openly praising Colombia and other countries for their performance in the drug war, has claimed that Bolivia has been backsliding in the counter-narcotics effort.[17] Nevertheless, the United States agreed to send $34 million in anti-narcotics aid to Bolivia in 2007. Senate Majority Leader Harry Reid recently met with Morales along with five other United States senators in La Paz. Attempting to smooth over strained U.S.-Bolivian relations, he remarked that Morales had eradicated more than 12,000 acres of coca in 2006 and was "moving forward."[18]

Martín Condori Flores is a Quechua Indian who has no liking for U.S. drives to eliminate coca. He works for an indigenous organization called CONAMAQ (or *Consejo Nacional de Markas y Ayllus*), which has demanded the Indians' right to their own, original native government and territorial demarcation of lands. Flores wears a red poncho and speaks with his mouth full of coca leaves. As he chews, he talks about how the leaf is sacred to the Indians and serves medicinal purposes. It is important, he says, for the Indians to maintain their own health centers where they can practice ancestral medicine and incorporate coca leaf.[19]

Coca nationalism has become so pronounced in Bolivia that recently the country's constitutional assembly passed a resolution declaring that Coca-Cola should drop the name of Bolivia's sacred leaf from its trademark soda. The move was prompted by a commission of coca industry representatives who lobbied the government. The group also passed a resolution calling for coca leaf to be included in Bolivia's coat of arms, which currently depicts branches of olive and laurel, plants that are not native to the Andean region.

Though the commission is not formally affiliated with the Morales government, its activities are in keeping with the president's effort to rehabilitate the image of the coca leaf. The resolution it passed states that coca is part of Bolivia's "cultural heritage," and demands that Coca-Cola and other international companies refrain from using the name of the sacred leaf in their products. Coca-Cola dropped cocaine from its ingredients around 1900, although the company's secret formula still calls for a cocaine-free coca extract manufactured by a New Jersey-based chemical company.

David Choquehuanca, Bolivia's foreign minister, claims that coca leaf is so nutritious that it should be included on school breakfast menus. "Coca has more calcium than milk," he told the Bolivian newspaper *La Razón*. An eight ounce glass of milk contains 300 milligrams of calcium. According to a 1975 study conducted by a group of Harvard professors, a coca leaf weighing 3.5 ounces contains 18.9 calories of protein, 45.8 milligrams of iron, 1540 milligrams of calcium and vitamins A, B1, B2, E and C, which is more than most nuts.[20]

With government officials like Choquhuanca now leading the charge, how do the non-Indians perceive the rise of Morales? Xavier Albó is an anthropologist at the Center for Research and Promotion of the Peasantry, located just a couple blocks from my hotel on the Calle Sanjines. A Jesuit priest with a scraggly beard, he was born in Spain but came to Bolivia more than fifty years ago. Since the 1970s, he'd spent a lot of time in the Quechua region near Cochabamba, and later the Aymara areas. In the course of his work he'd learned both indigenous languages.

"I don't know your cab driver," he says, when I describe the opinionated *mestizo* driver who picked me up at the airport. "But it's possible he feels threatened by recent political developments." Albó says that while many non-Indians are not concerned by the rise of the Aymara, others feel "under siege."[21] Other experts agree that privileged sectors of society now feel like the tables are being turned upon them. The middle class has been excluded from the positions it occupied before and has seen a decline in its social standing.[22]

One radical indigenous figure who makes the elite cringe is Felipe Quispe, who was active in the indigenous struggle in Achacachi, a town 110 kilometers south of La Paz. Magdalena Cajías is a historian at the Upper University of San Andrés and producer of the 2002 documentary film, *Achacachi, the Aymara Insurgency.*[23] In conjunction with her film, Cajías spent two years gathering firsthand testimonials from *campesinos* linked to Quispe. In 2000, Quispe was Cajías's student in the history department. Cajías and her colleagues conducted visits and interviews with Quispe's followers and were able to sit in on key meetings on the course of the *campesino* and indigenous movement.

I ask Cajías how she perceived Quispe at the time.

"He was intelligent and skilled at cultivating a certain discourse at a precise moment. His ideology was based on recuperating ethnic and cultural elements within the larger social struggle. Quispe's struggle wasn't always so abstract: he and his followers would initiate a blockade so as not to pay for water service, or to reclaim lands. On the other hand, we noticed that no one could go to meetings without putting on a poncho."

Though Morales's rhetoric originally centered on anti-imperialism and coca, he later incorporated Quispe's emphasis on ethnicity. Cajías informs me that it's only in the last five years that the Bolivian president has been wearing a poncho, something he never used to do. According to Waskar Ari Chachaki, an Aymara historian, sociologist, and activist, the Aymara dream of creating a grand Aymara republic, governed by its own laws, language, and culture.[24]

Despite such pronouncements, however, it's unlikely that the Indians will seek to institute a radical cultural agenda. Indeed, Indians have frequently sought to integrate themselves into the Bolivian state and white or *mestizo* society. For example, they have linked up with populist parties, principally the Revolutionary Nationalist Movement (known in Spanish under the acronym MNR). Cajías downplays the idea of an Aymara state, remarking that Aymara nationalism is "more confrontational in its rhetoric than in actual practice." In fact, the idea of forming a separate Aymara nation does not enjoy much support, which is why Quispe no longer has much of a following. Aymara nationalism, Cajías tells me, "is nothing like Serb nationalism." The most the Aymaras might press for is a certain amount of autonomy—for example, the right to elect their own municipal authorities.

Nevertheless, racism persists, and while indigenous activists maintain that it will decrease now that Morales is in power, the old notions are not likely to die out completely. Flores remarks to me that because of racism it is "a little difficult" for a Quechua Indian to live in La Paz. "Colonialism had deep seated roots here," he says.

Morales has declared that one of the top priorities of his adminis-
tration will be to eliminate racism. The opposition in turn has accused
Morales of seeking to aggravate racial tensions in Bolivia. Because they
are in the government now, the Indians feel they have renewed clout.
Meanwhile, government employees are required to speak Aymara in the
Ministry of Foreign Affairs. Indeed, Morales has laid down the law, an-
nouncing that all officials and civil servants would have to learn
Quechua, Aymara, or Guaraní (a major language of Bolivia's Amazon
Indians), within two years.

Morales's speeches are full of phrases from Aymara and Quechua,
and the Bolivian leader refuses to wear a suit and tie at official func-
tions, opting for a casual brown jacket decorated with indigenous motifs. Even the playing of the national anthem has undergone a sea
change. At the opening of a constituent assembly not long ago, thousands waited while the choir sang the anthem in Spanish, Aymara,
Quechua, and Guaraní.[25] What's more, the Indians proudly hang the
wiphala on the streets of La Paz.

Meanwhile, music has become an important cultural marker. In El
Alto, hip hop songs written by Indian youth critique capitalism while
emphasizing racial pride and radical social change. The music is a fu-
sion of rap and traditional Andean music, and is sung in both Spanish
and Aymara. Today, the principal center of the Bolivian hip hop movement is Radio Wayna Tambo, which plays music of the younger generation. Cajías tells me that radio has been a great vehicle for cultural
awakening: it has become very common, she explains, to hear Aymara
spoken on the airwaves. Musicians, who acknowledge the influence of
gangsta rap and fallen idols such as Tupac Shakur, say they don't merely
want to imitate *cumbia* and tired old themes. Rather than simply sing
about lost love, today's Indian hip hop musicians seek to awaken indigenous consciousness.

Even as they appropriate hip hop, the Indians also seek important
changes in higher education. Though Indian faculty members were
regarded as backward when they first pressed for programs emphasizing ethnic identity, many scholars now conduct research on indigenous culture.

One example is the Andean Oral History Workshop, which draws
attention to the history and culture of Bolivia's indigenous peoples. The
research facility has amassed a collection of video and audio recordings

and a text archive. Though the program is lodged in a modest attached house, it has made a political impact by helping Indians to reconstitute the traditional *ayllu* structure of rural Andean communities, characterized by cooperative local governance under traditional leaders.

One of Cajías's colleagues at San Andrés, Silvia Rivera Cusicanqui, a sociology professor and a founding member of the workshop, is a passionate supporter of traditional Andean culture, including the chewing of the coca leaf. By interviewing elders in rural areas and consulting archives, she and her co-workers have documented the largely ignored history of Indian rebellions in the first half of the twentieth century. In the mid-1980s, the workshop produced a 90-part dramatization of the life of the Indian rebel leader Santos Marka T'ula. The program was broadcast on the radio in Aymara.[26]

According to the *Chronicle of Higher Education*, for many years education in Bolivian universities was the preserve of *mestizos* and whites. That, however, has changed under the Morales regime. The president, who himself never finished high school, has called for greater access to higher education. Experts now estimate that almost half of the students enrolled in Bolivia's 11 public universities are of indigenous descent. In the large cities where Indians live, such as La Paz and Cochabamba, that percentage rises to two thirds.

At San Pablo Catholic University of Bolivia, 2000 students are enrolled, 90 percent of them indigenous. Students study veterinary medicine, agricultural sciences, and nursing. In 2005, a student on one of the university's rural campuses elected to write and defend his undergraduate thesis, dealing with llama nutrition, in Aymara.

The *Chronicle of Higher Education* reports that "the event was historic, and the public defense, near the shores of Lake Titicaca, was attended by journalists and representatives of foreign embassies. The student was dressed in a traditional Andean Indian costume, including a woolen poncho and a cap with earflaps. The committee of professors questioning the student chewed coca leaves. There was simultaneous translation in Spanish."

Morales would like to go further. Officials are considering a number of ideas to expand access, including scholarships for indigenous students and even creating an "indigenous university."

In his quest to level the playing field for Bolivia's Indians and reduce the nation's 16 percent illiteracy rate, Morales has enlisted the help of

Cuba. The island nation has sent experts to help in a literacy campaign in cooperation with schools of education at public universities. The government recently announced that several indigenous languages would be added to the campaign. Chávez has also lent a hand by inviting 5,000 Bolivian high school graduates to study in Venezuela for free.

According to reports, indigenous students at university have become emboldened by the new political climate in the country. Officials report that since Morales was elected, more students have been signing up to take courses in Aymara and Quechua. Bernardino Huallpa Chura, head of the rural-students' center at San Andrés, remarked that overt racism is hardly an issue anymore: "We've overcome most of that problem by now."[27]

"When you speak with the Indians nowadays, do you notice any psychological shift?" I ask Cajías.

"Yes. I have noticed a change in my students in the history department, who have *campesino* origins. Ten years ago, it was difficult to get them to even say their last name. Finally they would say their name, but very slowly."

A case in point is Waskar T. Ari, a prominent Aymara scholar. When Ari was wondering whether to enroll in a university in the mid-1980s, his uncle advised him that it would be a waste of time to pursue his academic career with an Indian name. At the time, the first generation of indigenous scholars was just starting to acquire faculty jobs, and some professors reported facing subtle discrimination, particularly if they emphasized their ethnic origins. "If you become a lawyer, no one will take your advice," Ari's uncle told him.

Ultimately Ari did enroll at San Andrés, but under an assumed name: Juan Arias. "But now it's different," Cajías remarks. "People say, 'I am from such and such a town in the *altiplano*, and I am an Indian!'"

Other experts agree that the Indians have come into their own culturally. Victor Hugo Cárdenas is a member of the Tupac Katari Revolutionary Liberation Movement, and served as vice president under the Gonzalo Sánchez de Lozada government in the 1990s. A charismatic if somewhat slick-mannered Aymara dressed in a striped sports jacket, Cárdenas grew up in humble circumstances. His father was the only person to attend school in his region and later became a rural teacher. It was he who taught the young Cárdenas how to read and write.

With his father as a positive role model, Cárdenas went on to study at university in the early 1970s. As a student, he helped to create the Katarista movement, which emphasized indigenous class as well as ethnic identity. In 1985, he and other Quechuas and Aymaras were elected to Congress. Shortly thereafter he launched a presidential bid but only captured 3 percent of the vote. Once he joined a coalition with Bolivia's oldest party, however, he found success, becoming vice president in 1997. Cárdenas denies that the Indians feel any cultural hostility towards U.S.-driven globalization, though he personally had noticed a seismic psychological shift among Bolivia's indigenous peoples. "There's a great awakening and sense of pride here," he says. "One can sense it, it's plain to see."[28]

At times, however, the new cultural nationalism has provoked aggressive reactions. Choquehanca, an Aymara Indian, remarked that in the affluent *zona sur* neighborhood of La Paz people hated Morales and even wanted to spit at him.[29] Choquehuanca, who grew up on the shores of Lake Titicaca, didn't learn to speak Spanish until he was 7 years old. Educated in rural schools, he later won a scholarship to study in Cuba. Something of a cultural extremist, he has said that he doesn't turn to Western books for advice, and indeed boasts of not having read any books for years because he doesn't wish to cloud his mind with European concepts. Choquehuanca prefers the knowledge of Aymara elders. "When I say we have to read the wrinkles in our grandfathers' brows, it's to recover the wisdom that our grandfathers still have," he says.[30]

Choquehuanca has emerged as the principal spokesperson for the government's indigenous vision, speaking on everything from the cosmic bent of the Morales government to the supernatural qualities of coca.[31] According to the *Wall Street Journal*, Choquehuanca is close to Morales and has exerted a profound influence on the president. In 2006, the two attended a gathering of a Quichua Indian chief in Quito, where Morales vowed to reject Western concepts imported "in English," and to recover the wisdom of the elders.[32]

What's more, Morales tapped Félix Patzi, an Aymara, to be his minister of education. A young Aymara intellectual, Patzi has argued that the new government should use procreation to reverse the pernicious effects of colonization. Family planning, he claimed, was a failed conspiracy launched by the elite to keep the Indian population down. Indigenous women needed to understand this fundamental principle, he argued, and have five to eight children each. Only then would the white minority become inconsequential.[33]

Patzi wants to eliminate the "colonizing" national educational system and inject it with more cultural diversity. The Morales regime seeks to install Bolivian languages alongside Spanish in the country's school system, requiring all teachers to learn either Aymara, Quechua, or Guaraní. He has said that it was an "embarrassment" that whites and *mestizos* had little familiarity with indigenous languages.[34]

Some believe that the aggressive cultural nationalism espoused by members of the Morales regime will destabilize society. Cárdenas claims that when he was initially elected vice president, whites reacted positively. The Katarista movement, he says, was always inclusive and never adopted "ethnically driven rhetoric like Morales." The new Bolivian President, Cárdenas says, is "very confrontational," and relied on rhetoric and symbolism designed to appeal to the Aymaras who live in the *altiplano*. He fears that under the current administration racial polarization will increase. Since Bolivia returned to democratic rule in the 1980s, the country "had never been so divided."

On campus, stormy new racial politics had affected Cajías personally. "My father was very, very dark and my mother was rather white." She says. "If people don't know me, they say, 'She's a white professor' in a disparaging manner."

Compared to the Aymara in Bolivia, Brazilians are not nearly as culturally nationalist. Though the hawkish foreign policy of the Bush administration has done a lot to tarnish the international standing of the United States, fundamentally Brazilians are not very anti-American. Indeed, if Bush were to suddenly vanish from the scene, Brazilians might look differently on the United States. In particular, a president like Hillary Clinton or Barack Obama might elicit a lot of curiosity in Brazil.

Culturally, American influence is quite strong in Brazil, though the South American country has redefined U.S. culture on its own terms, for example, by creating *bossa nova* and its own forms of jazz. Meanwhile, Brazilian and American festivals exist side by side. In Brazil, children are quite fond of Saci, a one-legged black African Brazilian boy who smokes a pipe. The pagan Saci, who comes from a childhood fairy-tale, has the power to give one what one wishes. But now, though people still hold Saci parties, they also celebrate Halloween.

Daniel Buarque is an international reporter for O Globo Online, and formerly worked at Brazil's largest paper, *Folha São Paulo*. While cutting his teeth at the paper, he was employed at *Mais, Folha de São Paulo's* cultural supplement (similar to the *Times Literary Supplement*). According to him, the anti-globalization and anti-Bush forces are very vocal in Brazil, but there is also a "silent majority" that accepts global-ization. In Brazil, there is little opposition to the U.S.-led consumer lifestyle and fast food. Meanwhile, though Brazil has a growing film in-dustry, the latter models itself after Hollywood. In fact, some Brazilian directors, such as Fernando Mereilles (*The Constant Gardener*), have gone on to have success there.[35]

Because of Brazil's close cultural ties to the United States, Chávez's cultural nationalism hasn't resonated very well in Brazil. Though the Venezuelan leader was well received at the World Social Forum, a meet-ing of anti-globalization forces featuring pacifists, environmentalists, libertarians, trade unionists, and anti-establishment militants held in the Brazilian city of Porto Alegre, observers claim that he doesn't enjoy broad support in the country.[36]

"I think all the Chavistas in Brazil were present at that sole event," Buarque says skeptically. When Bush recently visited Brazil, there were protests all over the country. By contrast, when Chávez visited there were no protests because "people who don't like him don't take him seriously."

What's more, Chávez's constant references to Bolívar have fallen on deaf ears in Brazil, where the Great Liberator is not an important icon. Currently Chávez is building an oil refinery near Recife in the munici-pality of Abreu e Lima, an area that carries key symbolic importance for the Venezuelan president: during the wars for independence in South America, Abreu e Lima, a general, fought alongside Bolívar during the Liberator's military campaigns. "I grew up in an area located forty min-utes from Abreu e Lima," Buarque says. "No one in the town knows who Bolívar was."

On the other hand, though Brazilians are not too allied to Chávez's cultural project and hardly reject U.S. pop culture, Lula has proven quite adept at cultivating newly reconfigured cultural symbols. Indeed, to truly understand Lula's rise on the national stage one has to consider not just politics but culture. Lula, originally a poor northeastern migrant, understands the poor on an intimate psychological level. In spite of the fact that Lula has in many ways abandoned his radical labor politics as president, the masses regard Lula as one of their own. Like Chávez, who originally hails from the Venezuelan *llano* and speaks with a provincial accent, Lula stresses his own accent. Perhaps this is a conscious effort to confront elite culture. Within Brazil, says Paulo Fontes, visiting professor at the Program in Latin American Studies at Princeton University, many are strongly prejudiced against northeasterners, though few will openly admit it.

"The perception of northeasterners in São Paulo," Fontes says, "is similar to the English perception of the Irish. They are viewed as hard working but kind of backward."

Not only does Lula stress his provincial accent; he also emphasizes informal behavior. For example, the president holds soccer games in the gardens of government installations. The people, Fontes explains, don't feel as if Lula is pretending to be one of them. Meanwhile, the opposition always comes off as posh and upper class.[37]

Meanwhile, Lula has promoted disenfranchised people to his cabinet. For example, he appointed Marina Silva, a black woman who didn't learn to read or write until she was 16, as the head the Ministry of Environmental Protection. The president also appreciates *candomblé*, an Afro-Catholic voodoo-like religion. Indeed, he has attended *candomblé* voodoo rites, in the process helping to legitimize marginalized Afro-Brazilian culture. For Lula, it's a smart political move: on the outskirts of large cities, the poor have developed a sense of pride and a whole culture has sprung up in opposition to rich neighborhoods. Like Bolivia, the poor have adopted hip hop culture as well as *capoeira*, a martial art practiced by Afro-Brazilians.

In Brazil, blacks make up nearly half the population but are disproportionately represented among the poor, lagging behind whites in income, education, and living standards. It wasn't until recently that Brazilian authorities even acknowledged the existence of racism in their country. To his credit, Lula has created a state secretariat to promote racial equality and has made the study of Afro-Brazilian history compulsory in the public schools.[38] More controversially, Brazil has been experimenting with quotas that reserve a sizable number of places at some public universities for those students who are black or poor.

Meanwhile, in an effort to reclaim popular culture, Lula has made Afro-Brazilian musician Gilberto Gil as his minister of culture. Gil first attained notoriety as one of the founders of a pop movement called *tropicalismo*. The genre, which includes other well known musicians such as Caetano Veloso, sought to "cannibalize" foreign cultural ideas while remaining true to distinctively Brazilian culture. *Tropicalismo* became a link between *bossa nova* and international pop groups such as The Beatles and Rolling Stones.

Gil has never been content to merely perform his role as a major Brazilian entertainer. In 1969, for example, he was arrested and imprisoned for his opposition to the country's military dictatorship. *Tropicalismo*, he remarked in an interview, sprang from a "new left allied with existentialism and Sartre, with a belief in counterculture."[39]

After his release from jail he introduced reggae into Brazilian music, and later started to sport short dreadlocks. An avid fan of Bob Marley, Gil got interested in black politics through the legendary reggae musician. Later in 1976, Gil traveled to Africa where he met Stevie Wonder in the Lagos house of politically active pop star Fela Kuti. The visit made a big psychological imprint on Gil, and the Brazilian musician started to reflect on his own Afro-Brazilian heritage. "I was like a tree being replanted and able to flourish," he has said.

Gil began to record songs using Yoruba words and incorporating African high-life and juju music. He even became a priest of Xango, one of the gods worshipped in *candomblé*.

Gil explains that up until the past few decades, black cultural forms such as *candomblé* and *capoeira* were banned.[40] But the rise of Lula on the national stage will usher in cultural renewal. The president, he declares, "personifies this national spirit of solidarity, a people committed to pluralism, a mixture of races and customs, with a pacifist outlook on the world."

As minister of culture, Gil hopes to promote policies that will benefit the underprivileged. "Brazil's image abroad," he says, "is associated with popular culture: samba, the way we play football. But what we need to do is break the prejudice that popular culture is a lesser product. Blacks and Afro-Indians are the soul of the country. Brazil needs to come to terms with itself, different from the Brazilian elite, who want to be a copy of Europe or the United States."[41]

In an interview with the *Daily Telegraph*, Gil remarked that it was a good time for Brazilian culture, like the optimistic time before the military dictatorship in the early 1960s.

"There's a new energy in Brazil," he says. "You'll see."[42]

CHAPTER SIX

RED IS THE COLOR
OF REVOLUTION

Chávez routinely uses the word "revolution" to characterize his movement. But to what extent has his administration undertaken truly revolutionary programs? How responsive has the government been to the
public and social demands? Chávez has spoken about increasing political access for poor people through "participatory democracy" in contrast to the corrupt electoral democracy that used to prevail in the
country. Chávez arrived on the stage at a particularly delicate time in
Venezuelan politics. The two-party system had largely been discredited,
corruption was rampant, and a drop in world oil prices was causing
tremendous economic hardship.

One of Chávez's first acts as president was to call for a Constituent
Assembly to draft a new constitution that would transform the stagnant,
exclusionary character of Venezuelan society. His idea was to propose a
democracy based on participation, in which Venezuelans' rights were
defined not just in purely political terms but also encompassing social
justice and equality.[1] The preamble of the 1999 Constitution, in fact,
provides for a new "participatory democracy" based not only on elected
representatives but also votes by referendum and popular mobilization.
Social organizations were encouraged to draft their own proposals for
consideration by the new Constituent Assembly. Indeed, more than 50
percent of the 624 proposals brought to the table by civil society during

the drafting of the new constitution were eventually included in the document. The constitution's coverage of a broad range of issues reflects this participation: there are no less than 111 articles spelling out civil rights that address such issues as culture and education, indigenous rights, adequate housing, land distribution, worker safety, and priority of the environment.[2]

In theory, the new Constitution was a welcome development in Venezuelan politics. But what would it mean in practice? The Chavistas hoped that their electoral mandate would allow them to retool the state and its relationship to the rest of society. Since the passage of the constitution, pro-Chávez candidates have swept one electoral contest after another, including 20 out of 22 state governor positions in October 2004 and all 167 seats in the National Assembly in December 2005.

In the latter election, most opposition candidates withdrew before the elections after claiming voter secrecy concerns. The opposition charged that the country's electoral council was comprised of Chávez supporters, and that touch screen voting machines and a fingerprint identification system used at the polls would lead to breeches in voter confidentiality, even after the government agreed not to use the fingerprinting system. Prior to the election, the opposition went to the Organization of American States (OAS) with a long list of demands before it would participate in the election. When the electoral council agreed to its demands, the opposition pulled out anyway, though OAS observers had declared that "important advances" had been instituted to ensure clean elections. Even the *New York Times*, which originally supported the April 2002 coup, suggested that the opposition may have pulled out because polls showed that Chávez would have trounced them in the election.

Today, with the Chavistas in power, an interesting exhibit inside the National Assembly commemorates the death of Fabricio Ojeda, a member of parliament who founded a communist insurgent group called the FALN during the 1960s. Clearly, it's become symbolically important for the Chavistas to establish their ties to prior revolutionary movements.

All of the revolutionary symbolism, however, will be a mere smokescreen if the Chavistas fail to come through for a big group in society—namely, women. Once Chávez called for a new constitution, some women activists vowed to hold the new National Assembly to account. One organizer, Nora Castañeda, was particularly determined to carry out Chávez's authentic vision of participatory democracy.

Castañeda came up the hard way. Her mother, a domestic worker, raised six children without support from a male partner, holding down three jobs to feed her family of six children. At one point, she was taken to Caracas by Nora's father, a politically well connected landowner and lawyer. There, she was put to work in the house of a relative, where she was expected to cook and clean to earn her keep. Sadly, many women in Venezuela have had similar experiences. Castañeda's mother told her, "I don't have any money to leave you, but my inheritance to you is to provide you with an education." Nora was fortunate: she became an instructor at the Central University and grew determined to provide other women with the same assistance that her mother had given her.

Once Chávez came to power, Castañeda became a prominent advocate for the implementation of Article 88 of the new Constitution, which officially recognizes the unwaged work of housewives and provides a small wage for home duties.[3] Castañeda was joined in her lobbying efforts by thousands of other women including feminists, former guerrillas, housewives, and professionals. Historically, Venezuelan women have faced severe discrimination. Up until the early 1980s, for example, married and cohabiting women were relegated to inferior status by penal, civil, and labor laws. Women were not allowed to own property or sign official documents without spousal approval.

Chávez's arrival, however, ushered in big changes. Currently, political parties are legally obligated to field 50 percent women candidates. Venezuela is one of the few nations in the hemisphere to acknowledge that violence and discrimination against women forms an obstacle to the development of democracy. According to the *New York Daily News*, Venezuelan women's aspirations received strong legal backing in Chávez's Constitution of 1999. "Because of its language," writes the paper, "many call it the nonsexist Magna Carta."[4] With the approval of Chávez's Constitution, one of the most advanced in the world, women achieved an unprecedented social and political victory. The document addresses discrimination, sexual harassment, and domestic violence. It guarantees full equality between men and women in the workforce and is the only constitution in

Latin America to recognize housework as an economically productive activity.

According to an article on the Web site venezuelanalysis.com, "By allotting economic privileges to a job that was previously unrecognized as having an economic value, Venezuela is breaking down societal norms and capitalist ideology which exclusively associate value with producing revenue." Perhaps even more profound, Chávez's Constitution recognizes the sexual and reproductive rights of women and obliges the state to provide accurate information concerning family planning. Meanwhile, Chávez himself peppers his speeches with discussions of women and their problems. When he addresses the nation, he says, "*Venezolanos y Venezolanas*" ("Venezuelan men and women").

Within this mood of social and political ferment, Castañeda petitioned the National Assembly to create a new bank that would provide small loans to women.[5] In contrast to the earlier administrations that bestowed only a symbolic ministry to women, Chávez has recognized the severity and complexity of women's social and economic plight. In March 2001 he approved Castañeda's proposals and appointed her president of the new bank.[6] The Women's Bank, or Banmujer, the only state-owned women's bank in the world, is one example of Chávez's determination to eradicate poverty and create meaningful opportunities for all.

At one point, I pay a visit to the bank. All the employees are women. Housed along pollution-clogged Urdaneta Avenue in downtown Caracas, the bank has extended credit to working-class women so that they might form small businesses. The vast majority of those who receive the loans are women; men get support only if they are working in women-run business ventures.

The process all starts at the local level, where poor women hold meetings, determine their needs, and then contact Banmujer. The bank in turn is required to fund projects in the poorest areas and to let the community know what it has to offer. It employs a network of female promoters who fan out "Avon Lady-style" across the country, even to remote regions like the Amazon, to offer financial assistance in the form of loans. The promoters then inform the women that the Women's Bank, unlike a traditional institution, operates under the principle of "popular economy," which is meant to benefit everyone. The promoter proceeds to outline the requirements the women must meet in order to receive bank assistance. One important condition is that the women must form a group of between five and ten people and decide what kind of business they will create. Later, the bank provides technical support to local women, not based on what the bank official wants to teach but rather what the community wants to know.

Since it got under way in 2001, Banmujer has issued tens of thousands of credits for a number of small enterprises, ranging from cleaning co-ops and fashion design businesses to beauty salons and candy manufacturing plants.[7] Banmujer funds some economically unorthodox but socially progressive projects. A promotional calendar handed out by the staff features glossy pictures of women harvesting coffee. According to the government, Banmujer is organizing a pilot project called Plan Café, an "agro-ecological" effort to farm organic coffee.[8] The bank has even sponsored recycling workshops for women employed in sanitation cooperatives.

But Banmujer, like PdVSA, might be conceived of as a social instrument as well as a financial institution. In line with the goals of the 1999 Constitution, the bank's promoters provide information to their clients about sexual and reproductive health, in addition to business and legal advice, while they're speaking to clients about the bank. What's more, Banmujer works in cooperation with the Ministry of Health and the Barrio Adentro program of Cuban doctors. Together, the three work to guarantee compliance with articles 75–77 of the Constitution, dealing with sexual and reproductive rights. They seek to ensure that women have access to free medical services, appointments, and contraceptives throughout Venezuela.[9]

Meanwhile, Banmujer promotional literature touts the bank's support for programs designed to combat domestic violence against women.[10] Castañeda herself has remarked that she wants the Women's Bank to "transcend economics." She seeks to empower women to exercise their rights and duties as citizens in accordance with social justice as enshrined in the 1999 Constitution. Indeed, some of the tasks carried out by the bank seek to encourage personal growth and the cultivation of a political consciousness. For example, Banmujer provides workshops and training on gender perspective and how to improve women's self esteem.

Another example of a feminist initiative is in Catia, a district located on the outskirts of Caracas. The space had formerly been a pumping station belonging to PdVSA. There, working-class women organized themselves into a cooperative within a so-called "Endogenous Center of Development." The women work busily on sewing machines, producing red T-shirts. Peering closer, I glimpse an image on the shirts: a profile of the Communist revolutionary and arch nemesis of the United States, Che Guevara.

The Catia complex houses a Módulo de Mercados de Alimentos, also known as Mercal. Since their creation in 2003, the nationwide Mercals have sold staples such as coffee, powdered milk, pasta, rice, and beans to the people. Within the market, local residents can buy discounted items including cooking oil, beans, ice cream, and shampoo. A young woman who is showing us around the facility remarks proudly that the public can save up to 50 percent on discounted high-quality items.

I am taken aback at the scale of the Catia complex. In addition to the Mercal, we also visit a textile cooperative. The facility had two male workers but otherwise was staffed solely by women. In Venezuela, explains our eager young leader, poverty affects women hardest because they have to shoulder the responsibility of raising children when men abandon the family. On the other hand, our guide continues, the women working in the cooperative had undergone a profound psychological shift. Before, they had always been ordered around but now they had all become part owners in the cooperative and took great pride in the Che Guevara T-shirts they produced at the plant.

All of these efforts are complemented by a new state entity, the National Institute for Women, or INAMUJER, which seeks to educate women to defend their political rights. The Institute, led by a former guerilla fighter named María León, seeks to promote a democratic society, not just politically, but also socially and culturally. In order to achieve this, the Institute organizes educational campaigns on sexual and reproductive rights and prevention of violence against women. INAMUJER has also created a free telephone hotline for victims of domestic violence as well as a shelter, Casa de Abrigo, for women who fear for their lives. The Institute is also organizing programs to sensitize police officers, lawyers, and doctors to gender and domestic violence issues so as to ensure that women receive proper support and services.

On the other hand, not all state institutions have stood up for women's rights. For example, the Constitutional Chamber of the

Venezuelan Supreme Court voted five to two in favor of a petition striking down legal provisions permitting the detention of domestic abusers without charges. The five judges who voted for the petition were men, and the judges who opposed it were women. The law at the center of the controversy dates to 2000 and gave the police the power to detain domestic abusers for 72 hours, in order to allow the victim, usually the wife or children, sufficient time to arrange for a safe place to go.

For Venezuelan women, it's not a petty legal question. Domestic violence in Venezuela is widespread: in 2005 the Public Prosecutor's Office registered 36,000 cases of domestic violence; many more incidents went unreported. Many women die at the hands of their partners, and rape, including marital rape, which is a crime in the country, remains a major problem in Venezuela. In one week alone in 2006, 52 women reported being raped. One publicized and extreme case involved Alexandra Hidalgo. For 14 years, she was married to a former military commander in Caracas. When she returned to school, her husband began to beat and harass her. In May 2004 she was kidnapped and raped by a group of men, including her husband. "The sexual abuse was horrific—they were savage," she remarked.[11] Her husband was held in custody from September 2004 to April 2005, but then released without having to post bail. He is now a fugitive. Two men were sentenced to eight years in prison for the attack, and two others were acquitted.

One of the female Supreme Court judges expressed dismay at the decision striking down provisions allowing for the detention of abusers. The decision cannot be overturned. "This means abusers are free to return home, beat their wives or children again and make them pay for the police charge, if there was one," she remarked. María León herself blasted the Court: "It's unbelievable that police or administrative authorities have to wait for a judge to act while an abuser is killing his wife." León expressed incredulity that society, which was supposedly getting better at protecting women, was now apparently going backwards to the days when domestic violence was accepted.[12]

Despite such reversals, women have advanced in many key respects. They have, for example, played a key role in drafting, advancing, and reforming a wide variety of legislation in diverse fields. What's more, Chávez officials claim that new social programs have integrated women into the political system. Rubén Águila Cerati is the director of electoral politics for Chávez's MVR party in the western State of Mérida and a former member of the Venezuelan Communist Party. A colorful and jolly man, Cerati was once a guerrilla fighter. He gesticulates wildly in the air as he speaks. In his over-the-top rhetorical style he is reminiscent of Chávez.

Cerati claims that the Bolivarian Revolution has transformed gender relations. "Today we have 153,000 *merideños* [inhabitants of the state of Mérida] registered in the MVR [Chávez's political party]. Fifty three percent of these people are women. In the political assemblies, women are the dominant force. I can't say there is no *machismo* here in Mérida, but women have been liberated."[13]

Still, not all is as rosy as it might seem at first glance. Only a minority of poor women has received access to Banmujer's services,[14] and a huge percentage of loans granted by the bank have not been repaid. Indeed, by hard-nosed banking standards, Banmujer has been a colossal failure.[15] Meanwhile, though women are encouraged to participate fully in politics, they have been underrepresented in recent years in leadership positions within government. Chávez initially did not appoint any women to his government, but recently has promoted a number of women to cabinet positions. Another obstacle is that, while the Chávez administration has placed some importance on the feminist agenda, gender has taken a back seat to the Bolivarian Revolution's emphasis on race and class. Despite advances in the law, the reality is that discrimination against women continues to be an ongoing fact in wider society, as Castañeda has frankly admitted in public statements.[16]

While Chávez's victory in 1998 held out the possibility of overcoming traditional social problems, many hopes have still not been satisfied. "There are some policies that are very positive," remarks Mariño Alvarado, Director of Provea, a human rights organization in Caracas. However, he adds, "in other areas things are pretty much the same." Though there has been a great willingness within the government to help the poorest and historically most marginalized sectors of society, bureaucratic inefficiency has been a consistent problem. Unfortunately, the government's willingness to implement progressive policies is not enough to make the policies succeed.

Venezuela is awash in oil money, and people's expectations are high. However, public discontent over inefficiency is mounting, not just among the opposition but among sectors of the population that support the Bolivarian Revolution. People are calling for the right to health care, the right to housing, and the right to work. Leaning forward, Alvarado confides, "If you go to the presidential palace right now I'm sure you'll find people there. Every day there is another protest."[17]

Chávez has been fortunate in that he's enjoyed a kind of cult of personality. Indeed, so popular has he become that vendors hawk Hugo Chávez dolls, dressed in full military regalia. At the touch of a button, the dolls deliver a speech on the Bolivarian Revolution.[18] When something goes wrong, the poor tend to blame inefficient government bureaucrats and not the president. The problem is that cases of corruption are mounting at the highest levels of government. Though it might seem unlikely at first glance, Venezuela might get to a point where people start to blame Chávez for government inefficiency, and if real solutions aren't found right away to social problems, Alvarado says, "It would not be strange to think that there might be a popular uprising against the president."

One of the most daunting problems has been the dire shortage of housing in the country. All over Caracas and its surroundings, brick houses lean precariously off the side of steep and eroded hillsides. "The housing problem is one of the most serious that Venezuela faces," Chávez has remarked. "Our revolution has provided some answers but they're really not enough."

One of the more ambitious housing projects launched by the Chávez authorities is called Ciudad Miranda, which consists of dozens of tall apartment blocks and smaller houses. People had been relocated to Ciudad Miranda from unsafe housing elsewhere. Once residents have been awarded an apartment in Ciudad Miranda, they have 20 years to pay back government housing loans. Many residents have set up cooperative businesses with start-up money from the government, and the authorities have almost finished constructing a local school.

Ciudad Miranda's uniform rows of apartment buildings are bland and unattractive, but in the hills surrounding the town of Charallave the authorities have built housing on a much smaller, human scale. Local residents have traded in their *ranchitos* or rudimentary shacks for charming houses freshly painted on the outside in red and white. They have modern kitchens and bathrooms. A local woman who is about to move into her new home beams proudly as she guides us around the premises. The residents deny there has been any favoritism in the allocation of housing.

Despite these local successes, the housing problem constitutes an acute embarrassment for the president. In response to the government's offer of low-interest credits and subsidies for interested home owners, people have mobbed the state mortgage bank, *Banco Hipotecario Latinoamericano*, which was providing subsidized long-term loans. Still, however, housing has proved to be scarce.

"Just as we say 'Homeland or Death'," Chávez remarked to his ministers, "it's 'Homes or Death.'"[19]

According to the Venezuelan newspaper *El Nacional*, the government needs to build 150,000 houses every year if it wants to overcome the housing shortage; during Chávez's eight years in power only 204,000 houses had been constructed.[20] Meanwhile, experts decry the lack of planning in the construction of new housing. Moreover, the housing that has been built should have been more conveniently located close to services, employment, and medical facilities. The housing minister was sacked after only one year. Each new minister who has been appointed has brought a different agenda and separate programs, thus encouraging bureaucratic inefficiency and waste.

Located about an hour from Caracas by car, the state of Vargas spans the coast and has a brutal tropical climate. Efrén Figuera heads Codeva, a non-governmental organization that has been working on development projects in Vargas. He's accompanied by Anelis Morales, who owns a house in the area and works with the organization.

"Venezuela is very centralized," Figuera explains, "so the farther away you live from Caracas, the fewer benefits you'll receive. Unfortunately, it's often the most remote areas that are most in need of resources."[21]

A big problem in Venezuela is that, as a result of the oil-driven culture that reigned for many years, there is little tradition of community organizing. Oil money gave rise to a bloated state bureaucracy and state-owned companies such as PdVSA. Chávez has shown every indication that he will continue with the country's pattern of nationalizations: for example, he has threatened to nationalize banks as well as the cement and steel sectors so as to boost the government's role in the economy. He has also nationalized the country's largest private telecommunications and electricity companies.

Most people have grown accustomed to simply requesting the state bureaucracy to do things for them instead of organizing themselves to pursue their interests together. "This creates a situation in which the community doesn't get together to express collective needs. When you have this one on one relationship between the individual and the government, it's much easier to buy people off," Figuera remarks. The government has called on the community to organize itself in an effort to break with the earlier, dependent mindset

Nearby is a carved-out gully, the result of a catastrophic downpour that occurred in late December, 1999. For four days, intense rains fell across the state. Massive landslides shook the area, destroying homes and killing tens of thousands. Even worse, the disaster exacerbated a long-running housing shortage in the country.

Walking around the gully is a bizarre experience. On the one hand, workers are incredibly jocular with us and pose for photos. It seems odd however to be joking around within a landscape of such desolation and hopelessness. To the side of the gully, there are people living in rudimentary cinder-block houses. There is no garbage pick up, forcing local residents to burn their refuse in a gigantic pile. Looking up the side of the hill, I fear that the earth might collapse on top of the houses in the event of further heavy rains. A middle-aged Afro-Colombian woman whose house was severely damaged by the disaster says that the landslide took everything away; anything left by the rains had to be sold in order to eat.

Seven years after the fact, local residents here complain that the government still has not processed the paperwork that would allow them to relocate to safer housing away from the disaster area. One young man with three children says that he and his family are ready to relocate, but the authorities continue to delay. "Chávez has never come here to see what's going on," he complains bitterly.

According to Figuera, many people are still awaiting housing. Vargas is a narrow little state, flanked by the ocean on one side and mountains and rivers on the other. The vast majority of its territory is at risk for natural disasters.

As a result of the Vargas tragedy, the local development agency Corpovargas has been busy designing new engineering projects in the area to reduce the risk posed by torrential rains. However, residents are unconvinced by the new measures. They are still nervous that another natural disaster might endanger their livelihoods.[22] Recently hundreds of Vargas residents occupied a local building in protest of their conditions; they were later dislodged by the authorities. According to *El Nacional*, the 105 families had been waiting for a year and a half for new housing. Some had been obliged to live with family members, while others continued to live in high-risk areas. The paper reported that residents' patience had "run out," but at long last the governor of Vargas and the vice minister of housing had finally agreed to meet with the protesters.[23]

Even as it struggles to solve severe housing shortages, the Chávez administration confronts other thorny social issues such as health care. In Venezuela, most who can afford to pay for it opt for private health care, usually paid through health insurance. Chávez, however, has declared that prices for basic services in private hospitals have increased to "ridiculous" levels. The Venezuelan leader has led an assault on what he calls "medical capitalism," which in his words is "the most perverse thing in this world." In an effort to halt the soaring coasts of medical care, Chávez has threatened to take control of private clinics if they refuse to drop their prices. He is following through on his pledge to put private facilities under strict regulations that would cap profits made by doctors and clinic owners.

As Chávez continues his war of words against the private system, he seeks to improve the public health care system with help from Cuba. He has turned to Cuban doctors who operate out of so-called "octagon modules," mini-clinics like the one I'd seen earlier outside of Caracas. The clinics are popular and attend to patients free of charge.[24] Within the Barrio Adentro program, the vast majority of doctors are Cuban, with some Venezuelans.[25]

But even here, there have been obstacles. Anelis explains that a Cuban woman doctor had been practicing in Vargas for some time. However, the doctor wasn't very familiar with the area and the way things were run in the community. She lacked proper facilities and had to live in someone's house. It was extremely awkward for her to see patients in the house, and ultimately the arrangement didn't work out. The doctor had left five months ago, and unfortunately no one had taken her place.

Nevertheless, public officials remain upbeat. According to Rubén Águila Cerati of the MVR, Chávez's "mission" programs stressing health and education have transformed the countryside.[26] "*Campesinos*," he notes, "who had never seen a doctor now have them right at their side. The Cuban doctors have incorporated themselves into the peasantry. The *campesinos* are not suspicious of communism."

Even at the level of primary care, however, the system has been plagued by deficiencies. Cerati would do well to tour health facilities in the Andes Mountains around Mérida. Though poor *campesinos* have gained welcome access to Barrio Adentro clinics, sexual health services are not equally distributed, and it is poor women who face disproportionately high rates of STD infection. To an extent, this is a lingering problem having to do with previous administrations. However, Chávez must do more to address sexual and reproductive health.

In clinics around Mérida, doctors do not have condoms for their patients and must tell their patients to go buy them at local pharmacies, which charge more for a small package of condoms than many families spend on food for one day. Indeed, the lack of condoms is not isolated to one specific clinic: across the state of Mérida, in urban barrios as well as rural clinics, doctors simply do not have condoms for distribution. At its root, the problem in extending and improving sexual health care has to do with an ingrained machismo. Women continue to die because, in spite of the governments' rhetoric promoting health care as a human right, sexual health is still marginalized.[27]

What's more, it's unclear what the future has in store for Barrio Adentro. Around 5,000 of the 20,000 Cuban health personnel sent to Venezuela in 2005 have reportedly returned to Cuba, as the island's restive population becomes increasingly worried about the absence of key health workers. The Venezuelan Medical Association, which opposes Barrio Adentro, claims that 45 percent of the program's clinics have stopped operating.[28]

Public hospitals are confronting even more daunting problems than the primary care system. Public health care in Venezuela pits two systems, divided largely by politics, against each other. Though Chávez has spent millions on the Barrio Adentro program, he has largely ignored the traditional public hospitals. *The Miami Herald* profiled one public hospital in Catia where ceiling tiles were missing, patients were crammed into small waiting rooms, and some even carried their own needles. "Problems are not simply aesthetic," noted the paper. "Four patients in the critical care unit died earlier this year when the hospital ran out of oxygen."[29]

Chávez has underfunded the traditional hospitals because the physicians' association supported the 2002 coup and oil lock-out of 2002–03. Doctors complain that Chávez wants to "trample" the old system by not supplying adequate maintenance or resources.[30] Doctor Federico Janai of the Venezuelan Medical Federation has complained that Chávez equips Barrio Adentro clinics but does not supply Venezuelan hospitals. The government shouldn't pay Cuban doctors, Janai says, when Venezuelan doctors working in public hospitals make barely $300 a month.[31] Those who defend the Cuban presence in Venezuela counter that Venezuelan doctors do not practice in poor neighborhoods and tend to service the rich.[32] Chávez himself frankly admits that public hospitals are in poor shape, but blames previous governments. He says he wants the hospitals to become the flagships of Venezuela's health care system, and recently announced a $111 million plan to upgrade dozens of hospitals.[33]

Monsignor Alfredo Torres, general vicar of the archdiocese in the city of Mérida, agrees to discuss how the Church has perceived Chávez's Bolivarian Revolution. A long-time fixture of the local church establishment, Torres went into the seminary when he was fifteen years old. The priest is careful not to criticize Chávez's social programs directly, yet he complains that Mérida's *barrios* are still wracked by poverty and that "change for the better has not reached the people, who continue to search for a means of survival." Though the Cuban doctors had helped, overall the health situation hadn't changed. Conditions in a local hospital were still horrible, he claims, and people needed to buy sheets, medicine, and other necessities.[34]

Even as the traditional hospitals face decline, other health clinics like the sizable one in the Endogenous Center of Development are on the upswing. The facility services local people from Catia. There are separate divisions on the premises for gynecology, pediatrics, and dentistry. Doctors and nurses run to and fro. Walking outside, I even spot a pharmacy on the grounds. According to the guide, some drugs from Cuba are sold at the facility, along with some generic AIDS drugs.

To its credit, the government tackled the country's AIDS problem early on, increasing its HIV/AIDS budget more than five-fold in the

first three years of the Chávez administration. The authorities continued to fund the program, even in the midst of a severe economic crisis
in 2001. Despite the funding, however, conditions within AIDS units of
local hospitals remain unhygienic and run down. Because of the stigma
surrounding AIDS in Venezuela, patients were being kept in a separate
ward at one hospital to the west of Caracas.[35] Despite these problems,
Venezuela has made important strides. In 2004 the country purchased
generic antiretroviral drugs from India for the 12,000 HIV/AIDS patients in care of the government. Altogether, Venezuela provided patients with six antiretroviral products from India and two from Cuba,
distributed free of charge. The government undertook the commitment
to care for the patients and provide the antiretroviral "cocktail" after the
Supreme Court in 2000 found that patients had a right to coverage
under the public health system. Every year, the government spends $30
million on the program.[36]

I've been invited to attend an environmental conference in Maracaibo,
organized by a state agency, Institute for Conservation of Lake Maracaibo (known by its Spanish acronym ICLAM). The conference doesn't
start for a few days, but I arrive early to evaluate the course of the Bolivarian Revolution in Zulia. In particular, I am interested in learning
more about environmental politics in Zulia and determining whether the
Chávez government is truly pushing a progressive ecological agenda.

The trip is uneventful except for the ghastly view over the bridge
once we pass over Lake Maracaibo, Latin America's largest lake. Much
of the lake is covered with green patches of duckweed, the notorious
lemna acuática, or "water lentil." In 2004, duckweed covered almost half
the surface area of the lake.[37]

According to experts, duckweed has contributed to the contamina-
tion of the already polluted lake. Tragically, duckweed could alter the
habitat of various species of fish by exhausting their oxygen supply while
cutting off light from the depths of the lake. Scientists are not sure why
the duckweed appeared in the first place, but some claim that freshwater
from torrential rains favors the spread of the weed.[38] Experts also warn
that nitrogen and phosphorus from sewage discharge serve as nutrients
for the duckweed.[39]

While the authorities have debated how best to eliminate it, concerned members of the fishing community have taken matters into their own hands by raking the *lemna* out of the water with rakes and poles.[40] Try as they might, however, local residents have had trouble eliminating the pesky duckweed, which has been known to duplicate in size every 48 hours.[41]

The environmental crisis in Lake Maracaibo has cast the Chávez regime in an unflattering light. ICLAM officials have asserted that duckweed is not toxic and could even be used as animal feed and fertilizer. But researchers at the University of Zulia refuted that view, saying that *lemna* contained mercury, lead, and other toxic metals.[42]

The environment could prove to be Chávez's Achilles heel. If he wants to demonstrate that he is a leader with true progressive stripes, he must show results in tackling environmental problems. In his 2005 address to the United Nations, Chávez derided what he called "a socioeconomic model that has a galloping destructive capacity." The Venezuelan president expressed concern about "an unstoppable increase of energy" and added that "more carbon dioxide will inevitably be increased, thus warming our planet even more." On other occasions, Chávez has argued that powerful nations are responsible for causing global warming. What is more, he has publicly regretted pollution resulting from traditional sources of energy. It's rather ironic that Chávez, as the leader of one of the world's leading oil producing nations, would emphasize global warming at the United Nations.

Is Chávez an environmental hypocrite? To its credit, Venezuela has ratified the Kyoto Protocol reducing greenhouse gas emissions. The country emits only 0.48 percent of the world's greenhouse gases and according to officials Venezuela is in fourth place in Latin America regarding greenhouse emissions after Brazil, Mexico, and Argentina. Nevertheless, Venezuela exports 1 million barrels of oil per day to its northern neighbor and thus contributes to global warming more than its own emissions statistics would indicate.[43]

If Chávez demonstrates that he can resolve environmental problems like duckweed, he may assuage his progressive environmental critics. Before visiting Lake Maracaibo, I'd read some articles about the growing duckweed phenomenon, but it's certainly another matter to see it up close. Thinking that I will probably hear a lot about the issue during the ICLAM conference, I do my best to put the depressing spectacle out of sight and out of mind for the time being.

What I find strange is that the conference features not just scientists but a representative from the local development agency, Corpozulia. At one point, the man gives a rosy presentation about new port and infrastructure projects planned for the state of Zulia. For me the discussion, which is all about industrial development, seems entirely out of place here.

That's not the only strange thing about the conference. Outside the dining hall where participants eat lunch, mining companies have set up promotional booths. Scantily clad women working for mining and oil companies ply me with glossy pamphlets and even candy as I walk through an adjacent hallway,.

Jorge Hinestroza is a sociologist in the University of Zulia, a longtime activist and a former general coordinator of the Federation of Zulia Ecologists. I'm betting that he, more than anyone else, can give me a sense of the local activist scene and the readiness of the Chávez authorities to address pressing environmental concerns.

Hinestroza promptly lays into ICLAM, calling the organization "elitist." "The conference," he says, "was comprised solely of experts. It is all rather ironic because supposedly in Venezuela we are living in an era which has opened the doors of science to the community. But as this event makes clear, there is no link between the people and science."[44]

One of Hinestroza's colleagues, Elio Ríos, the vice president of the Zulia Association of Environmentalists (AZUL), has made a name for itself by resisting coal exploitation in the Sierra of Perijá, a mountainous area near the Colombian border. Recently, Ríos sent out an e-mail accusing ICLAM of excluding poor communities from the conference. Ironically, Ríos himself is a fervent Chávez supporter and in fact participates in meetings of the Bolivarian Circles. However, he has been one of the most vocal critics of the regime when it comes to the environment. The son of an oil worker, Ríos grew up in Maracaibo and was involved in politics from an early age. In 1973, for example, he took part in demonstrations in support of Chilean President Salvador Allende, who was overthrown that year by Pinochet with the help of the United States. He later went on to help form AZUL and got involved in left-wing student activism at university.

The Bolivarian Revolution could ultimately be ground down by inefficiency, corruption, or excessive paternalism from Chávez. But another danger is that the government might become alienated from the base over the question of the environment. For the moment, environmentalists like Ríos are supporting Chávez because they believe that he embodies many aspirations of a progressive social agenda. However, Ríos also fears that Chávez and his circle are pushing a development model that does not adequately take the environment into account. Zulia inhabitants, Ríos charges, are now paying the price with the emergence of the *lemna*.[45]

Following the emergence of the water lentil, the authorities declared an "environmental emergency" in Lake Maracaibo. Fishermen met with local authorities, who agreed to invest $1.5 million to stop reproduction of duckweed and to bring machinery from Canada to help in the massive cleanup.[46] In 2004, Chávez himself declared that he would "save" the lake from duckweed. Chávez accused previous governments of not doing enough to control pollution in the lake, but admitted that his own regime "could have done more" to protect the area.[47]

Hinestroza criticizes the Chávez authorities, whose policies had been "far from desirable." Though the president has revolutionary pretensions, the Ministry of Environment only trusted "experts" to handle the duckweed issue, "while the communities are passive observers, assigned to pick up duckweed, which provides employment for the community."

With the spread of duckweed, lakeside inhabitants have been exposed to a public health hazard. *Lemna* increases the mosquito population, causes intestinal and skin infections, and serves as a bridge for disease-carrying rats that make their way to local houses. Curiously, however, the spread of duckweed has not resulted in a groundswell of opposition from local inhabitants, who hold the government in high regard and have been patiently awaiting the authorities' contingency plans. Ironically, the government's revolutionary pretensions have made people less politically active; they expect Chávez to solve all their problems for them. Environmental activists in Zulia are skeptical that fundamental political change might be driven from below. Despite the growth of Bolivarian Circles, popular struggles have been "frozen," according to Hinestroza.

Chávez, like other left-wing leaders, has assumed the discourse of change and adopted revolutionary rhetoric. It's unclear, however, what Chávez means by revolution. Some believe that Chávez will not institute radical socialism, preferring instead to carry out gradual change while placing more and more stringent restrictions on private capital. Meanwhile, Chávez will continue to press for his socialism for the twenty-first century, characterized by grassroots mechanisms of political empowerment and more cooperative firms.

The engine of change will be Chávez's new United Socialist Party of Venezuela, though some wonder how the party ought to function. William Izarra, an ideologue of Chávez's Bolivarian Revolution, says that the United Socialist Party will not resemble other left parties such as the Communist Party of Cuba. Chávez's party, he declares, should be based on popular power and citizen assemblies.[48] The true role of the party, he argues, is to win elections, take power, and then transfer it back to communities. It is fundamental, he argues, to keep the revolution going and to have "constant movement," like a centrifuge that never stops.[49]

While it's unclear where the Bolivarian Revolution is headed or how far Chávez will actually go, one thing is clear: most of the left has gone along with the Venezuelan president. Indeed, left-wing governments encourage high expectations, and activism may decrease as a result.[50] Perhaps Chávez is more a skilled populist than a revolutionary. Populists generally assume power in Latin America during periods of crisis or perceived crisis. The people in turn look upon them as saviors. Like other populist leaders, Chávez emphasizes leadership as the glue holding his movement together. In such a way, he is able to gloss over the contradictions, problems, and failures of his regime.

One manifestation of the "glue" holding the revolution together is the color red. In front of my hotel in Caracas, Chavistas dressed in red paint a new mural. What's more, many of the workers wear red in Catia's Center of Endogenous Development as well. Indeed, color has always been a means of political identification in Latin American politics.[51]

Umberto Silvio Beltrán is the Zulia regional coordinator of the Bolivarian Circles. A true believer for whom Chávez can do no wrong, Beltrán goes on and on about the virtues of the president and his revolution.[52] The Bolivarian Circles seek to organize civil society, to raise political consciousness, to spur the community to participate in government, to mobilize against the opposition, and to press for the fulfillment of social needs. The participants are told not to provide social services, but to aid in the planning and implementation of such services within the community. In theory then, they act as a sort of planning, information, and referral center for state programs which seek to em-power ordinary Venezuelans.[53] The Circles serve as liaisons between local neighborhoods and the government and encourage support for Chávez. The president's opponents accuse the groups of functioning as armed gangs, whose job is to intimate the opposition. The Chavistas vehemently deny the charge.[54] Organizers say there are approximately 180,000 people involved in Bolivarian Circles in Zulia. Each comprises ten people and a spokesperson. In Zulia, organizers hope the Circles will help to promote the advancement of true, democratic socialism.

Beltrán is a Paraguayan native and theater director who fled the re-pressive political climate in his country in the 1970s and wound up liv-ing the life of an expatriate in Venezuela. He lives in an affluent section of Maracaibo but has worked in dodgy areas of the city, including one neighborhood known as a "red zone." Nevertheless, he has never had any problems and has established warm friendships with local residents. Beltrán and his colleagues conduct ten meetings per day in poor *barrios* and show videos about the political evolution of oil company PdVSA under Chávez. The Bolivarian Circles, moreover, have helped to con-struct new housing and schools. In Zulia, local priests understand what Chávez is trying to accomplish and are sympathetic to the Venezuelan leader. Protestants and women also have a formidable presence in the Zulia Circles.[55]

Some experts such as Steve Stein believe that Chávez's Bolivarian Circles and communal councils have encouraged the growth of a more democratic system. The danger, however, is that these mechanisms might become nothing more than "tribalistic arms" of the Chávez state. The real question is, where does the economic and decision-making power lie? If power is concentrated in the state, then the organizations can only ask for things, and maybe get them because they are perceived as loyal. If that is the case, then the Bolivarian Circles and the like are prone to become anti-democratic, creating a kind of vertical depend-ence around the cult figure of Chávez and replacing democracy with in-stitutionalized charity. What, then, are we likely to see in Venezuela: more authoritarian rule or more participatory democracy? Paradoxi-cally, we see both tendencies in the Bolivarian Circles.[56]

For William Izarra, the man military expert Domingo Irwin loves to hate, Chávez can do no wrong when it comes to spurring so-called participatory democracy. In a recent interview, he touched on the emergence of the communal councils, the "first unit of direct democracy." Izarra hopes that the councils will become something more than mere instruments to "execute a budget." He frequently delivers his indoctrination workshops to participants in the councils, hoping to establish a more direct link with the people and bypass political parties and the municipal authorities.[57] Indeed, Izarra hopes that the communal councils will lead to "popular power," in which the community will interact directly with the government. "These councils," Izarra has remarked, "now take up the work which used to correspond to municipalities." For Izarra, municipal structures are part of an ossified system that needs to be overhauled. In line with these aspirations, a government commission will design the new socialist state, and proposed structural changes will be submitted to a referendum. In the long-term, Izarra seeks to create "a new socio-political cultural model, which responds to our historical roots and the revolutionary process." "We need a new culture to create a new human being," he remarks.[58]

Izarra is not alone in these sentiments: in Venezuela, workers are tutored on socialist values, and officials frequently call for the creation of a selfless and patriotic "new man."[59] Since he was elected in 1998, Chávez has promised a revolution, and since his third electoral victory in December 2006, he has pledged to accelerate social change. In Venezuelan society, Chávez says, the "new man" ought to be free of selfish urges and devoted to the common good.[60] Recently, speaking to cattle ranchers in central Venezuela, Chávez warned against the evils of capitalism and called on the ranchers to forge socialism through the creation of a "new man."[61]

The term "new man" harks back to the Cuban Revolution and Che Guevara, who thought that the common citizen should undergo a profound psychological change so as to serve humanity selflessly. Indeed, Chávez has placed great value on Che as a political figure: as early as 2000, a government foundation invited young students to write an essay on the Argentine revolutionary. Essay topics for the competition included: Che and the "new man"; Che's economic thinking; and Che, the "complete" or well-rounded citizen.[62] Somewhat bizarrely, Izarra refers to Jesus Christ, Simón Bolívar, Che Guevara, and Hugo Chávez as the icons of Venezuela's "socialism for the twenty-first century."[63]

For Chávez, the key to creating the "new man" is improving education.[64] Chávez officials are not just talking about constructing hundreds of new schools, but also about indoctrinating the population. Speaking before thousands of educators from across the world recently, Adán Chávez, Hugo Chávez's brother and the country's current minister of education, declared that teaching is the motor driving Venezuela's Bolivarian revolution. "To construct socialism, it falls to us to dismantle the old economic and social structures and form a new man with teaching that agrees with the current process of socialist revolution in Venezuela," Adán said.[65]

In Caracas today, one finds "socialist formation centers" where Venezuelans study socialist ideals while undergoing job training. In the new public Bolivarian University in Caracas, students see themselves as forming a socialist vanguard, envisioning Chávez's "new man" not as a mere technocrat but someone focused on both professional development and community well-being. In sum, students see themselves as humanists who value community service over individual advancement.[66]

Analysts, however, are skeptical about the prospects of a classless utopia in Venezuela any time soon. "Venezuelans are individualists," says Luis Pedro España, director of the Economic and Social Research Institute at Venezuela's Andrés Bello Catholic University. "They are not inclined to work for the community. They are very consumerist, even the (Chávez) faithful."[67] Indeed, while hardcore Chávez supporters would surely not object to further radicalization, it's unclear how many Venezuelans support the forging of a radical socialist state. According to a recent survey conducted by the Pew Research Center, a solid majority of Venezuelans approve of Chávez's influence on national events, though 72 percent believe that the country is better off with a free market economic model.

It's not as if Venezuela is marching towards the Cuban model anyway. In today's Venezuela, social and economic contradictions abound. Excess liquidity has, ironically, helped to spawn unbridled capitalism in construction, banking, and other sectors enriched by government spending. "In a money-fueled, go-go consumer culture," remarks the *Washington Post*, "inflation is elevated, cars sell for $100,000, elegant shopping malls thrive, a black market for American greenbacks is growing and fashionable art galleries sell paintings for tens of thousands of dollars." The economic contradictions reportedly worry Venezuelan policymakers.[68] Even as poverty declines, Venezuela's class divisions have stubbornly remained and a new class has even sprung up, the *"boliburguesía."* The phrase is a compound of the words "Bolívar" and "bourgeoisie," a riff on Chávez's Bolivarian Revolution and the new class of elites it has created. According to government critics, the *boliburguesía* includes Venezuelans working in the black and gray markets, government bureaucrats who impose "surcharges" on routine services, oil deal middlemen, money launderers, and drug smugglers. While Chávez has largely vanquished the old opposition, this new class could form an impediment to the advancement of socialism.

CHAPTER SEVEN

THE PONCHO REVOLUTION

Even as Chávez ostensibly seeks to prop up grassroots mechanisms such as Bolivarian Circles and communal councils, Andean nations too are seeking to redefine the state and its relationship to society. Throughout the region, Indian groups have long expressed impatience with corrupt and incompetent political systems. This frustration has spurred indigenous movements to adopt more direct forms of action, such as mass street protests and road blockades. If President Correa wants to succeed in Ecuador, he must forge links with major social movements and establish popular legitimacy as Chávez has done in Venezuela. While it's probably a mistake to speak of a South American "bloc" of countries allied to Chávez, there are some intriguing similarities between Correa and the Venezuelan leader.

"What's interesting," says political writer Saint-Upéry, "is that Correa is organizing his own base, something like Chávez's MVR party. He's trying to create local cells and family committees which are similar to the Bolivarian Circles in Venezuela."

In his rhetorical style, Correa resembles the brash and colorful Chávez. Like the Venezuelan, Correa presents himself as an outsider crusading against "the oligarchy." Because civil society was not very well organized, Saint.-Upéry says, Correa might be able to make significant political inroads at the grassroots level. As in Venezuela, social movements in Ecuador had been relatively weak. In the late 1980s, labor was declining and the indigenous movement was replacing the unions as the principal mouthpiece for popular demands.

But, Saint.-Upéry argues, the indigenous movement today has become essentially "pragmatic" and social movements are hardly in a position to force Correa toward the left. Meanwhile, there has been very little popular mobilization at all on the coast, where the right wing continues to predominate with its "fashionable populists."[1]

But how much clout does Correa have with indigenous peoples?

The CONAIE, created in 1986, is perhaps the most important Indian organization in the country. It has led many mobilizations or "uprisings" against successive governments in Ecuador, blocking major roads and marching on cities in an effort to advance the interests of indigenous peoples. Indians have called forcefully for an end to neo-liberal structural adjustment. They played a key role in the protests leading to the removal of President Abdalá Bucaram in February 1997 and later, in January 2000, to the downfall of the Jamil Mahuad government, whose "dollarization" plans CONAIE opposed.

CONAIE Communications Director Manuel Castro says that his organization can mobilize hundreds of thousands, depending on the nature of the call. When I query him about the Correa government, he is lukewarm at best At one point he even accuses the president of representing the "oligarchy." Within the current Correa cabinet, he says, older figures from earlier administrations still hold sway while representatives of Ecuador's social movements have been excluded.

Indeed, since Correa's meteoric rise on the national stage, CONAIE has been somewhat wary of the maverick politician. Though the organization supported the president's call for a new Constitutional Assembly, there has reportedly been a certain amount of "mutual distrust" between the two, and during talks disagreements surfaced about how best to form the new legislative body.[2]

Another prominent member of the CONAIE, Luis Macas, has said that the Indians' support for Correa is not "unconditional." Macas wants Correa "to govern with the people and not through political parties," and has criticized Correa's handling of the foreign debt.[3] After startling Wall Street by threatening not to pay the country's $10.3 billion debt, Correa has continued to pursue debt negotiations, a cautious approach that Macas has flatly opposed.

The indigenous movement wants true land reform, nationalization of natural resources, and redistribution of wealth. Yet Castro says that CONAIE doesn't want a revolution from one day to the next, but merely an administration that would meet social needs and end corruption. If Correa does not pay attention to these goals, Castro remarks ominously, then his regime might fall prey to the same kind of demagogic populism which characterized the earlier Abdalá Bucaram government.[4]

That's hardly a flattering analogy: Bucaram's regime, which was marred by accusations of flagrant corruption, ended abruptly after only six months in 1997 when Congress ousted the flamboyant leader. Bucaram was known for his unpredictable behavior. Known as "El Loco," or "The Crazy One," he was dismissed on grounds of "mental incapacity."[5]

To what extent does Chávez exercise any kind of ideological influence over Ecuadoran politics? Macas himself has used Chávez's term "participatory democracy,"[6] and the Indians have a long tradition of pushing for greater autonomy in local indigenous communities. While Castro is aware of political developments in Chávez's Venezuela, the Quichua Indian says that indigenous peoples have not discussed the possibility of setting up cooperatives in Ecuador. While the concept might have some validity, the Ecuadoran people would have to design proposals in accordance with local political conditions.

Nevertheless, CONAIE is hardly parochial in terms of outlook: Castro says that CONAIE has been in touch with other indigenous movements in South America, as well as the MST in Brazil and the *piqueteros* in Argentina. He downplays the differences between the movements, remarking that in South America everyone confronted "the same types of problems."

The real question, however, is how much influence CONAIE might wield in future. Experts agree that the CONAIE's "ideological presence" has exerted an impact on Correa's thinking as well as on his team. In contrast to what Castro has told me, however, sociologist and American expatriate Waters says CONAIE can't deploy many people on the streets.

"CONAIE likes to claim that it represents 45 percent of the population. That figure is overstated: my guess is that it's more like 10 percent. You also need to remember that lots of indigenous people do not identify with CONAIE. Similarly, not all Indians identify with Patchakutik [the Ecuadoran political party], which would explain why the political party garners only about 2 percent of the national vote."[7]

How can we explain this dismal track record? Some observers claim that the indigenous movement's prestige was "dented" as a result of CONAIE's participation in the Lucio Gutiérrez government. After the Indians helped stage protests against Mahuad in 2000, a representative of the indigenous movement became a member of a short-lived ruling triumvirate that replaced him.

Indigenous leaders were later awarded posts in Foreign Relations and Agriculture in the new Gutiérrez government. But when Gutiérrez, an army colonel, jettisoned his progressive agenda and moved towards market-driven policies, CONAIE withdrew from the regime. Gutiérrez himself fell in 2005 following protests. In light of the Indians' previous missteps and political miscalculations, it's understandable that Castro and others would proceed cautiously with Correa.

The Indians are not alone in their ongoing political struggle. In recent years, Ecuador has seen the emergence of a vibrant environmental movement. When I was first in Ecuador in the early 1990s, the environmental movement was still in its infancy. I recall interviewing environmentalists at an organization called *Acción Ecológica* for my articles about the Huaorani Indians. Located in a house not far from where Saint-Upéry lives, the NGO was composed, to my memory, entirely of women. I'd even heard the staff referred to as the "*eco-chicas.*"

I think about going back to *Acción Ecológica* to get a sense for where the environmental movement is headed and what links it might have to the Indians. But then I meet Icaza, a long-time environmentalist, in the cocoa bar and figure that I might as well talk to him.

Icaza had first gotten involved in ecological issues as a young man of 22. "Fate intervened," he tells me during our conversation on Avenida Amazonas, "when I got the opportunity to work as a volunteer at the Charles Darwin station in the Galapagos Islands. From that point onwards, I felt a great calling to work on environmental issues." Since the late 1990s he'd worked on conservation, most recently as an employee of a Swiss NGO which sought to protect Andean forests.

Icaza explains that environmentalism didn't really take off until the 1990s. *Fundación Natura*, an early group with links to the political establishment, had once been influential.[8] In the late 1980s, *Fundación Natura* and World Wildlife Fund had carried out a supposed "debt-for-nature swap," under which World Wildlife Fund purchased a portion of the debt at a discount from commercial lenders. Proceeds from the deal went to benefit a variety of conservation activities in Ecuador.

Recently, however, the organization has been outgrown by other groups that have adopted a more combative political approach. Unfortunately, the environmental movement is still only capable of mobilizing about 1,000 to 2,500 people to go to protests. "How much of an environmental consciousness exists here?" I ask. "Oof!" Icaza exclaims, as if to underscore the uphill struggle which lies ahead. "It's an issue which has been discussed only recently," he says.

In the short term, the environment surely won't be a huge priority for the Ecuadoran people, who are more concerned with immediate survival. On the other hand, Icaza adds, people might start paying greater heed to the environment if their lives are affected in some significant way by ecological problems. As if on cue, a man approaches from the next table. He apologizes for interrupting our conversation, but says that he's overheard the interview and would like to get more involved in environmental politics. Could Icaza let him know when there's going to be an upcoming protest? My contact gratefully takes the man's card, pledging to e-mail when the next opportunity arises.

Given that the environment is likely to become more important in future, what steps is Correa taking to address the issue? In Venezuela, the environment has proven to be Chávez's Achilles heel, and ignoring the issue could likewise prove perilous for the young Ecuadoran president. During his presidential campaign, Correa issued lime-green posters emblazoned with the slogan "Citizen Revolution." Once elected, Correa appealed to the Indians by backing a $6 billion lawsuit against U.S.-based Chevron that accuses the energy giant of polluting a large swath of the Ecuadoran Amazon.

But the ambitious president didn't stop there. Recently, he requested that the international community compensate Ecuador for its decision not to drill for oil in ecologically-rich Yasuní Park.[9] Wealthy nations, he asserted, should pay Ecuador $350 million a year in exchange for leaving oil under the ground in Yasuní.

To the delight of environmentalists, Correa, on a visit to the ugly oil-boom town of Coca, said, "I think oil has brought us more bad than good. We need to do something about it." The statement came at a time of growing popularity for so-called "carbon offsetting" schemes, which would allow First World residents to make donations to environmental groups to compensate for the environmental damage caused by their own wasteful habits.

Minister of energy and mines Alberto Acosta himself has also sought to build a bridge with environmentalists in an effort to head off development-minded technocrats. A couple months after I leave Quito, I read that he has resigned his post in the government to run for the membership of an assembly to rewrite the constitution.[10] My contact had relinquished his duties due to disagreements with other officials about the development of new oil fields in ecologically sensitive Yasuní National Park. The area is home to some of the world's most diverse populations of birds, amphibians, and trees.[11]

Acosta had supported Correa's scheme to spare oil development in the area. Not surprisingly, his principled stand put him at odds with other figures in the government, for example the president of Petroe-cuador, Carlos Pareja, who wanted to attract private investors to extract oil in Yasuní.

Sitting in our café, Icaza says that during the presidential campaign environmentalists had a dialogue with Correa, but now the regime has other, more pressing concerns. "I don't think Correa's first priority is dealing with conservation NGOs at the present time. On the other hand, we aren't putting pressure on him. The first order of business now is getting a progressive majority in the Constituent Assembly, an important platform from which we may launch an environmental agenda."

Unlike in Ecuador, civil society has traditionally been relatively well or-ganized in Bolivia, where grassroots democracy has emerged in re-sponse to tough physical and social conditions. In the barren highlands, indigenous farmers have survived by sharing what little they've grown in the rocky soil. If one family is starving, the mayor typically collects po-tato, prickly pear, and coca leaf to help out. When local residents die, everyone in the village helps pay for the funeral in the cemetery. When decisions need to be made, all sides argue until consensus is reached.

What is so compelling about the Bolivia story is Morales's pledge to adhere as president to many of these traditional values, such as common ownership and consensus decision-making. According to Morales, in his home village there is no private or individual property. He himself has stated that "The indigenous communities have historically lived in community, in collectivity, in harmony not only with each other as human beings but with mother earth and nature. We have to recover that."[12]

The problem, however, is that Indians were marginalized in society. Upon assuming power Morales was confronted with a stark social situation. According to a report issued by the UN Economic Commission for Latin America and the Caribbean, prior to Morales's election indigenous children still fell behind and dropped out of school far more than the general population, despite the provision of bilingual education. Educational services were negligible or non-existent, and illiteracy rates were far higher for indigenous people than other racial groups.

Most glaringly, infant mortality stood at 7.6 percent in the indigenous population, compared with 5.2 percent in non-indigenous Bolivians.[13] Health care was either rudimentary or non-existent. Indeed, in the south of the country mortality rates were among the worst in the world outside of sub-Saharan Africa.[14] Morales can ignore such inequities only at his political peril.

Upper University of San Andrés historian Magdalena Cajías argues that her country soon might see the emergence of the most combative social movements on the continent. "In Bolivia," she says, "the state has never been able to function without social pressure from below. That's to say, civil society is permanently organized and constantly exercises pressure on the government. At times, this pressure can become quite radical."

But radical in what sense? Historically, Bolivian political life has not been characterized by long-term armed struggle. On the other hand, there is a strong tradition of participatory democracy coming out of the *ayllu* [a pre-Inca form of political organization based on extended family groups] and the labor movement. Indeed, the Aymara have a long tradition of collective government and direct democracy, and are not accustomed to simply sitting on the sidelines and voting every four years: they demand constant participation in decision making.

Even before the meeting of Morales' new Constitutional Assembly, high-level government figures openly discussed incorporating indigenous principles into government. "What kind of society do we want?

Pre-capitalist or communal? That's the decision we face," said Félix Patzi, Morales's radical Aymara minister of education.[15]

Even as Patzi pondered the underlying basis of the new indigenous state, the MAS was drafting its own proposals to the new Assembly. Under one provision, the branches of government, including the executive, legislative, and judicial, would be selected "through universal suffrage and through traditional community systems of decision-making and forms of election." Under another intriguing provision, national juridical structures would incorporate the forms of administering justice of the indigenous peoples, and decisions imposed by indigenous authorities would be effective and valid before the courts and police.

And what kind of economic philosophy would the new state pursue? That's a question that Patzi took up himself. In a somewhat humorous but telling aside, he remarked, "One thing the new Bolivia won't need is competition. Competitiveness? I ask myself why. Why study business in a country with no businesses?"[16]

In the spirit of Patzi's comments, the MAS has proposed defining Bolivia as having a "communitarian social economy with private property," while natural resources would be declared "social property" to be managed sustainably by the state. The MAS demonstrated its radical credentials yet further by declaring that indigenous peoples have the right to "self determination and territoriality." MAS also sought to recognize the Indians' political systems, their right to select their own authorities, and the right to manage their own collective resources.

Such a program would indeed be quite radical. But it is by no means clear that Morales will be able to carry out his peaceful revolution. Unfortunately for MAS, the party failed to achieve the prized two-thirds majority in the Constitutional Assembly. As a result, the body has gotten bogged down in endless partisan disputes and procedural debates, achieving little. Morales has been much more hamstrung than Chávez, whose party, the MVR, pummeled the opposition and rammed through a new constitution in Venezuela during the first years of the Chávez administration.

The danger for Morales, of course, is that Bolivia, a volatile and unstable country, could come to a boil if MAS fails to carry out its promised agenda. Restive forces have already demonstrated that they're perfectly capable of toppling governments: for example, in 2005 dynamite-throwing tin miners and peasant women in traditional dress forced out President Carlos Mesa. On that occasion, 80,000 protesters surrounded the presidential palace and Congress, calling for nationalization of the gas industry and greater representation for indigenous peoples in government.

Mesa himself succeeded Gonzalo Sánchez de Losada, forced to resign in 2003 after Morales led violent protests against the government, which had pursued unpopular market-oriented policies.

In order to head off protest and the fate of his erstwhile predecessors, Morales announced a plan to improve public education, particularly in low-quality rural schools, by extending teacher-training programs from three years to five. He's also pursued a program of free health care with the help of Cuban doctors, much as Chávez has done in Venezuela. What's more, he's carried out agrarian reform, distributing land not to individuals but to traditional communities. The president has also increased the minimum wage by 50 percent,[17] surely a relief to Bolivians, 65 percent of whom survive on an income of less than $2 a day.[18]

Thus far, Morales's policies seemed to go over well amongst the Indians. "Evo Morales is a brother," says indigenous activist Martín Condori Flores, chewing coca leaf during our interview in La Paz. On the other hand, he adds, one has to look at the "whole picture." Politicians, he says, still marginalized indigenous peoples. Despite MAS's roots in social justice movements, Flores says the party's political establishment still looks down on Indians.[19]

Indeed, just before my arrival in La Paz, the relationship between Flores' indigenous federation to the Morales regime was put under strain over the issue of the Constituent Assembly. Though the indigenous group initially supported the formation of the new legislative body, it later claimed that the Assembly represented political parties and not social movements. Therefore, claimed the Indians, the Constituent Assembly should be considered "preconstituent" and a new Assembly convened.[20]

Flores says his organization, CONAMAQ, might be able to marshal some 30,000 Indians from all over the country to La Paz to engage in marches and hunger strikes. The group has contact with labor, he says, and the country's Indians and *campesino* farmers are united. What's more, his organization has ties with other indigenous movements, such as CONAIE.

When I ask him directly about being more confrontational, Flores says the Indians were not currently considering any kind of mobilization against the Morales government. If the regime did not live up to popular expectations on energy policy or coca, the Indians would first "reflect" amongst themselves, says Flores.

Unfortunately for Morales, not all of civil society shares Flores's patience toward the government. Perhaps more than any other issue, energy stands to tarnish Morales most. Shortly after he took office, the president confronted a protest launched by Guaraní Indians, who claimed that a joint gas venture in their territory had failed to result in development projects. Morales was obliged to send in troops to quell the protest, which briefly disrupted gas exports to Argentina.

Even more serious, Morales has suffered in the court of public opinion due to the widespread perception that he had not carried out a "real nationalization" of the gas sector. Nationalization of gas is an emotional issue in Bolivia; many people say that too many of their resources were stolen, sold off to foreigners at dirt cheap prices, hoarded by a small clique of rich Bolivians, or wasted through massive corruption.

In May 2006 Morales placed the energy sector under state control, giving foreign energy companies six months to sell at least 51 percent of their holdings or depart from the country. With the money garnered from gas nationalization, the president hoped to develop small-scale industry and create jobs.

Several months later, the state increased its stake in the nation's two giant gas fields from 50 to 82 percent, but took only a 60 percent share from Bolivia's minor deposits.[21] But according to *The Oil and Gas Journal*, one year after nationalizing the oil and gas sector, Morales had yet to place a single *boliviano* in the people's pockets. Analysts assert that the nationalization has yielded more political rhetoric than actual improvement in people's lives.[22]

During my conversation with Carlos Arze, the economist tells me that the government had not conducted a true "nationalization" of the gas industry, and everyone in society is aware of this fact. He says that the government is already struggling to satisfy local gas demand, something I was able to verify later while riding in a cab outside of La Paz, where I saw throngs of Indians carrying large canisters, waiting in line to buy gas .

Arze tells me that the situation has recently escalated, with people blockading roadways in protest over the scarcity of liquid gas. This, he adds, might lead social movements to press for a true nationalization. "The people say, the gas should belong to us, we're Bolivians and it should be cheap," he explains. "But who is going to oblige the companies to bring gas from Santa Cruz to La Paz, and not export it to Brazil or Argentina?"[23]

Judging from recent events, Arze is not off base in his observations. In early 2007, some of Morales's more radical supporters rose up in Camiri, in the Chaco region. In a sign that social forces were not about to let go of their struggle for control over natural resources, the protesters demanded a "real nationalization" of the gas industry.[24]

CHAPTER EIGHT

PENGUINOS, PIQUETEROS, AND THE PT

Compared to the dynamic and fluid relationship between Morales and Bolivia's social movements, governments of the Southern Cone and Brazil have proven far less innovative. But in Chile, Argentina, and Brazil, social movements, which for years were repressed, tortured and disappeared by the military, have captured the popular imagination and electrified politics. Not content to merely exercise external pressure on their political leaders, some activists have entered government in hopes of advancing socially progressive agendas.

Like her counterparts elsewhere in the region, Chilean President Bachelet has paid attention to hot-button issues such as health care. Judging from my experience seeking treatment for a stomach infection in a local Santiago hospital, medical attention is in need of some improvement: the doctor I saw failed to diagnose my infection, which persisted for weeks. To counter criticism that her government is simply interested in fiscal conservatism, Bachelet, herself a former pediatrician, has announced that her government would seek to improve the quality of health care afforded to all Chileans.[1]

During the first 100 days of her administration, Bachelet announced her new Community Family Health Care initiative, designed to bring health care facilities closer to where people live. The program seeks to develop a new model of more personalized care, establishing

60 new health centers, which will serve as satellites for larger medical clinics.

At the opening of one of the new health centers, Bachelet made reference to the Health Ministry's Code of Conduct campaign, which sought to improve coordination among all levels of the health care system. "What is the Code of Conduct about?" Bachelet asked. "It's about respect . . .for people who are vulnerable due to poverty, illness, age or any other factor."[2]

Another pressing issue for Bachelet is education. Addressing weaknesses in the educational system has become a political necessity for the president, as new social forces, including high school student activists, come to the fore in Chile.

In his *Punto Final* office, veteran activist and journalist Cabieses discusses the emergence of the students on the national scene with me. Quite frankly, he says, there hasn't been any movement like it for many years, and it had taken political observers by surprise. Referred to as *penguinos* (penguins) for their trademark blue and white uniforms, Chilean students oppose a measure that would lower the age at which offenders can be tried and sentenced as adults. Students also seek repeal of a Pinochet-era law governing the country's educational system. Under the law, responsibility for education was transferred to municipalities, which critics charge leads to a deep gap in the quality of education between Chile's richest and poorest regions.[3]

The students have also demanded free use of public transit and protested against a new transportation system that has polarized the country. Bachelet has seen her political base erode as "transit reform" has become a dirty word in Santiago. The new network was designed to modernize a fleet of notoriously polluting orange buses. As a result hundreds of routes were canceled and the subway system became overloaded. I personally observed the problem while waiting for the subway one morning during rush hour. Commuters were crammed into subway cars, and I had to let eight trains go by before I could find space on the subway.

The "Revolution of the Penguins" got jump-started in May 2006, shortly after Bachelet's inauguration. At the peak of the protests, as many as 700,000 students took to the streets in demonstrations that frequently turned violent.[4] "When these penguins march," notes the *Stanford Daily*, "Chileans get out of the way."[5]

Hoping to galvanize Chilean society, high school students are attempting to raise the student movement from its ashes. Chile has a history of student radicalism going back decades. Student organizations have long been identified with national political movements and reformist leaders, many of whom started their political careers as student activists themselves. It was no accident, then, that Salvador Allende's first speech after winning election in September 1970 was delivered from the balcony of the Student Federation building in downtown Santiago. The Allende years were a "euphoric" time for students. The president himself exhorted the young to help him transform the political and economic structure of Chile within a peaceful context. There was a sense that capitalism was giving way to a new order of state-guaranteed equality and social justice. Student brigades taught janitors to read. Campuses were abuzz with revolutionary rhetoric and even began to attract college students from abroad who sought to learn more about Allende's socialist experiment. With the Pinochet coup, however, the student movement was dealt a severe blow: the secret police did its utmost to harass, intimidate, and discredit students who were critical of the regime.

Given this history, it's perhaps no surprise that the Bachelet government has sought to placate the restive student population. In response to mounting pressure, Bachelet provided $200 million to satisfy some of the students' demands, including low fares in public transportation, more food rations for poor students, and the repair of dilapidated school facilities.[6]

Several months later, however, students took to the streets in a national strike designed to serve as a "warning to the government." The president, they charged, needed to speed up reforms of the Pinochet-era education law. Police used water cannon to disperse the students, who marched to the Education Ministry. Bachelet in turn admitted that the "education that our children receive is not as good as it should be. It's not everything that families hope for, and it's not as good as they deserve." Hoping to appease the students, she urged Congress to approve an education super-intendancy to oversee use of financial resources.[7]

But protests have continued to dog Bachelet's presidency. In early 2007, demonstrations began during the annual Day of the Young Combatant, which marks the death of two students killed by the Pinochet police in 1985. Police used water cannon and tear gas to break up the protests. In referring to the demonstrations, Deputy Interior Minister Felipe Harboe called it the "day of the young criminal." Officials claimed that the majority of those detained were school-aged students under 16.[8]

Clashes continued recently as students occupied many Santiago high schools, leading to confrontations with Chile's militarized police, known as *carabineros*, who sought to dislodge the protesters.

The question, however, is whether the *penguinos* will become a mere footnote in Chilean history or spark the rebirth of the country's political left, so decimated during the Pinochet years. Many Chilean college students, only a few years removed from "*penguino*-hood," reportedly do not sympathize with their younger peers.

Though Cabieses claims that the student movement isn't very organized and is unable to mobilize at the national level, one gets the sense that change could be afoot. According to the *Stanford Daily*, the protests have struck a chord in the country and have become "a sign of acceptance toward public expression as much as discontent with the public transportation reforms that have left much of downtown Santiago in gridlock."[9]

Bachelet, in an effort to appear sensitive to the rising tide of social discontent, has said that while she personally sympathizes with the right to free self-expression, the protests must be carried out in a constructive and non-violent manner.

But in the long-term, can Chilean governments contain the unrest as civil society, so long muzzled under Pinochet, starts to assert itself?

In Ecuador and Bolivia, it was the Indians who were at the forefront of social struggle. If social movements are to effect real change in Chile, they will have to take the country's Indians into account. According to Cabieses, Mapuche Indians were politically active after the Pinochet dictatorship, though only on a sporadic basis.

Currently, the Mapuche number some 600,000 in a country of 15.6 million and comprise the largest indigenous group in Chile. According to Amnesty International, the Mapuches lack serious access to justice and protection of their rights, and have been subject to police brutality. The London-based human rights organization reports that *carabineros* raided a Mapuche community in July 2006, supposedly looking for livestock stolen from local ranchers. The community, however, denied that stolen animals were being held on their land. According to reports, the police shot tear gas, rubber bullets, and live ammunition at the unarmed community.

Nibaldo Mosciatti, a press officer for the Bío-Bío radio station, remarked that "the power of the logging companies [which have displaced indigenous people from their land] is so strong that in the end you have the sensation and suspicion that part of the state apparatus is placed at their disposal."[10]

Unfortunately, Cabieses tells me, the Mapuches, like the rest of society, are "atomized," and the most radical Indians had been beaten back and repressed. Sadly, he says that Chile is unlikely to develop potent social movements like those that have emerged in Bolivia.

Meanwhile, labor unions had suffered a severe decline since the 1970s, suggesting that civil society has a long way to go if it wants to pressure Bachelet to endorse a more ambitious social and political agenda. "Social movements are very weak," Cabieses says. "The dictatorship, through repression and imposition of its economic model, were able to fracture social movements and almost succeeded in liquidating any kind of left political movement."

After my rather uninspiring week in Chile, I'm hoping to find evidence of more vibrant politics in Argentina. I am particularly interested in the *piquetero* movement, which emerged in the 1990s as a means of giving voice to workers laid off as a result of the government's privatization of state-run industries. The *piqueteros* demanded welfare payments and attracted some attention from the international left for their daring tactics, including blocking traffic.

After Argentina's economy collapsed in 2002 and the country's flirtation with neo-liberalism was completely discredited, the ranks of the *piqueteros* swelled. Many middle-class Argentines, who had had their bank accounts frozen and devalued by the government, began to sympathize with the movement.[11]

The martyr of the *piquetero* struggle is Teresa Rodríguez, a janitor in the oil town of Cutral-Co who was fatally shot by the police on April 12, 1997. At the time, she was crossing a bridge being blocked by unemployed workers. The blockade was one of the first *piquetes* (road blocks), which later became a standard tactic adopted by *piqueteros* across Argentina.

Though Rodríguez continues to be a potent symbol to many, her murder has gone unpunished: the four police officers charged with her killing have been released and pardoned.

For the incoming Kirchner administration, the *piqueteros* represented something of a challenge. The new president entered office in 2003, at a time of widespread public disgust with politics and the neoliberal model. A scant year and a half earlier, Argentina had seen 38 people killed during rioting and looting in protest over the economic crisis.[12]

In the first months of the Kirchner administration, government officials were paralyzed with fear that the *piqueteros* might turn the streets into a battleground. Kirchner personally told his ministers to avoid confronting or repressing street protesters.

At the same time, Kirchner opportunistically sought to divide the *piqueteros*, opposing hard-line activists such as Raúl Castells, while pursuing dialogue with more moderate factions related to the labor federation CTA, or Central de Trabajadores Argentinos.

Over time, the *piquetero* movement began to fragment. As the economy showed signs of improvement, the Argentine middle class, impatient with constant *piquetero* roadblocks, started to withdraw its support for the movement.

Kirchner's strategy of co-opting the *piquetero* movement eventually bore fruit. By 2006, some *piquetero* groups had pledged their political allegiance to Kirchner and agreed to offer support at political rallies. Meanwhile, more militant *piqueteros* failed to rally large numbers of protesters to participate in street demonstrations. In 2005, Castells ran for office in the midterm congressional elections. Though he was defeated, some lesser-known *piqueteros* allied to Kirchner were elected to Congress. The failure of the independent *piqueteros* perhaps indicates that they are more skilled at exercising pressure from without than competing with the well-oiled Peronist electoral machine.

Despite the electoral defeats and eclipse of the *piquetero* movement, some observers claim that the militants changed Argentine society. Psychologically, the country is now a *"piquetero"* nation; for example, rather than carry out conventional strikes, workers now conduct pickets of their own and block roads. Indeed, like the *piqueteros*, workers responded to the political and economic crisis of 2001 by adopting innovative tactics. In August of that year, angry Argentines put up roadblocks to protest public spending cuts affecting the salaries of civil servants and pensions. The demonstrators, who included public and private sector workers, rejected structural adjustment measures by the government of Fernando de la Rúa. In an unpopular move, the regime had sought to slash the fiscal deficit in an effort to avoid defaulting on the international debt. The protests were attended by at least 150,000 people and were backed by labor groups representing the country's public employees, teachers, doctors, and legal-system functionaries.[13]

As Argentine society radicalized, the workers finally seemed to find their backbone and their will to resist after years of inaction. Unfortunately, the unions, including the CTA, had failed to prevent the dismantling of worker protections, first under the 1976–1983 military dictatorship and later under the neo-liberal governments of the 1990s.

Disaffected, many workers have turned away from union bureaucracy and carried out radical new strategies such as factory takeovers. In one of the more noteworthy developments on the domestic social and political scene, the takeovers have inspired a whole new culture of worker resistance.

Takeovers first started in 2000 and later spread as a result of the economic crisis, when thousands of factories closed and millions of jobs were lost. It was a difficult time for most Argentines: during the recession leading into the late-2001 collapse and subsequent default on the international debt, thousands of businesses failed. The ranks of the unemployed and underemployed swelled to more than 40 percent at times.

The factory takeover movement today accounts for some 250 "recuperated" enterprises, providing jobs for more than 10,000 workers. Though businesses initially experienced tough times under self-management, many later achieved financial stability. Indeed, since being occupied in 2001 many of these firms have lived up to the capitalist ideal, becoming productive and profitable and even creating new jobs and investing. Within the firms, everyone gets the same salary, even for different jobs within the same company.

At the local level, worker-owned factories have become a symbol and inspiration to many, demonstrating that workers can indeed participate in all management decisions through direct democracy. The businesses show that employees can service communities, rather than simply obey the profit-driven laws of the free market. What's more, they have established important mutual solidarity networks with other Argentine labor organizations, such as subway and public health workers. Indeed, one expert claims that "worker self-management in Argentina is helping plant the seeds so that future generations can reverse the logic of capitalism." At long last, the Argentine working class seems to be fighting back after thirty years of intense neo-liberalism, first under the military dictatorship (when 30,000 labor activists and students were disappeared) and later under civilian administrations.

To get more information about the worker takeovers, I contact Andrés Ruggeri, an anthropologist at the University of Buenos Aires and an expert on worker-owned factories. We meet at Hotel Bauen, a hotel that had been taken over by the workers. Since 2003, the workers had operated the cooperative hotel with no legal standing or government subsidies.

The neighborhood is full of booksellers, theaters, magazine kiosks, and cafés. The hotel is located right next to the headquarters of the Communist Party and seems nondescript from the outside. I walk inside the lobby and order some spaghetti at the hotel restaurant. Presently Ruggeri shows up, a man in his thirties or forties with a close-cropped black beard, moustache, and wiry build. He is an avid cyclist who has biked all over South America and written a book about his experiences.

Ruggeri explains that he'd initially gotten interested in the worker-owned factories in 2002, when Argentina was in desperate economic and political straits. Even the media, which had always been pro-capitalist, took a decidedly neutral stand when the workers took over the factories. "You have to put yourself in the context of 2002," Ruggeri declares. "There was a lot of unemployment. People wanted to work, and because the workers were merely seeking to reclaim this right it was difficult for the media to go on the offensive."[14]

Most of the takeovers had occurred in Buenos Aires, but there had also been some others in outlying provinces. Despite worker militancy, investment had not gone down in the country as a result of the takeovers, perhaps because managers, acutely aware of the rising power of workers, feared that their firms would be taken over if they looked like they might go belly up.

I am under the romantic impression that workers were challenging the underlying tenets of capitalism through the takeovers, but Ruggeri says that they were merely adopting a defensive strategy, hoping to ensure their own survival. In most cases, the workers did not directly confront the owners, who had either abandoned the factories or gone bankrupt.

Like the declining *piquetero* movement, the worker takeovers have also decreased. They still take place on occasion, but improved economic conditions have made them much less frequent. It would be unlikely, Ruggeri says, that many more will occur.

Interestingly, he adds that the workers had changed psychologically, but "not all in the same way": while some laborers came to regard the worker-owned factories as a radical experiment and had developed quite a political consciousness, others had not become politicized. The latter simply saw their work there as another job that had to get done. The more politicized workers had assumed more managerial roles and complained that their peers had not taken enough responsibility. The apathetic group had shot back that their counterparts had become oppressors and were acting as the "new bosses."

Clearly, even worker-run businesses have their own dilemmas and internal politics. But the workers have been fortunate in one sense: in general, the Kirchner government has not openly repressed them. When the first takeovers occurred, the Argentine state was extremely weak and had little institutional authority.

Ruggeri says that Kirchner is unlikely to change his policy and become more confrontational in the future—unless, of course, a large and important company is taken over; in that event, the government would have to act. But otherwise, the regime will probably continue to adopt a "passive" attitude.

It is possible that the Argentine cooperative workers had initially acted in self-defense and were not necessarily trying to strike a blow at the heart of the capitalist system. But they still became a potent ideological symbol. With a couple of exceptions, most Argentine unions looked on the takeovers with disfavor. Some within the labor movement fear the influence of the cooperatives, since workers in the new businesses have severed their ties to the unions and no longer pay dues. Technically, the workers are no longer even workers, since they have no bosses.

Unconstrained by traditional labor, many leaders of the cooperative movement have waded into the arena of national politics, and some have even become deputies in Congress. But overall, the cooperative workers have not been able to spark the creation of a truly national, grassroots movement with real political clout.

Though there have been some cases of cooperative workers collaborating with *piqueteros*, in general these remain separate movements. Indeed, some cooperative workers even look down on the *piqueteros* as people who had failed to secure and defend their own employment.

Despite these internal conflicts, however, the worker takeovers represent an ideological challenge to the United States, a country with very different ideas about free trade and economic development. "There's a kind of domino effect which I don't think the U.S. likes very much," Ruggeri remarks. He goes on to relate how he and others in the cooperative movement had met personally with officials of the Inter American Development Bank (IADB) in 2003. One woman said that the bank might be inclined to help out the worker-owned businesses, but there was a slight linguistic problem. It turns out that on the IADB board in Washington, there was a certain amount of unease about the term "recovered factories" (in Spanish, *"empresas recuperadas"*), which implied that capital was being stolen.

Perhaps the apprehension of IADB officials was not entirely misplaced: the Venezuelans had been inspired by the Argentine example, and now the Argentine workers have become a symbol to many. Ruggeri had traveled to Venezuela twice, in 2005 and 2006, for meetings about the direction of worker-owned cooperative factories in South America. He was struck by the different perspectives at the gatherings. In Argentina, the state never steered the direction of the cooperatives, and workers had carried out dramatic actions as a reaction to economic crisis. But in Venezuela, it was the state and the Chávez authorities that had taken a direct role in promoting the cooperatives. For them, the businesses formed part of a larger political project.

There were many participants from other South American countries at the conferences, and so far workers had taken over companies in Brazil and Uruguay. In those cases it had been the same as in Argentina: companies had gone broke and workers had acted defensively to preserve their livelihoods.

What kinds of linkages might exist between the cooperative worker movement and other social struggles on the continent? On the one hand, many workers have been focused on their own factories and economic survival. The workers' movement remains heterogeneous, and though some people have developed a dialogue with wider social movements in South America, the majority have not. On the other hand, for those workers that have become politicized, a whole new world of international politics has opened up. Some factory takeovers in Argentina have become so famous that the leaders were now sharing round tables with the Brazilian MST and the indigenous Zapatistas from Mexico.

Hotel Bauen played a role in the struggle. After it was taken over by its employees, it attracted patrons who were interested in supporting the workers' demands. Gradually, however, the hotel began to attract a more mainstream clientele.

The musician playing old Beatles tunes on the piano turns out to be one of the "revolutionary" workers. Ruggeri graciously introduces me. Guillermo Pflujer explains that for much of his life he was apolitical. But then, President Carlos Menem, Washington's darling and free-market advocate, privatized the state gas company, *Gas del Estado*,[15] where Pflujer was employed, and he found himself in dire need. One day in 2003, he was walking down the street just outside Bauen looking for work as a pianist. The front of the hotel was blocked off by the police, but Pflujer was allowed to go inside, where he introduced himself to the workers. "I found myself at that very same piano where you saw me with Andrés," he says.

The workers urged him to stay, and Pflujer cleaned up the dirty piano. Hotel Bauen's first owner had bankrupted and abandoned the place, and workers were just starting to occupy the premises. While the police patrolled outside, workers dug in for the long haul. They got by on *polenta*, heating up their food on a small oven downstairs. It was dark and musty inside the hotel, where spiders had become the only guests.

A judge eventually ruled that the workers could reopen the hotel, and the new staff held a dance in celebration. Pflujer donated his own sound equipment. After about a year and a half, the workers started to earn a modest living.

At the time of my visit, there were 160 partners, and none worked more than 40 hours per week.[16] Before the takeover, the hotel had 70 workers, who frequently worked overtime to keep the place up and running.[17] Currently, the business is managed by an administrative council, president, vice president, and treasurer. Today, in the formerly dilapidated and boarded-up lobby, patrons can order drinks at a modern bar, and waiters wearing white shirts and friendly smiles attend to the public. The hotel has even opened a bookstore offering books by Marx and Lenin.

Despite improvements in the everyday lives of the workers, the hotel continues to exist in a kind of legal limbo. Since December 2005, employees have rallied to pressure the Buenos Aires city government to veto a law that would restore the hotel to its previous owner; indeed, the workers would like to see the hotel expropriated. It's by no means clear, however, that the employees will prevail. The city government has refused to veto the law, and if the Bauen cooperative fails to push through more favorable legislation it risks losing the hotel.[18]

Many workers hope to overcome the legal hurdles. Bauen, a three-star hotel, has become an inspiration to other laborers, and the cooperative offers assistance and lodging to others hoping to set up their own worker-owned businesses. Moreover, it offers discounted rooms to poor families from the provinces who have a child undergoing surgery in Buenos Aires hospitals. "A firm must . . . have a social usefulness," Gerardo Pensavalle, spokesman for the Hotel Bauen, remarked.[19]

Bauen's hospitality is repaid by other workers' organizations. Indeed, the hotel's floor is covered with beautiful porcelain tile, acquired in a trade between Bauen and Zanon, a worker-controlled ceramics factory.

Zanon, the largest recuperated factory in Argentina, was occupied in 2001. Located in the Patagonian province of Neuquén, it now employs 470 workers. Zanon workers frequently organize events at Bauen and stay at the hotel during sojourns in Buenos Aires.

Meanwhile, there has been a great deal of contact and reciprocal exchanges between Bauen workers and "Chávez and his people in Venezuela," who have been impressed by the hotel and the professionalism of its staff. Some Hotel Bauen workers have traveled to Venezuela to speak about their experience in setting up a cooperative system. Pflujer himself has not been, but he is enthusiastic about cooperatives and the cooperation with the Venezuelans.

"Do you like it here?" I ask.

"Yes," he says without much hesitation. "It's a challenge to be here, but it's a beautiful fight. My plan is to stay here."

What does the future hold for the workers' movement in Argentina? Six years after Argentina's worst economic crisis, popular participation in political and social struggle is going strong. With recuperated enterprises at the vanguard, Argentina has developed a vibrant and new working-class culture.

On the other hand, the economic outlook has been mixed. Though the economy stabilized after 2002 and grew steadily at around 9 per cent a year from 2003 to 2006,[20] Kirchner has failed to raise the standard of living. What's more, unemployment still stood at 12.5 per cent in 2006, with more than 5.2 million people unable to acquire enough paid work to meet their monthly needs.

Despite Kirchner's pledge to reform the political system, little has been done on this front. Though the president likes to portray himself as different from other Peronist leaders, this claim has appeared less and less convincing over time as Kirchner relies on traditional tactics of patronage.

Meanwhile, serious questions remain about the authenticity of Kirchner's commitment to the underclass. Given the government's success in reducing unemployment and raising pensions and wages, Kirchner would seem to be a more progressive leader than Lula for example. On the other hand, though salaries have increased, growing inflation reduced real earnings for public employees. Additionally, he has renewed a regressive mining law which limits royalty payments to the state at just 2 percent. Meanwhile, though salaries have increased, growing inflation reduced real earnings for many public employees. Kirchner moreover moved to pay off the foreign debt at the expense of funding deteriorated health and educational facilities and providing improved salaries for workers in these vital public sectors.

Though the Kirchner administration has not pursued a policy of repression toward worker-owned firms, the government nevertheless has an abysmal labor record. In today's Argentina, trade unionists are routinely threatened and even attacked. Activists face police brutality, political arrests, and criminalization of social protest.

One particularly jarring incident involved Carlos Fuentealba, a 41-year-old chemistry teacher who was injured on April 4, 2007, when a policeman fired a tear gas canister at his head from six feet away. He died a few days later.

Coincidentally, the death of Fuentealba coincided with the tenth anniversary of the killing of *piquetero* martyr Teresa Rodríguez. Like Rodríguez, Fuentealba was involved in a protest in Neuquén, in this case a road blockade organized by the provincial teachers' union. The action followed a month-long strike demanding pay raises and public education grants. Though the wage increase had been approved at the national level, the measure had still not been applied in Neuquén.

Further outraging the teachers, Jorge Sobisch, the governor of Neuquén, justified the police's actions. A right-wing politician, Sobisch has confirmed that he gave the order to call in the security forces and declared that he would give the order again. The governor justified the police action by claiming that the teachers were blocking roads and transit. In response, the unions and teachers called for a demonstration against police brutality. Meanwhile, the subway unions of Buenos Aires expressed their solidarity by conducting a strike that brought the city to a standstill.

The very day that the protest erupts, I'm eating a plate of gnocchi in a restaurant on the Avenida de Mayo. On TV, newscasters are talking about the Fuentealba case. They announce that later that day, the workers would be marching downtown to call attention to the death of the teacher. I stroll out on to a huge boulevard, sporting many lanes and an obelisk at one end of the street. I notice that young students have already taken over one of the lanes and are marching through the city. I continue along my way down the Avenida de Mayo, arriving several minutes later at the Casa Rosada. I am engulfed by crowds and can hardly move. Down one long street, the dense crowd extends as far as the eye can see. Young protesters file past me with placards decrying political repression. At one point, a group of anarchists passes by, waving their characteristic red and black flags.

Ramón Lucero, a long-time activist with a bushy moustache and glasses, fills me in on the aims of the protest as we stand in the Plaza de Mayo. He estimates that there are at least 30–40,000 marchers on the streets of Buenos Aires. I can't verify the figure, but it doesn't seem an unreasonable guess given the endless streams of people flooding into the Plaza de Mayo.

My activist contact is cynical about Kirchner's progressive pretensions: when the government deemed it politically expedient, he says, the president criticized the military. A skillful politician, he had been able to co-opt many popular leaders and thereby dilute the independent strength of social movements. At other times, however, Kirchner employed armed force for purposes of repression.

On the other hand, incidents such as the death of the Neuquén teacher have served to unite the left. One sign of the rising power of the left, Lucero says, straining to speak to me over the din of the crowd, is that the unemployed were now organizing side by side with workers and *campesinos*.[21]

I

When Brazilian president Luiz Inácio "Lula" da Silva spoke before the January 2004 Summit of the Americas in Monterrey, Mexico, his words were music to the ears of the activists in the audience. Neo-liberalism, he said, was "a perverse model that mistakenly separates the economic from the social, stability from growth, responsibility from justice." "We in Brazil have begun the war against hunger," he added. "The starving cannot wait."[22]

Many, however, suspect that Lula's radicalism is more style than substance. João Pedro Stédile, an economist and activist with Brazil's landless-peasant movement, remarked in an interview that circumstances surrounding Lula's ascendancy were a far cry from those that brought Chávez to power. In Venezuela, Chávez was elected close on the heels of popular struggle, at the hands of which "neo-liberalism has been clearly defeated." For that reason Chávez has been able to talk about creating alternatives to capitalism. In Brazil, by contrast, social movements were on the decline by the time Lula was elected, and the government opted to ally itself to the forces of neo-liberalism.

In 2003, wages fell by 7 percent, while unemployment ran as high as 28 percent in cities such as Salvador. Yet Lula, slapping the face of his party base, prioritized debt repayments, which accounted for a staggering 10 percent of the nation's economic output.[23]

Some have wondered how the Workers' Party, which started out a quarter of a century ago as a vibrant, democratic organization supported by workers, activists, and socialist intellectuals and politicians, eventually morphed into a corrupt elite party backed by financial speculators and agro-mineral interests and run by "greedy upwardly mobile professionals."[24] Indeed, in a system called *mensalão*, Workers' Party leaders even bribed opposition legislators to informally join their alliance in Congress. The lawmakers were paid in monthly allotments for their votes.[25]

Lula's ideological backsliding has led to a fractious struggle over the heart and soul of the Workers' Party. In December 2003, three PT congressional deputies as well as a highly respected senator, Heloisa Helena, were expelled from the party. Their crime? Opposing legislation demanded by the IMF to open up Brazilian pension funds to privatization and simultaneously slash workers' benefits. Lula was absent from the meeting but argued that the new legislation provided a solid basis for the rest of his government. Helena shot back that she had not devoted her life to the PT in order to cut workers' pension rights once in power.[26]

In its first years in office, the Lula regime accomplished many "firsts." No government moved so far and so fast to the right. In such a brief span of time, no government party had more top party leaders, congressional representatives, ministers, and officials placed under investigation for fraud; no government had paid more in foreign debt interest and principal; no government had created more multi-millionaires; and no government had disillusioned more poor voters.[27]

In the wake of the PT expulsions, the party rank and file started to discuss their options. While most decided to stay in the party, members began to press for a change in direction. For example, Valter Pomar, the PT's secretary of international relations, has been calling for his party to get back in touch with its roots. Pomar, who is also the general secretary of the São Paulo Forum, a body formed in 1990 to bring together left-wing parties from across the hemisphere, has warned against the Lula government's alienation from the so-called "bases." He has argued that the PT should concentrate less on legislative alliances and more on the "socio-political, institutional and social network of support for the government."[28]

While in São Paulo, I figure it might be instructive to talk with Pomar about the future direction of the PT. He's a busy man, but I finally manage to catch up with him in the lobby of a Jardins hotel where he is participating in a conference. Not only does Pomar want to take the party in another direction domestically, but he also has ambitious plans on the international level. For instance, he routinely travels throughout South America meeting with members of Chávez's party, the Venezuelan Communist Party, and Evo Morales's people in Bolivia. In the long term, Pomar hopes to establish contact with local governments as well as labor unions, rural farmers, and youth.

But the PT man wants to go even farther, establishing links between the party and international campaigns for social justice. For example, the PT has had contact with something called the Jubilee 2000 campaign, a group that advocates for debt relief.[29] What's more, the PT has participated in key political discussions and learned from the experiences of other activists from across the hemisphere during the World Social Forum. Even more impressively, the PT has had contact with the Brazilian worker-owned factories that, inspired by the Argentine example, have recently begun to spring up. The party favors public, and not state-owned, forms of property. The PT supports the notion of cooperatives, though there is still no clear consensus within the party about what kind of cooperative might be best, and no concrete model has been established.

Pomar has painted a more fluid picture of the PT than one might get from reading international critics on the left. Still, I wonder how independent social movements can support the PT in light of the president's backtracking on key issues such as land reform.

According to the last agrarian census carried out a decade ago, 1 percent of Brazil's owners controlled 45 percent of the farmland. As democracy returned to Brazil, farmers organized and founded the MST in 1984. Its activism and land occupations have helped to change life in the countryside: since 1995 various governments have settled about 900,000 families in farming colonies, albeit often in appalling conditions.[30]

One of the most successful movements opposing neo-liberal doctrines in South America, the MST seizes unused land to provide real, workable alternatives for the neediest. The movement's daring land occupations, which have made it something of a *cause célèbre*, usually involve some 300 families. In a typical action, farmers identify idle plots of land and squat there until legal ownership is provided. Once the occupation is complete, however, the MST founds schools and lucrative cooperatives in its settlements. The movement, which is decentralized, provides its members with the basic social services that the Brazilian government is unwilling or unable to supply. For example, the MST has set up medical clinics and even training centers for health care workers. What's more, the MST has established thousands of schools, teacher training programs, and even a college.

But these bold actions have, not surprisingly, come at a cost: wealthy landowners and elites routinely use force to halt land expropriations, and attacks by the military and private militias have caused the deaths of thousands of farmers.[31]

The PT has been a long-time ally of the MST, and in fact the land-less farmers provided crucial support to Lula's presidential campaign. Officials of the Lula government boast of having settled 381,000 families during the president's first four-year term, which ended in 2006. MST activists, however, paint a different picture: they claim that 140,000 families are still encamped under plastic sheeting awaiting land. What's more, they argue, so-called "monocultures" like sugar cane for ethanol degrade the environment, drive farmers off the land, and reduce the food supply.

While many MST sympathizers within the government share the landless farmers' suspicion of big farming, it's unclear how much clout they have. As *The Economist* magazine has remarked, these officials must "answer to a president who is enthusiastic . . .about ethanol."[32]

Could it be that Lula had been somewhat successful at co-opting the MST, thereby neutralizing the challenge from social movements, much as Kirchner has co-opted the *piqueteros* in Argentina?

It's not as if Lula's retrograde policies have gone unchallenged. For example, Stédile of the MST remarked in an interview that Lula had merely adopted "a kinder, gentler, neo-liberalism," a recycling effort that has failed the country.[33]

One political observer and scholar, James Petras, has disdain for Lula's social policies. "The biggest loser in the debacle of Lula's regime," he writes, "has been the Landless Workers Movement, which has continued to support the government even as scores of peasant activists have been killed [and] tens of thousands of land squatters have been forcibly evicted." By supporting Lula, Petras claims, the MST made a serious tactical misstep: activists had severely weakened the struggles of the landless peasants and divided the opposition, to the benefit of the Brazilian right.[34]

With the MST playing a somewhat less combative role in Brazilian politics, I wonder whether organized labor might step in to fill the vacuum. For some political context, I ask labor expert Paulo Fontes at Princeton about the situation confronting labor prior to Lula's election.

In the 1990s, he tells me, labor was suffering as a result of globalization and the opening up of the economy. Moreover, industry became more decentralized and relocated to regions of the country where labor had not been historically strong—a process in many ways reminiscent of what happened in the United States during its own de-industrialization process. Meanwhile, high unemployment, a growing informal sector, new technologies, and lack of labor law reform also weakened organized labor.

Nevertheless, the labor movement in Brazil had been able to withstand this battering, and by the beginning of the Lula administration it was still in better shape than its counterparts throughout Latin America. What's more, despite the fact that the MST had siphoned off informal workers from the traditional unions, the two maintained warm ties.

"All these movements are much more connected than they seem to be," Fontes tells me. "In reality they have been together for 20 years. When I was working in the labor movement, I remember the Landless Movement asked us for a truck and material things."[35]

Despite these advantages, Lula's election posed a thorny political dilemma for the labor movement. On the one hand, having a PT leader in the presidency raised expectations that a new day was at hand. Lula himself was a founder of the CUT (*Central Única dos Trabalhadores*), the country's largest union federation, and indeed nine ministers and another 56 high-level officials in the executive branch hailed from union ranks, nearly all from the CUT.[36]

"As a movement," Fontes remarks, "labor is now weaker. But now, these people are running things, they have power."

The question, however, is whether that power actually translates into a real change in economic orientation for the country. The left wing of the CUT has been critical of Lula's economic policies, which probably would have a less neo-liberal direction if labor had been stronger in the country.

There have been fierce debates in the labor movement about Lula. While many argue that the president has not done much to advance formal labor rights, others concede that things are much improved for the working class in general. Lula has shown consideration for the plight of the masses by instituting the Bolsa Familia (Family Basket) program designed to aid the 44 million Brazilians who are unable to provide sufficient nutrition for themselves. The program provides cash transfers to families for food, based on their current income level. By May 2006, it had benefited 9.1 million families, not quite the total target population of 11.1 million but still a sizable number of Brazilians. Most of the people benefiting from Bolsa Familia lived in Lula's native northeast, a dirt-poor region of the country.[37]

The program has not been immune from controversy, however. Though the government claims that it has reached millions of people, Bolsa Familia has suffered from a lack of funding. What's more, the program advocates unsustainable cash transfers as a solution to poverty, which merely creates a cycle of dependency on the government. Lula announced that he would expand Bolsa Familia to the landless, an "insufficient swap" considering that Lula had failed to provide property to the desperate farmers living in makeshift tents along many roadsides in Brazil.[38] While some on the Brazilian left feel that Bolsa Familia is not really designed to combat poverty and is a mere band-aid, others argue that the program is important and that it is paving the way for improvements.[39] The left-wing *Monthly Review* points to another problem with Bolsa Familia: under the law, only those whose income falls well below what minimum-wage earners make—itself a meager sum—are eligible to receive benefits.

On the other hand, through Bolsa Familia, Lula has been able to build up a new base of political support. By circumventing the unions and social movements, he has cemented his relationship with the poorest sectors of the population.

Tarcisio Secoli is a prominent member of the metal workers' union in the industrial ABC region of São Paulo. Originally an employee of Daimler Chrysler, Secoli has worked with the metal workers' union since 1982 and participated in various strikes within the ABC region. He explains that the well-established metal workers' union, founded in 1943, played an important role in the struggle against the military dictatorship in the 1980s.

Judging from all of the Lula posters plastered up around the union headquarters, the metal workers have warm ties with the government. Indeed, Secoli tells me that the union's ties to Lula go way back: in 1989, after the return of democracy, the metal workers supported Lula's failed presidential bid.[40] Currently, the union, with its membership of 80,000, was still going strong, organizing workers not only against U.S. firms such as Ford, but also foreign companies such as Toyota and Volkswagen. According to Secoli, the president of the union conferred with Lula once every two to three months.

Given all the Lula posters, I initially figure that the metal workers union is probably politically compromised. But Secoli is no labor hack, and he paints a vibrant picture of the labor movement. Hardly a fan of government nationalization of industry, he remarks that "this would just give rise to a new owner. The owner would be someone from the government. We don't want to go back in time. We want self management."

Indeed, Secoli is quite aware of the worker-owned factories developing in Argentina. He explains that the phenomenon had spread to Brazil, where there are now 25 worker-owned factories. What's more, the country had seen the emergence of more than 200 cooperatives run by the likes of artisans and farmers.

The cooperatives were in turn grouped into a larger union that pledged to fight for a new kind of "solidarity" economy. The metal workers' union was interested in providing political support for the worker-owned factories, and would even seek to purchase products from these firms.

I cannot say that I felt as politically inspired at Secoli's union as I did in the radical Argentine hotel. And yet, the metal workers' union hardly conformed to my stereotype of old-guard labor. From my conversation with Secoli, I gained the sense that the labor movement here might be sufficiently dynamic and flexible to change with the times, and to form new alliances.

CHAPTER NINE

SOUTH AMERICAN MEDIA WARS

It's Caracas, summer of 2006, and I'm struck by the changed media atmosphere in the country. Turning on the TV in my hotel, I watch Venezolana de Televisión, or Channel Eight, a state channel. I am treated to an outlandish and bizarre sight: a pro-Chávez host sporting a beard and wearing a baseball hat and sweatshirt.

Waving his hands wildly in the air, he blasts the political opposition. Flipping the dial, I see opposition pundits scurrilously insulting Hugo Chávez in a fashion that would be unthinkable on mainstream U.S. media. Welcome to Venezuela's media wars, which have become particularly vitriolic in recent years.

Like TV, print media has also taken on a much more belligerent tone. In the upper-class Caracas neighborhood of Altamira, I find a newsstand and buy two papers, *Diario VEA*, a pro-Chávez paper, and *El Nacional*, which is against the regime.

Taking care not to let anyone see my pro-Chávez paper in this anti-government neighborhood, I head to a café. On the front page of *VEA*, a headline screams, "General Baduel Warns: Foreign Aggression is Possible."

It would seem as if Chávez has now gotten the upper hand on his enemies through state-funded media and a new satellite news station called Telesur, Television Station of the South, which is beamed throughout the hemisphere.

Since 2005, Telesur has provided 24-hour satellite programming. The station, which is supported by Argentina, Bolivia, Cuba, Nicaragua, and Venezuela, is beamed to 20 Latin American and Caribbean nations and has an audience of some 5 million viewers.[1]

Telesur, which is an effort to counteract the influence of U.S. media such as CNN, is an important instrument in the drive towards hemispheric integration. The station aims to build cultural awareness by showing South America "through South American eyes."

Another interesting state-sponsored channel is Vive, which provides a more thoughtful dialogue than Channel Eight. When I tune in to watch one night, some intellectuals are discussing different approaches to documentary film making. The moderator is a hippie-looking man with long hair and a beard. During a pause in the program, Vive shows stark images of bombed out Iraq and a caption reads, "Imagine if your city was invaded and destroyed by a foreign army?"

More roundtable discussion from the panelists is followed by another program break. This time images of oil equipment flash by as a solemn voiceover intones, "It's up to you to protect the oil. Venezuela: now it belongs to everyone." Later, I see a critical documentary about Operation Just Cause and the 1989 U.S. invasion of Panama.

Before long, Vive turns to Chávez speaking live in the western Plains state of Barinas. He stands before loyal Chavistas dressed in red, talking of the need to create communal banks. For the most part, he has the stage to himself, maintaining total control over the discussion. Once in a while the president pauses, calling on his followers to answer his questions. It's as if he's playing the role of a stern rural schoolteacher testing his adoring pupils.

From a psychological perspective, Chávez's manipulation of the Barinas event is fascinating if not particularly surprising: for years, the president has demonstrated complete mastery over the media. His hallmark TV show, *Aló, Presidente!*, was immensely popular. During the weekly program, Chávez spoke on politics and would take telephone calls from people around the country.

Feeling restive, I go downstairs to reception where I talk up the humble and pleasant night watchman. He explains that he's a Chavista, but not a fanatic, diehard supporter. He appreciated some of the *cinéma vérité* programming on Vive but didn't like *Aló, Presidente!*, which he found uninformative. He believed, moreover, that Chávez's appearances on TV had failed to instill much anti-U.S. feeling in the middle class.

I had to agree with my new acquaintance: for me, Vive was most interesting when it was not didactic. I was particularly taken with the station's footage of rural life without any narrative voiceover. I liked one segment, a kind of reality-style video of the *llano* or Plains region. The scene showed children performing a popular dance called the *joropo*, farmers making cheese, and cowboys rustling cattle.

The next day my peace delegation arrives and I'm pleased to hear that Jess, our tour leader, has seen fit to arrange an interview with Carlos Correa, a media expert. We crowd into our blue van and head to the offices of the human rights organization Provea near the National Library. As our group gathers around a large table, Correa breaks down the pro- and anti-Chávez media for us. "Without a doubt," he explains, the media is one of the chief battlegrounds of the Venezuelan political conflict."

In print media, the Chávez government could count on the support of *Últimas Noticias*, a daily paper. There were dozens of other pro-government papers, including the tabloid *VEA*. The government didn't own these papers outright, though it provided them with office space and advertising. Arrayed against the government were *El Nacional* and *El Universal*.

After the 2002 coup, the government strengthened state-sponsored media in response to the private media's assault on the Chávez regime. The government had, for example, made major investments in Venezolana de Televisión, the channel featuring the bombastic host in the baseball hat. Venezolana de Televisión's focus is mainly on political "preaching to the choir," though recently the station has incorporated some sports programming and morning shows directed at housewives.

Meanwhile, Venevisión and Televen are either neutral or leaning toward Chávez. Pitted against the government is Globovisión, a news channel similar to CNN and broadcast in Caracas and Maracaibo, and a second station, Channel Two.

Despite the new, more pro-Chávez media environment, Telesur faces significant technical as well as stylistic challenges. Venezuelans are accustomed to U.S. media and a level of production values that Telesur has difficulty matching. Moreover as a cable channel in a nation where many cannot afford to pay for TV, its audience remains small.[2]

Some regard Chávez's manipulation of the media as a classically populist strategy. With *Aló, Presidente!*, Chávez is following in the footsteps of previous Latin American leaders. For example, Lázaro Cárdenas, president of Mexico from 1932–38, would answer telegraphs from ordinary Mexicans in a weekly radio address, making himself accessible to the people, at least symbolically, in the same way as Chávez is now doing on television.

But there might be limits to Chávez's media strategy. Though *Aló, Presidente!* has worked beautifully up to now, the president's style does not necessarily go over well in other countries. Peruvians, for example, dislike Chávez's media presence. "They find his way of speaking weird and pretentious," Stein declares. Part of the problem is that his style is distinctively Venezuelan, exhibiting characteristics that are "perhaps not so favorable in another environment."[3]

Besides TV, I am also interested in Web sites and other electronic media which had proven particularly influential during the 2002 coup. I figure that Wilpert, the publisher of venezuelanalysis.com, should know something about this subject, and during our interview I ask how he started the site.

In 2003, Wilpert hooked up with Martín Sánchez, one of the founders of a pro-Chávez site called Aporrea, which represented the Popular Revolutionary Assembly, or Asamblea Revolucionaria Popular in Spanish. One of the most important Web sites after the attempted coup, Aporrea provided key information and continuous updates on developments in Venezuela. Impressed with Aporrea's impact, Wilpert was inspired to create a news site in English, hoping to bring to the international community information that was not controlled by the existing corporate media.

When I ask Wilpert where the funding for the site comes from, he chuckles. "That's always a tricky issue," he says.

The site receives some grassroots donations, but also gets support from Chávez's Ministry of Culture. This had led the opposition to claim that venezuelanalysis.com is "100 percent government." But Wilpert denies that the government has ever interfered with the site's content and claims to be looking for advertising and more funding from foundations. He confesses that it has been "kind of hard" to find people to work on the site; at the high point he had four or five people, but the number has fluctuated as reporters come and go. It is somewhat difficult working as a journalist in Caracas, he says, because the government is not always forthcoming with information, and "you're generally regarded with a lot of suspicion." Nevertheless, electronic media has indeed made an impact. Wilpert's venezuelanalysis.com reaches about one thousand people every day. What's more, the site is read by journalists and academics, and reporters who view it pass along the information they find there to the other, mostly anti-Chávez journalists based in Venezuela.[4]

Electronic media has certainly made a difference in countering the anti-Chávez forces, but to my mind it's really Telesur that has made the biggest impact. One day in Caracas, I take a cab to the Telesur station, located in the same building as Venezolana de Televisión.

Seen as South America's answer to Al Jazeera and CNN, Telesur is spearheaded by Andrés Izarra, the station's president. A rising star in the Chávez administration, Izarra is the son of diehard Chavista and retired air force officer William Izarra. Andrés started to work as a journalist while living in France, writing for a magazine published by an uncle who was jailed in Venezuela in the 1970s for left-wing political activity. "Still," writes *The New York Times*, "Mr. Izarra seems an unlikely Chavista."[5]

As a young man, Izarra had a privileged upbringing, attending an elite school in Caracas. He speaks impeccable English, having studied in Massachusetts while his parents pursued graduate studies at Harvard. What's more, Izarra worked for almost five years in the United States at CNN and NBC.

As a news director at RCTV, an anti-Chávez media outlet that provided pro-coup coverage of Chávez's ouster in 2002, Izarra was at the heart of the media wars in Venezuela. Founded in 1953, RCTV is a veritable Venezuelan institution, the producer of a long-running political satire program and a famous nighttime soap opera.

After Chávez was elected in 1998, RCTV, under the direction of the country's wealthy oligarchy and the likes of station chief Marcel Granier, came out strongly against Chávez. For two days prior to the April 11, 2002 coup RCTV preempted normal programming and provided wall-to-wall coverage of a general strike that sought to topple Chávez. A series of commentators voiced vitriolic attacks against the president, and the station allowed no time for a response from the regime, instead airing nonstop ads encouraging Venezuelans to participate in an April 11 march designed to oust Chávez. RCTV provided blanket coverage of the event. When the march ended in tragedy and violence, RCTV ran manipulated video blaming Chavistas for scores of deaths and injuries. "After military rebels overthrew Chávez and he disappeared from public view for two days," remarks *The Los Angeles Times*, "RCTV's biased coverage edged fully into sedition."[6]

When thousands of Chavistas poured into the streets to demand the president's return, RCTV refused to cover the protests, instead choosing to run cartoons, soap operas, and old movies. To top it off, Granier personally went to Miraflores, the presidential palace, on April 13 to pledge support to Dictator-For-a-Day Pedro Carmona, who had abolished the nation's Supreme Court, Constitution, and National Assembly. Izarra resigned from RCTV during the coup and later testified before the National Assembly that he had received an order from his superiors at RCTV: "Zero pro-Chávez, nothing related to Chávez or his supporters . . .. The idea was to create a climate of transition and to start to promote the dawn of a new country."[7] At the time, Izarra was not a Chávez sympathizer; the reporter later remarked that his decision to resign had more to do with concerns about the lack of journalistic ethics and objectivity at RCTV.[8] Cast out of Venezuelan private media, Izarra returned to CNN as a field producer during the oil lockout of 2002–03.

"Andrés was far from being a Chavista when I met him," remarked Lucia Newman, a senior Latin America correspondent for CNN and Izarra's former boss at the network. "But he found himself in a position in which he had to choose sides," she added. "In a general sense, I think he's now a true believer."[9]

After handling media relations for the Venezuelan Embassy in Washington, Izarra's rise within the Chávez regime was nothing short of meteoric: at the age of 35, he was put in charge of *Aló, Presidente!* and also enjoyed a stint as Venezuela's minister of communications.

Now at Telesur, Izarra has become a passionate defender of Chávez's controversial decision not to renew RCTV's license.[10] While Amnesty International, Human Rights Watch, the Committee to Protect Journalists, and members of the European Parliament, the U.S. Senate, and even Chile's Congress denounced the closure of RCTV, Venezuela's oldest private television network, others claim the move is justified.

Writing in *The Los Angeles Times*, for example, Bart Jones wondered, "Would a network that aided and abetted a coup against the government be allowed to operate in the United States? The U.S. government probably would have shut down RCTV within five minutes after a failed coup attempt—and thrown its owners in jail. Chávez's government allowed it to continue operating for five years, and then declined to renew its 20-year license to use the public airwaves. It can still broadcast on cable or via satellite dish." Granier, continues Jones, should not be viewed as a free speech martyr. Radio, TV, and newspapers continue to be uncensored in Venezuela and are unthreatened by the government.[11]

"RCTV practiced a form of media terrorism," Izarra has remarked. "The families that own RCTV hate my guts for saying that, but the oligarchy that once controlled Venezuela is finally coming apart."[12]

As I head to Izarra's Telesur station in Caracas, I'm wondering what I'll find. Despite the station's newfound stature, the facilities are pretty modest. There's no elevator, so I make my way up the four flights of stairs. As I arrive on the third floor, I notice a kind of makeshift café lodged in a dark, industrial room where a few people sit drinking coffee.

In the Telesur waiting room, a man offers me some pro-Chávez papers to read. Presently Telesur's director, Aram Aharonian, shows up. A small Uruguayan man, he dresses informally, sports a gray ponytail, and has a kind of steely, playful expression. We conduct an interview in his office, which is barely larger than a cubicle.

The Telesur director acknowledges that the station has been critical of the United States, but denies that it's a pro-Chávez mouthpiece. I point to a photo on his wall, showing Aharonian and Chávez joking together. "Does he ever call you?" I ask bluntly.

"Never," Aharonian says categorically.

He says the photo was taken in 2001 when Chávez came to a meeting of the foreign correspondents association. Aharonian says he hadn't spoken to Chávez since November 2005, when the president came to observe Telesur's installations. Moreover, the Chávez government had never expressed discontent with the station's coverage. Aharonian then goes on at length about Telesur's independence.

"We're providing information that's not available on local TV," he continues, sipping espresso. "We actually provide context so that people know what the news is about."

He complains that the news business has gone through a process of dumbing down since the Gulf War. Journalism has become instantaneous but also devoid of any investigation, analysis, or debate. Telesur by contrast is "rescuing" journalistic ethics by providing context and opinions about goings-on.[13]

Telesur is no stranger to controversy, however: in 2006, when the station announced a content-sharing agreement with Al Jazeera, Connie Mack, a right-wing Republican congressman from Florida, remarked that the decision was designed to create a "global television network for terrorists."[14]

Again and again, Aharonian, who speaks in a Uruguayan accent that I find difficult to understand, says that I am starting from a "false assumption" in viewing the station as an essentially anti-U.S. media outlet. If Michele Bachelet said it was important to encourage economic ties to Japan and the United States, Telesur would cover that.[15]

If Izarra can be believed, the station is not necessarily staffed exclusively by Chavistas, either. Speaking to *The New York Times*, Izarra said that he was tolerant of different opinions at Telesur. According to him, 120 of the station's 400 employees were opponents of Chávez. Izarra kept tabs on the figure by using lists of voters and their political sympathies, available on pirated software.[16]

What's more, the station had run into problems with South American governments, casting doubt on the thesis that Telesur was strictly anti-U.S. In a revealing aside, Aharaonian confides that the station's Haiti coverage had proved controversial with the Chilean, Argentine, and Uruguayan governments. One of the first stories that Telesur had broadcast, in fact, concerned the MINUSTAH force in Haiti. In the report, the Haitians said that the Latin American soldiers were repressing the Haitian people. Though the reporting had ruffled feathers and "some officials in various countries" had even called him, Aharonian stuck by his story.

Telesur will face significant challenges in its efforts to expand its coverage throughout South America. In some of the larger Latin American countries, for example, Telesur lacks access to cable networks which are controlled by the owners of private stations who have not been cooperative with Aharonian and his staff.

On the other hand, Telesur might be able to do business with small cable providers operating in the interior of countries. Another option would be to sign agreements with regional and national TV stations, either private or state-owned, to broadcast Telesur segments.

While CNN still has three or four times Telesur's audience share, the station, Aharonian claims, has achieved "a lot of credibility" in just a year and a half, to the point that CNN now recognizes the need to adapt and compete.

In the meantime, Aharonian is looking for ways to finance the station without relying on the state. I am pleased to hear that Telesur is shortly planning to move out of the Venezolana de Televisión building to new headquarters provided by the state, thus ending its visible association with the rabidly pro-Chávez Channel Eight. The station also has ambitious plans to open branches in Quito, Lima, and Montevideo.

Now that it has become a force in its own right, many Latin American TV stations have requested images from Telesur. What's more, Telesur has established a presence in Cuba.

"Cubans historically have had a very siege-like mentality," Aharonian says. "The U.S. has been trying to transmit its media to Cuba for forty years, and it has done it poorly—Radio Martí for example. We have a different approach. We see our presence in Cuba as an opportunity to get the Cuban people more informed about what is happening in Latin America and in the world. We now get three hours on prime time on Cuban television. In a certain sense, we have a captive audience, as there's not a lot of opportunities to change channels."

Speaking with Aharonian, I get a sense of the many challenges involved in launching a new TV station. And yet, it is undeniable that the station had made great strides and might eventually have a hemisphere-wide impact.

"To what extent does Telesur contribute to South American integration?" I ask.

"The problem in Latin America is that we don't know anything about each other, we are blind to ourselves. We always saw ourselves through the lens of Madrid, London, New York. We begin with the idea that first we must get to know ourselves. Our problems are similar, the expectations are similar. Telesur is merely a tool so that people get to know what's happening in Latin America, so that people recognize, 'Oh, that's Ecuador,' or 'Oh, that's Chile.' And this may spur the process of integration, as you say."

Judging from the reports, Telesur is indeed a station on the move. In May 2007 it held an International Communication Conference in Caracas with noted journalists, media executives, and intellectuals. The two-day event, which was open to the public, featured interesting roundtable debates on such topics as: "Impunity and power of major media outlets"; "The responsibility of national governments"; "The use of radio and TV airspace as a public asset"; and "Social ownership of the media."

Participants included Danny Glover, movie directors, and journalists from across South America, including Tariq Ali, editor of the British magazine *New Left Review*. Glover remarked that in the United States, the issue of media control and citizen participation in the media was off the table.

"People (in the United States) don't participate in a dialogue that allows them to see that they have the power of information," he said. "We see the positions that the media take, and people should take that power back and make themselves the architects of the media."

At the end of the conference, participants agreed to promote the creation of independent, community-based alternative media outlets as a counterbalance to the corporate media. In a manifesto approved by Telesur's advisory council, participants declared that radio and television were an "asset for humanity" and should be administered by national governments, not by corporations. Furthermore, national governments should use their authority to revoke, concede, or renew licenses in accordance with their various constitutions. The participants applauded recent decisions taken by Argentina, Brazil, and Uruguay to reclaim public air space.[17]

In Ecuador, very few people have access to the internet, and digital media has not taken on the same political significance as in Venezuela. On the radio, however, there is some limited space for alternative views. One station, Radio La Luna, is openly supportive of the Correa regime and is readily available over the internet.

Judging from my conversation with Manuel Castro at CONAIE, however, TV is more politically conservative. The TV media, says the Quichua Indian, typically ignores indigenous proposals, paying attention only when violence breaks out. Castro adds that indigenous festivals, such as *inti raymi* (the Festival of the Sun, which dates back to the era of the Inca), or special harvests are met with a virtual media blackout.[18] The CONAIE hopes to break up entrenched monopolies, making the media more democratic and open like Telesur, a channel Castro endorses.

But over at *El Universo*, Saint-Upéry's wife, Mónica Almeida, tells me that Ecuador is very different from Venezuela. Her own paper had taken a measured tone toward the incoming administration. It's unlikely, she explains, that Correa will seek to build up government media to the same degree as Chávez has done, though the regime is clearly interested in a state-run television station. Currently, Channel One is in economic straits, and the government has shown some interest in buying it.[19]

I leave Quito with the impression that Ecuador is hardly embroiled in an intense media war like Venezuela's. But after I return to the United States, the situation starts to become more polarized. If recent news reports are any indication, Correa just might follow in Chávez's footsteps. According to Dow Jones International News, the Ecuadoran leader plans to regulate Ecuador's media ownership through the Constituent Assembly. "One of the things that the Assembly must do," Correa commented, "is bar economic and financial powers from having communication media because this is an incestuous relationship, ill-fated for a democratic society."

Speaking in Cayambe, north of Quito, Correa proposed that the constitution disallow bankers from financing media outlets. According to the president, Ecuadoran television is controlled by powerful interests, and the Association of Television Channels is nothing more than a "bankers club."[20] A 2006 study by Ecuador's Central University reports that many television stations, including Teleamazonas, Telecentro, Gamavisión and Cable Noticias, are funded by recognized bankers who also own newspapers, radio stations, and magazines.[21]

"Here there are groups that own two or three TV channels and 40 or 50 radio stations, and so they are owners of the truth," he added. Correa went so far as to accuse certain media outlets, which he did not name, of being "corrupt" and "lacking seriousness." These outlets, he claimed, broadcast "lies" and had "slandered" him personally.[22]

Some observers of the media, such as my contact Efrén Icaza, believe that there are substantial conflicts of interest within the media.

For example, the corporate media failed to report on Ecuador's banking scandals, which had cost the impoverished nation a whopping $8 billion.[23]

Correa says that the media "does not inform, it defends the pockets of its owners. Laws must be established to stop information from being managed by economic groups, as it has been up until now."[24] Economy Minister Ricardo Patiño has brought tensions to a boil by denouncing a supposed campaign by the banks and media to "take President Correa out of power." Correa has remarked that he would "cancel the license of any television station that conspires against its government."[25] The following month, during his first visit to Spain as president, Correa said that it was "necessary to tell the whole truth" about RCTV. "If I had been President of Venezuela, in that moment [that RCTV incited the coup] I would have cancelled the frequency." Correa has argued that the media is irresponsible and says whatever it feels like, usually to defend the economic status quo.

Correa, who has never shied from rhetorical flourishes, added that "the only problem that the Ecuadoran media has is that, since the 15th of January, there's an actual government and they're not accustomed to that, they're accustomed to ordering governments around."[26] Such broadsides are certainly combative, but as Correa sympathizers point out, the president hasn't closed any papers.[27]

Not surprisingly, though, Correa seems to be doing his utmost to increase the clout of state media. Communication Secretary Mónica Chuji has reportedly been seeking to set up a state television network.[28] A state channel, Correa has asserted, would not be a "mouthpiece" for the government, but rather an independent entity that would "guarantee transparent information, not linked to private interest groups."[29]

While it's unclear how the issue of state TV will get sorted out, Correa has wasted no time in seeking to get closer to the people. His Communication Secretariat announces presidential activities via a multi-station radio program entitled, "The President Talks to His People." The show, reminiscent of U.S. President Franklin Roosevelt's famous "fireside chats," airs every Saturday. Reporters from various radio stations and representatives from civil society are generally invited on the show, which is moderated by well known media figures. The program lasts an hour and a half, of which Correa uses 45 minutes to report on his activities during the week. During the rest of the time, journalists are free to pose whatever questions they wish.

With Correa apparently seeking to emulate many aspects of Chávez's media policy, it seems possible that Telesur might take root in Ecuador. During our conversation back in Caracas, Telesur Director Aharonian had expressed some regret that there was no state TV channel in Ecuador. In 2005, he had traveled to Ecuador to "symbolically inaugurate" Telesur's signal in the nation. But UV Televisión, a private station located in Loja, 600 kilometers southeast of Quito, was the only channel in the country to transmit Telesur on open signal. UV's Director, Omar Burneo, remarked that "We believe that Telesur is the best alternative in order to develop television with pluralistic and diverse content." Burneo said he would broadcast three to four hours of Telesur programming per day on UV, whose signal reached only the south of Ecuador.[30] Since that time, Aharonian tells me, Telesur has developed excellent broadcast exposure in the Ecuadoran interior on regional, private, and university TV channels. But he still wanted more visibility in Quito itself.

If the Correa government ultimately creates a state channel, Telesur will gain a more powerful outlet for its news broadcasts. According to the Ecuadoran paper *El Comercio*, Telesur has been advising the Ecuadoran government on how best to set up a new state channel.[31]

Meanwhile, Correa has looked to cultivate closer media links with Venezuela. Chuji herself reportedly visited Venezuela recently in an effort to work on a communications agreement between the two countries, which would include arrangements for Telesur to operate in Ecuador.[32] In August 2007, Correa and Chávez signed an agreement of understanding that Ecuador should form part of Telesur, and a couple of weeks later the Andean nation committed to putting up 5 percent of the station's capital.[33]

With the political ferment in Ecuador, I figure it will take a while for the media question to sort itself out. But Morales has been in power for longer than Correa, and Bolivia has been Venezuela's strongest regional ally. If any country was likely to embrace the kind of media strategy that Chávez has pursued, it was bound to be Bolivia. Indeed, just prior to my arrival in La Paz, Bolivia was formally incorporated as a partner in Telesur.

Baldwin Montero, editor of the conservative paper *La Razón*, resembles a younger Evo Morales, despite his English first name. A media veteran, he'd been working as a journalist for eighteen years.

I'd heard that the media was very critical of Morales during the last election, and Montero says there's a fair degree of truth to the reports. Constant media attacks had led the president to adopt a more aggressive stance toward some journalists and to become a frequent critic of the country's privately owned newspapers and television stations. He often complains that the media treated his government unfairly. "My parents taught me to pray in church with my eyes closed," he has said. "But when I do it some media say that Evo is asleep."[34]

As in Ecuador, in Bolivia relations have been heating up between the government and the media. Morales frequently has accused the press of deceiving the Bolivian people about his government's intentions, and even described it recently as the main "adversary" of his administration. Some observers predict that Morales, like Chávez, may intervene to deprive certain media outlets of their broadcast licenses.[35]

Furthermore, Morales might enlist Chávez's support by buying up some media with Venezuelan capital. Additionally, Telesur has a correspondent in Bolivia, and Bolivian state TV broadcasts segments from the South American station. Morales was also interested in creating a program similar in format to Chávez's *Aló, Presidente!*[36]

Indeed, after my departure from Bolivia, Morales launched a weekly radio show in which he talks about his administration and takes questions from callers. The show, "The People Are News," airs for two hours each week on the Patria Nueva (New Fatherland) state network, whose signal covers all of Bolivia.

Few people watch TV in the Bolivian countryside, where radio is more prevalent. Fortunately for Morales, the government enjoys a certain amount of support on the radio. There has been a great move towards community radio in the country, and the regime is now able to broadcast its activities on local stations.

According to the Associated Press, there are now more than 20 community radio stations supportive of Morales;[37] the Venezuelan government has provided $1.5 million to finance the stations.[38] What's more, "Radio del Sur" or "Radio of the South" a radio station that forms part of Chávez's ALBA plan based on reciprocal trade and solidarity between nations, recently began operations with help from such countries as Cuba, Nicaragua, and Venezuela.

Having shored up political support through radio, Morales is now moving on to television. Community TV, he has said, is the next frontier. "In the years to come we will have television for the poor," he declared, "so they can tell their own truth and can educate us through their own media."[39]

Print has also become a battleground in the media wars. According to Montero, some weeklies are now being managed by Morales sympathizers.[40] During a conference in the Bolivian city of Cochabamba, Journalists for the Truth, a pro-Chávez organization of some 5,000 Venezuelan media professionals, presented a proposal to form a "newspaper of the south," as an alternative to the traditional South American press. The idea of the paper, explained Marcos Hernández, president of Journalists for Truth, is to give voice to those who have been invisible to the traditional media. In each country, reporters would form cooperatives, which would write their own stories. The articles would then be revised by a central editing committee. Hernández said that the proposal was enthusiastically received in Cochabamba, because it stood to open the door to new forms of communication and challenge traditional media monopolies in South America.[41]

The media climate in Chile is much more conservative than in the Andes. Indeed, speaking with *Punto Final* editor Cabieses in his modest Santiago office leaves me with the impression that progressive media in the country might face daunting challenges ahead.

In contrast to Venezuela, Chile has no television station that espouses the views of the left. According to Cabieses, the situation in the mainstream press is no different. There are two left-wing bi-monthlies, *El Siglo*, of the Communist Party, and his own *Punto Final*, but both have notoriously low circulation and Cabieses complains that his paper suffers from distribution problems and a lack of publicity.

In radio, the situation is a bit more hopeful, though still difficult: the Communist Party owns one station, and there are a few other progressive stations. On the internet, there is more political diversity than in TV and print, but digital media is still incipient in Chile, where most people lack internet access.

With Venezuela as my constant reference point, I ask Cabieses whether the Chilean government might sponsor more state media and whether this might generate an information war as we'd seen under Chávez.

Cabieses does a double take. "You mean, *here?*" he asks, incredulously.

"Yes," I say, chuckling. "Are you surprised by my question?"

Cabieses explains that in Venezuela, state media emerged because the government actually wanted to confront the private media. In Chile by contrast, the political differences between the government and media were negligible.

The situation is all the more challenging, because CNN and other U.S. media outlets are quite strong in Chile, though strictly among the middle and upper classes. It's relatively easy to watch Telesur in the center of the country, but elsewhere only those who have access to Direct TV and a long-range antenna can receive the signal.

That's a far cry from the media climate in Argentina, which is one of the state sponsors of Telesur. Not only that, but Argentina's state news agency, Télam, recently signed a cooperation agreement with Telesur whereby the two organizations will share journalistic material in various forms.

In Brazil, on the other hand, large media conglomerates like O Globo predominate, presenting a rather discouraging picture for left-wing journalism. According to observers, news reports tend to be conservative, typically savaging Chávez, for example, as a "proto-dictator." Indeed, with the exception of some small and not particularly influential magazines, Brazilian media is even more anti-Chávez than the U.S. corporate media.[42] It's thus not surprising that the Brazilian media has been critical of Evo Morales for his nationalistic policy toward the gas industry and Brazil's Petrobras and hostile toward domestic social movements, such as the MST.

To get an inside perspective on the mainstream media, I speak with Daniel Buarque. A young reporter who cut his teeth in the city of Recife, Buarque later moved to São Paulo where he got a job at *Folha de São Paulo* and later O Globo Online.

He tells me that in general the media tends to bash the Lula government. Most papers "came out against everything the government did" and tried to "hone in on problems." When he worked at *Folha de São Paulo*, he even detected a desire to "take down" the Lula government.[43]

"It wasn't like, 'Let's lie, let's come up with things that aren't real,'" he says. "But there was this attitude of trying to find real issues to bring down Lula."

Buarque adds that *Folha de São Paulo* was not even the most rabidly anti-Lula paper: that prize fell to another paper, *Estado São Paulo*.

While TV has been somewhat less critical of Lula, magazines, which are controlled by powerful economic interests, are firmly against the government. *Veja*, for instance, publishes columns every week accusing Lula of corruption and arguing that he should step down .

Radio, meanwhile, takes its cue from TV and the print media, and "isn't very independent." Globo owns the three main radio stations, and Buarque tells me that to his knowledge there is no truly progressive radio station in the country. In contrast to Venezuela, the internet remains largely irrelevant.

Nevertheless, the Brazilian media has not shied away from criticizing Bush. "There is a sense that he has turned his back on South America, and is only interested in fighting useless wars," Buarque remarks.

Meanwhile, despite its hostility to Chávez and Lula, the mainstream media does not identify with the right as it does in Venezuela. In Brazil, no one says they are on the right because this term is associated with the earlier period of military dictatorship. "If you say you're on the right," Buarque explains, "it implies you are against democracy. There's no media outlet that openly advocates for a right-wing government."

Though Globo initially supported the military during Brazil's dark days of dictatorship, it would never support a coup against the current government. Nor would any other outlet, not even the rabidly anti-Lula *Veja*, support a return to military rule.

Nevertheless, Lula clearly sees the need to bolster state media in order to enhance his position. On Monday mornings, he broadcasts a show on state radio called *Breakfast with the President*, which splits time between hard-hitting economic issues and lighter fare. During one broadcast, Lula himself interviewed Ronaldo, a soccer star, as well as other players on the Brazilian national team. The discussion centered on problems faced by soccer players early on in their careers before they achieved international status. Ronaldo remarked that, despite his upbringing in poverty and a recurring injury, he was able to overcome adversity through perseverance. According to one report, the interviews seemed to be "tailored for Lula's recently launched campaign to promote national pride."[44]

Buarque says the government wants to go beyond *Breakfast with the President*, and create a state-run TV station. Lula has hired a well known media figure and political analyst to set up the station. Meanwhile, Telesur is reportedly interested in beaming its programming to Brazil in Portuguese.[45] Because of the prominence of U.S. media, however, Telesur might find it difficult to gain acceptance in Brazil.

"CNN is really the main source of international news for media in Brazil," Buarque says.

While Lula has clearly not pursued such a confrontational stance towards the media as, say, Chávez, clearly many South American leaders have recognized the political importance of media. In asserting greater state control over media, today's governments have signaled to the corporate media that they are indeed a force to be reckoned with.

MOVING FORWARD

SOUTH AMERICAN COMMUNITY OF NATIONS

Many have long proposed closer South American political and economic integration, but the time to move forward has never seemed more propitious. Despite their many political, cultural, and economic differences, South American nations share a commitment to harnessing their energy resources for the good of the people and overcoming the legacy of brutal military rule. Some have managed to overturn neo-liberalism and are now moving towards a more socially responsive form of economic development. The region's governments face varying levels of social pressure from below, but all must contend with a revived civil society fed up with political repression and tired of the economic proscriptions offered up by the United States and its elite South American allies.

Fermín Toro, Venezuela's former ambassador to the United Nations, tells me that Chávez's emergence revived the hope that Venezuela "might follow its destiny" by encouraging greater unity with Ecuador, Colombia, and Panama.[1] These nations had once formed the Republic of Colombia, which was dissolved in 1830 when the Great Liberator, Simón Bolívar, died.

Despite Chávez's Bolivarian aspirations, however, the Venezuelan leader has been critical of the type of integration being pursued in the Andes. In April 2006 he withdrew Venezuela from the Andean Community, citing objections to Colombia's and Peru's proposed free trade

agreements with the United States.[2] Diplomatic friction like this stands
as an obstacle to closer South American integration. Countries in the
Andean Community want Venezuela to return, and while Chávez hasn't
ruled out the possibility, such a move would prove logistically problematic given Venezuela's current membership in Mercosur. A possible solution would be for Venezuela to become an associate member of the
Andean Community, like Chile.

Toro believes that Venezuela will return to the Andean Community
when the political situation has changed within the wider region. "The
Andean Community has been our political home in the past and will
continue to be in future. Venezuela will rejoin the bloc when we are all
Bolivarians."

One way to consolidate integration efforts might be to dissolve the
Andean Community of Nations and merge it with Mercosur. As far back
as December 2004, Mercosur nations declared their intention to form a
South American Community modeled after the European Union. The
proposed union would join Mercosur with the Andean Community,
Chile, Guyana, and Suriname.

Bolivia's Morales has called on his colleagues to speed up the
process of launching this South American Community of Nations because, in the words of his Presidency Minister Juan Quintana, it is "not
possible for one nation to end poverty alone." Quintana has blamed friction between the Andean Community and Mercosur for inhibiting the
development of a balanced regional strategy in such fields as international competition and communications.[3]

While it's unclear how such problems will ultimately be resolved,
Mercosur has made important strides as of late. The bloc is beginning
to take on political projects, rather than pursuing economic objectives
alone. For example, Mercosur now has a European Union-styled regional parliament in Montevideo, and many Uruguayans hope their
capital might evolve into the "Brussels of South America."

The Mercosur Parliament, or Parlasur, comprises 18 active congressional delegates from each member country, who will be able to
issue resolutions and to commission studies but not to legislate over national congresses.

For Cuba, the rise of a unified and fortified Mercosur comes as
good news indeed. A recent Mercosur summit held in Córdoba, Argentina, was notable for the presence of Cuban leader Fidel Castro.

"This must be the only meeting in which they did not try to attack me," Castro remarked ironically.[4]

Taking advantage of the changed political climate in South America, Castro signed a Complementary Economic Accord with Mercosur, an agreement that would benefit the island state in its trade with South American countries.[5] A few months later, ambassadors of the Mercosur nations announced their intention to carry out other joint initiatives with Cuba dealing with tourism, energy, and medicine. Such a rapprochement between South America and Cuba must be regarded as a setback for Washington, which has for decades sought to isolate the island nation.

But many obstacles to South American unity remain on the horizon. Kirchner, for example, has stressed that Mercosur must transcend its mere emphasis on economic growth. "We are not interested only in economic integration," he said. "We are not interested in a region of the world where integration is full of poverty, exclusion and unemployment," he added, referring to the stark differences between strong economies such as Argentina, Venezuela, and Brazil on the one hand, and smaller economies like Paraguay and Uruguay on the other.[6]

Kirchner's concerns are not unfounded. Indeed, since its inception in 1991, Mercosur has shown little willingness to address the relative disadvantages suffered by small nations, and Paraguay and Uruguay have pointed out that most economic growth is accounted for by bilateral trade between Argentina and Brazil. True regional integration, the smaller nations complain, is "not going anywhere."[7]

In fact, Mercosur is still not even a true customs union, even though its member nations agreed to form one as long ago as 1991, under the Treaty of Asunción. Core members did start to reduce tariffs at first, but it soon became clear that complete tariff elimination was too ambitious and could lead to a political backlash given that it threatened to undermine certain industries. Consequently, in 1994 Mercosur nations signed the Ouro Preto Protocol, under which they agreed to exceptions protecting sensitive national industries, such as the automotive and sugar industries, which became subject to special accords.

What's more, Uruguay complains that Argentina and Brazil are inhibiting the export of Uruguayan bicycles, rice, and many other products, causing Uruguay's exports to fellow Mercosur nations to fall

precipitously since the 1990s.[8] Mercosur's inability to solve such underlying problems has hindered the continental integration process.

The list of intra-regional conflicts goes on. At a recent Mercosur
summit, for example, Argentina tried to stop Uruguay from building
two potentially polluting pulp mills on the Uruguay River that serves as
a border between the two nations. The two sides have become entrenched, with Argentine environmentalists frequently blocking bridges
between the two nations to protest construction of the plant. The Argentine authorities have taken no action to prevent the protests, and the
Uruguayan tourism industry has suffered as a result.

Andrés Oppenheimer, a columnist at the *Miami Herald* and a Mercosur skeptic, concedes that the new Parlasur will be able to make some
political headway. Parlasur legislators are also members of their respective national congresses, which means that they might push the integration agenda at home. "That would be important," he says, "because
about 60 percent of Mercosur's trade rules have not been ratified by the
congresses of the bloc's member countries."

Oppenheimer concludes that Mercosur is stuck in "limbo," as it tries
to build political institutions without having implemented even its most
basic economic agreements. If Parlasur finally succeeds in persuading
each member country to remove trade barriers, this could be a welcome
development. But if it fails, Oppenheimer adds, Mercosur could become
yet another "Latin American integration bureaucracy, and a joke."[9]

A recent Mercosur summit in Rio de Janeiro revealed underlying
geopolitical fissures, chief among them a festering problem between
Brazil and Uruguay. Uruguay, a small nation of 3.2 million, is completely dwarfed by Brazil with its 188 million inhabitants, and although
it forms part of South America's "pink tide"—having recently elected a
center-left government under the Broad Front of Tabaré Vázquez—its
economic conflicts with its bigger neighbors have been an obstacle to
political integration. Uruguayan authorities requested greater flexibility
to reach trade agreements outside of Mercosur in order to compensate
for such trade imbalances as their $495 million trade deficit with Brazil
in 2006, but their pleas fell on deaf ears. In response, Vázquez pointedly
refused to meet with Lula.

"We don't want handouts or charity from the larger countries,
but merely fair treatment for the smaller partners, so that all the

countries in this integration process can experience concrete benefits," Vázquez said.[10]

Reporting on the Rio summit, the Brazilian press had a field day. The inability of Mercosur nations to overcome their differences was a farce, they said, and the meeting as a whole proved to be "a complete waste of time."[11]

Unfortunately, the Bush White House has been able to exploit internal friction within Mercosur for maximum political advantage. For example, the United States has made progress in negotiating a Trade and Investment Framework Agreement (TIFA) with Uruguay, which may ultimately lead to a free trade agreement. Such a development would certainly undermine Mercosur, and Lula, in an effort to mollify Uruguay, traveled there to stress his desire for balanced trade within the South American bloc. It is necessary, he said, to seek balances and benefits "so that the aspirations of all of the countries are taken into equal consideration," regardless of the differences in size or economic power among Mercosur's member states.

The timing of Lula's visit seemed to underscore the important geopolitical stakes of South American integration. The Brazilian president arrived in Uruguay just two weeks before a scheduled visit by Bush, a trip that would mark a historic rapprochement between Washington and Montevideo.

Despite the missteps at the Rio summit, not everyone expects the friction between Uruguay and Brazil to fundamentally alter the course of future integration. Downplaying recent tensions, historian and political analyst Luiz Alberto Moniz Bandeira insists that Uruguay will not leave Mercosur. The country has a tiny population, and no one would invest there if it lost its access to the combined Brazilian and Argentine market of 200 million people.

Moreover, Bandeira predicted that George Bush's swing through the region "would not change anything." The Brazilian academic believes that Bush "went to Uruguay to try to get that country out of Mercosur," but Uruguayan resistance to closer ties with the United States would keep that from happening.[12] Despite economic and political rivalries between Argentina and Brazil, Bandeira expects the two nations to one day form the axis of a South American bloc capable of ending U.S. hegemony in the region. "Brazil," notes the historian, "understands that integration

with Argentina is necessary for there to be a globally powerful hub to negotiate with the other giants."[13]

Consolidating Mercosur, or even creating the South American
Community of Nations for that matter, will be no easy task. But most
experts are confident that the continent will become integrated, even if
it takes 30 or 40 years to complete the process. At this point, then, the
real question is not whether integration will occur, but how politically
progressive a form it will ultimately take. In contrast to Africa, South
America has seen a strong left emerge in response to poverty and social
inequality. Valter Pomar, Secretary of International Relations with
Brazil's Workers' Party, is confident that regional integration would
have a significant geopolitical impact, because it "would take place
within the context of a rising left movement. That is important, because
the European Union was pushed for and created under conservative
governments."[14]

If Brazil wants to solidify Mercosur, however, it must overcome its
own cultural tendencies as well as the economic and political differences
within the bloc. Many Brazilians are culturally oriented towards the
United States, studying English rather than Spanish as their second language. What's more, Brazil sees itself as very different from the rest of
Latin America in a cultural and linguistic sense.

"We don't see people in Argentina as equals," remarks Daniel Buarque of O Globo Online, "and we've had a lot of disputes with Argentines historically. We look on Uruguay, Chile, and Paraguay as really
separate countries." Nevertheless, a small minority of people in the
Brazilian south and São Paulo are beginning to change their perspective
and to develop "a sense of community," he says. "People are beginning
to see that we form part of Latin America and that we are equals, that
we are brothers."

South American integration is clearly a tantalizing prospect for the likes
of Fermín Toro. During his tenure at the United Nations, the diplomat
sought to reorient Venezuela's foreign policy and to garner support for
other South American nations.

A lawyer by profession, Toro also worked as a professor for many
years at the Central University, where he specialized in international

law. He also taught Venezuelan diplomatic history and is currently writing a book about Venezuela's first experiences at the United Nations between 1946 and 1948.

Originally from one of the oldest and most established families in Venezuela—the "oligarchy," as he puts it—Toro later became a Communist through self-education. Later, in 2002, he joined the Office of the Presidency and worked at Chávez's Directorate of International Relations.

If South American countries train future diplomats who share Toro's vision, the region could see integration develop along socially and politically progressive lines. Working at the Presidency, Toro helped to coordinate Chávez's foreign relations, not just with other heads of state but also with popular organizations in South American countries such as Argentina and Ecuador. He and his colleagues would typically contact social movements in advance of Chávez's trips, ask them what they thought of Chávez, and try to encourage solidarity with the Bolivarian Revolution.

The veteran Communist left Venezuela for New York in December 2003. Toro tells me that when he first got to the United Nations, he became acutely aware of Venezuela's insignificant role within the world body. "We had no presence there," he laments. Venezuelan career diplomats had always cultivated a close alliance with the United States, and as a result his country had no independent voice on the world stage. Observing this sorry state of affairs, Toro was determined to "make a 180 degree turn" at the Venezuelan Mission to the United Nations.

"We wanted a foreign policy more in line with Latin American integration of the Bolivarian Revolution," he explains.

By the time Toro arrived in New York, Venezuela had, surprisingly, still not officially condemned the U.S. invasion of Iraq.[15] Bush's decision to press for war had proven controversial in South America. In fact, Chile, at the time a temporary member of the UN Security Council, sided against the invasion. South American countries expressed concern that war in Iraq would take attention and resources away from famine relief and the AIDS crisis.[16] In Brazil, Lula sought to unite South American countries against the war, but failed to prevent outbreak of hostilities. Toro arrived at the UN after Iraq had been occupied by the U.S. militarily. He and his colleagues issued a strong statement, condemning the invasion.

Having made his country's views on Iraq clear to the White House, Toro went on to redirect Venezuela's foreign policy towards the rest of Latin America. Formerly, Venezuela had sided with Europe and the United States in criticizing Cuba's human rights record. But in a meeting of the non-aligned nations, Venezuela expressed solidarity with Cuba and reversed its earlier opposition.

Toro also made waves by opposing the MINUSTAH military mission in Haiti, which had been sent in to the Caribbean island in the wake of President Jean Bertrand Aristide's departure. Typically, it was customary to debate and vote on peacekeeping missions within the "Rio Group" of nations, but when Venezuela opposed the military mission it became impossible for the body to reach consensus. Toro acknowledges that the disagreement created some tensions with other South American nations, but these were largely insignificant.

When Venezuela sought to become a non-permanent member of the Security Council, Toro says 80 percent of the Latin American region supported his country's candidacy. "The empire" blocked Venezuela's aspirations, he says, referring to the United States. It had to rely mostly on votes from outside Latin America to do it, though—a victory of sorts for supporters of integration in the region.

To hear Toro describe it, the United States was still able to pressure a couple of Latin American countries to cooperate in its effort to isolate Venezuela. During the vote on Venezuela's Security Council bid, a handful of Central American countries, plus Colombia and Peru, backed Guatemala, Venezuela's rival for the seat. The pro-U.S. bloc was also joined by Chile, whose government Toro clearly disdains.

Such divisions, Toro says, will make it difficult to achieve genuine regional cooperation. Colombia remains squarely in the U.S. camp, and other nations, such as Paraguay and Uruguay, are "compromised" because they are small and weak. Yet the prospect of a South American Community of Nations, which would be far more formidable than the so-called Latin American bloc at the United Nations, remains a tantalizing one to Toro. Politically united and economically integrated, South America might finally come into its own as a major player on the world stage.

NOTES

INTRODUCTION

1. Nikolas Kozloff, *Hugo Chávez: Oil, Politics, and the Challenge to the U.S.* (Palgrave, 2007), 56, 37, 42, 45–6, 55, 18–20, 136.
2. "Background Note: Venezuela," U.S. State Department Web site, http://www.state.gov/r/pa/ei/bgn/35766.htm (accessed August 18, 2007).
3. Nikolas Kozloff, *Hugo Chávez*, 15–16.
4. Nikolas Kozloff, "Maracaibo Black Gold: Oil and Environment in the Era of Juan Vicente Gómez, 1908–1935," unpublished doctoral dissertation, Oxford University 2002, 163, 197.
5. Nikolas Kozloff, *Hugo Chávez*, 9, 10, 11, 13, 84, 46–8.
6. Rachel Coen, "Spotlighting (Some) Venezuela Killings," FAIR, July/August 2002, http://fair.org/extra/0207/venezuela.html (accessed September 15, 2007).
7. Nikolas Kozloff, *Hugo Chávez*, 109.
8. "Lula–Brazil's Lost Leader," Council on Hemispheric Affairs, June 21st, 2006, http://www.coha.org/2006/06/21/lula-brazils-lost-leader/ (accessed August 6, 2007).
9. Sue Branford, "Lula critics expelled from Brazilian Workers Party," *Red Pepper*, February, 2004, http://www.redpepper.org.uk/Feb2004/x-Feb 2004-Lula.html (accessed August 5, 2007).
10. "Background Note: Argentina," U.S. Dept of State Web site, http://www.state.gov/r/pa/ei/bgn/26516.htm (accessed August 18, 2007).
11. "Argentina risk: Political stability risk," Economist Intelligence Unit (research and advisory firm linked to *The Economist* Magazine providing country, industry, and management analysis), Risk Briefing, January 25, 2007.
12. "Slaking a thirst for justice—Human rights," *The Economist*, April 14, 2007; "FEATURE-Argentina to open notorious dirty war prison," Reuters Foundation, September 5, 2007, http://www.alertnet.org/thenews/newsdesk/N27453593.htm (accessed September 15, 2007).
13. Larry Rohter, "Recalling coup, Argentina vows 'never again,'" *The New York Times*, March 27, 2006.
14. Rohter, "Recalling coup."
15. "Slaking a thirst for justice."

16. Mark Almberg, "Chile's brutal past," Morning Star Online, June 21, 2007.

17. Patrick Fitzgerald, "Stanford: Chile's students emerge as remarkably potent political force," *The Stanford Daily* (Stanford), U-Wire, May 30, 2007.

18. "Slaking a thirst for justice."

19. "Background Note: Chile," U.S. State Dept Web site, http://www.state.gov/r/pa/ei/bgn/1981.htm (accessed August 19, 2007).

20. Fitzgerald, "Stanford: Chile's students."

21. "Background Note: Chile," U.S. State Dept Web site, http://www.state.gov/r/pa/ei/bgn/1981.htm (accessed August 19, 2007).

22. "Chile president asks Venezuela's Chávez for respect," Reuters, April 13, 2007, http://www.reuters.com/article/worldNews/idUSN1337876620070413 (accessed September 16, 2007).

23. "Bolivia: Morales backtracks to save constituent assembly," Latin American Special Reports, March 1, 2007.

24. Judy Rebick, "Peaceful revolution is taking shape; A rare interview with Evo Morales as he begins a profound transformation of his country," *The Toronto Star*, August 8, 2006.

25. Rebick, "Peaceful revolution."

26. "Background Note: Bolivia," U.S. State Dept Web site, http://www.state.gov/r/pa/ei/bgn/35751.htm (accessed August 19, 2007).

27. "ONU.- Evo Morales exhibe ante el plenario de la ONU una hoja de coca y defiende su uso terapéutico," Europa Press—Servicio Internacional, September 20, 2006.

28. Rebick, "Peaceful revolution."

29. Peter Kammerer, "A ray of hope to some, a new thorn to others," *South China Morning Post*, May 6, 2006.

30. "Background Note: Bolivia," U.S. State Dept Web site, http://www.state.gov/r/pa/ei/bgn/35751.htm (accessed August 19, 2007).

31. "Ecuador: Indigenous movement seems to be changing course," Latin American Special Reports, July 12, 2007.

32. "Andean Countries: Attempting to shape region-wide policies," Latin American Special Reports, July 12, 2007.

33. "Ecuador: Indigenous movement seems to be changing course," Latin American Special Reports, July 12, 2007

34. "Ecuador: More anti neoliberal posturing," Latin American Economic and Business Report, May 3, 2007.

35. Monte Hayes, "Leftist nationalist assumes presidency in Ecuador, promising major changes," Associated Press, January 15, 2007.

36. "Correa, un cristiano amigo de Chávez que promete revolucionar a Ecuador," Agence France Presse, October 15, 2006.

37. "Correa, un cristiano amigo."

38. "Ecuador: Correa's team," Economist Intelligence Unit—Business Latin America, January 15, 2007.

39. Hayes, "Leftist nationalist."
40. Susana Madera, "Un economista sin bagaje político," *La Voz de Galicia*, November 28, 2006.
41. "Correa, un cristiano amigo."
42. Hayes, "Leftist nationalist."
43. "Ecuador: More anti neoliberal posturing," Latin American Economic and Business Report, May 3, 2007.
44. Hayes, "Leftist nationalist."
45. "Una revolución constitucional," *El Comercio*, January 16, 2007.
46. "Ecuador: More anti neoliberal posturing."
47. "Ecuador's Correa says looking at Repsol oil deals," Reuters, July 11, 2007, http://www.reuters.com/article/companyNewsAndPR/idUSL1135 271820070711 (accessed September 16, 2007).

CHAPTER 1

1. AHC (American Heritage Center, a historical archive located at the University of Wyoming in Laramie, Wyoming), John Douglas Collection, Box 1 Acc #6017, "John Douglas' Letters From A Wildcat Well, Venezuela 1924–1925," 37, letter, June 3, 1925, Douglas to his father.
2. AHC, John Douglas Collection, "John Douglas' Letters From A Wildcat Well," 37.
3. *El Farol* (magazine published by Creole Petroleum Corporation, Caracas), "Historia del Petróleo en el Estado Zulia," August, 1949, 7.
4. Lee, "Rush For Oil in Venezuela," *The World Today*, March, 1926, 366.
5. "John Douglas' Letters From A Wildcat Well," 37.
6. *The Lamp* (magazine published by Exxon Corp, New York), "Snuffing Out a Half-Million-Dollar Blaze," August, 1925, 27–29.
7. Lee, "Rush For Oil in Venezuela," 366.
8. *El Farol*, "Snuffing Out a Half-Million-Dollar Blaze," 28.
9. José M. Salas Ramírez, *De una venezuela rural al mundo de los hidrocarburos* (Impresora Nacional, 1992) 24.
10. *Boletín de la cámara de comercio de Caracas* (Caracas, Chamber of Commerce of Caracas), "El Gran Incendio de La Rosa," July 1, 1925, No. 140, 2913.
11. Interview with Bernard Mommer, February 25, 2007, Lieuwen, "Petroleum in Venezuela, A History" (University California Publications in History Vol 47, 1954) 49, National Archives (College Park, Md), Record Group 59, Internal Affairs of Venezuela, 831.504/20, George Jones, Standard Oil of New Jersey, to Secretary of State, New York October 1st, 1926, Judith Ewell, *Venezuela and The United States* (University of Georgia Press, 1996), 135
12. Karin Strohecker and Brian Ellsworth, "PERFIL—Discreto europeo lidera estatización petrolera Venezuela," Reuters—Noticias Latinoamericanas,

June 20, 2007. In my account of Mommer's life and career, I have relied heavily on Strohecker and Ellsworth.

13. "ENTREVISTA—Cumplan o váyanse, dice a petroleras venezolano Mommer," Reuters—Noticias Latinoamericanas, May 16, 2007.

14. Nikolas Kozloff, "Venezuela Launches Hemispheric 'Anti-Hegemonic' Media," Council on Hemispheric Affairs report, April 28, 2005, http://www.coha.org/2005/04/28/Chávez-launches-hemispheric-%e2%80%9canti-hegemonic%e2%80%9d-media-campaign-in-response-to-local-tv-networks-anti-government-bias/ (accessed August 30, 2007), Securities and Exchange Commission report on Venezuelan National Petroleum Co., July 20, 2005, Securities and Exchange Commission Web site, http://www.secinfo.com/d11MXs.z1ZCa.htm (accessed October 12, 2007)

15. Greg Wilpert, "Financial Statement of Venezuela's State Oil Company Shows Profits Up by 44%," venezuelanalysis.com (Web site offering news and analysis from Venezuela), October 3, 2006, http://www.venezuelanalysis.com/news.php?newsno=2096 (accessed August 30, 2007).

16. María Elena Monroy, "Social Districts, PdVSA and The People United For Integral Development," *Sowing The Oil* (International Magazine of PdVSA), Year 1, No. 2, May-August 2006, 35–37.

17. Greg Wilpert, "Financial Statement of Venezuela's State Oil Company Shows Profits Up by 44%," venezuelanalysis.com, October 3, 2006, http://www.venezuelanalysis.com/news.php?newsno=2096 (accessed August 30, 2007).

18. Jesús Rodríguez, "The Miracle of Seeing Again," *Sowing The Oil* (International Magazine of PdVSA), Year 1, No. 2, May-August 2006, 39–40.

19. Marion Barbel, "Oil Companies Move Forward with New Contracts in Venezuela," *Global Insight Daily Analysis*, January 4, 2006.

20. "Govt to replace op agreements with mixed companies," *Business News Americas*, April 14, 2005.

21. Marion Barbel, "Oil Companies Move Forward with New Contracts in Venezuela," *Global Insight Daily Analysis*, January 4, 2006.

22. "Chávez Nationalizes Venezuelan Oil Fields," NPR *Morning Edition*, May 1, 2007.

23. Interview with Mommer.

24. "Hugo Chávez's Future," Nikolas Kozloff interviews Greg Wilpert, Z Net (progressive political Web site), http://www.zmag.org/content/showarticle.cfm?ItemID=12301 (accessed April 30, 2007), "Venezuela Takes Over Control of Extra-Heavy Oil Projects," *Global Insight Daily Analysis*, undated, http://www.globalinsight.com/SDA/SDADetail9134.htm (accessed October 14, 2007), Peter Millard, "Venezuela Govt Disputes Value of Orinoco Heavy Oil Projects," Dow Jones Newswires, April 24, 2007, posted at Rig Zone Web site (providing news and analysis on the petroleum industry), http://www.rigzone.com/news/article.asp?a_id=44280 (accessed October 14, 2007)

25. "Chávez Nationalizes Venezuelan Oil Fields," NPR *Morning Edition*, May 1, 2007.

26. "Venezuela, Cuba to begin oil exploration off the Caribbean island," Associated Press, July 31, 2007, http://www.iht.com/articles/ap/2007/07/31/business/LA-FIN-Venezuela-Cuba-Oil.php (accessed September 1, 2007).

27. Hampden Macbeth, "The Not So Odd Couple: Venezuela's Hugo Chávez and Cuba's Fidel Castro," Council on Hemispheric Affairs, June 21, 2005, http://www.coha.org/2005/06/21/the-not-so-odd-couple-venezuela%e2%80%99s-hugo-Chávez-and-cuba%e2%80%99s-fidel-castro/ (accessed September 1, 2007).

28. César J. Álvarez, "Venezuela's Oil-Based Economy," Council On Foreign Relations, November 27, 2006, http://www.cfr.org/publication/12089/venezuelas_oilbased_economy.html (accessed September 1, 2007).

29. T. Christian Miller, "Ecuador: Texaco Leaves Trail of Destruction," *The Los Angeles Times*, November 30, 2003, posted at Global Policy Forum, http://www.globalpolicy.org/socecon/tncs/2003/1130texacoecuador.htm (accessed August 30, 2007).

30. U.S Energy Administration, Ecuador Country Analysis Brief, March 2007, http://www.eia.doe.gov/emeu/cabs/Ecuador/Background.html (accessed May 2, 2007).

31. U.S Energy Administration, Ecuador Country Analysis Brief, March 2007, http://www.eia.doe.gov/emeu/cabs/Ecuador/Background.html (accessed May 2, 2007).

32. Interview with Efrén Icaza, March 11, 2007

33. Nikolas Kozloff, "Como conviven las petroleras con los indios," *Hoy* (Quito daily), September 19, 1993.

34. Nikolas Kozloff, "The Rise of Rafael Correa, Ecuador and The Contradictions of Chavismo," Counterpunch (progressive Web site featuring news and analysis), http://www.counterpunch.org/kozloff11272006.html (accessed May 4, 2007).

35. Interview with William Waters, March 10, 2007

36. Gareth Chetwynd, "Fresh direction at Petroecuador," *Upstream*, March 23, 2007.

37. "Ecuador counsel should name representative to Oxy hearing: Palacio," *Platts Commodity News*, September 27, 2006.

38. Juliette Kerr, "President Claims 'Half Victory' with Occidental's Dropping of Arbitration Case Against State Oil Company in Ecuador," *Global Insight Daily Analysis*, October 5, 2006.

39. Chetwynd, "Fresh direction at Petroecuador."

40. James Brooke, "New Effort Would Test Possible Coexistence Of Oil and Rain Forest," *The New York Times*, February 26, 1991.

41. Chetwynd, "Fresh direction at Petroecuador."

42. Gonzalo Solano, "Ecuador Candidate Defends Chávez Ties," Associated Press, September 26, 2006.

43. Monte Hayes, "Antiestablishment leftist favored in Ecuador's presidential race," Associated Press, October 14, 2006.

44. "Ecuador Warns Polluters," *International Oil Daily*, February 6, 2007.

45. "General interest—Quick takes: Ecuador threatens environmental squeeze," *Ei EnCompass: Environment*, February 19, 2007, Bernd Radowitz, "A Yr Of Bolivia Gas Nationalization Brings Windfall, Worries," Dow Jones International News, April 27, 2007.

46. "Ecuador Warns Polluters," *International Oil Daily*, February 6, 2007.

47. Interview with Acosta.

48. For more on this question, see Nikolas Kozloff, "Hugo Chávez's Achilles Heel: The Environment, interview with Jorge Hinestroza," venezuelanalysis.com, http://www.venezuelanalysis.com/articles.php?artno=1847 (accessed March 4, 2007).

49. Aaron Luoma and Gretchen Gordon, "Turning Gas into Development in Bolivia, Will Evo Morales' attempt at re-nationalization bring real change?" *Dollars and Sense*, November/December 2006, http://www.dollarsandsense.org/archives/2006/1106luomagordon.html (accessed September 8, 2007).

50. U.S. Energy Information Administration, Bolivia background, http://www.eia.doe.gov/emeu/cabs/Bolivia/Background.html (accessed May 5, 2007).

51. Ben Dangl, "Bolivia's Gas War," Z Net, September 24, 2003, http://www.zmag.org/content/showarticle.cfm?ItemID=4245 (accessed August 31, 2007).

52. Ben Dangl, "Bolivia's Gas War," Z Net, September 24, 2003, http://www.zmag.org/content/showarticle.cfm?ItemID=4245 (accessed August 31, 2007).

53. Interview with Carlos Arze, March 23, 2007

54. Radowitz, "A Yr Of Bolivia Gas Nationalization."

55. "Gas mends frayed South American ties," *Energy Compass*, May 25, 2007.

56. "Tough times for Petrobras," *Petroleum Review*, June 13, 2007.

57. "Coca Growers' Leader Evo Morales Describes His Banishment as "Kidnapping," BBC Monitoring Service: Latin America, May 12, 1995.

58. "Morales' party falls short of two-thirds majority in assembly: exit polls," Agence France Presse, July 3, 2006.

59. "PdVSA and YPFB to sign new joint venture deal to operate in Bolivia," Alexander's Gas and Oil Connections, http://www.gasandoil.com/goc/company/cnl62375.htm (accessed May 6, 2007).

60. Interview with Cristian Folgar, April 12, 2007

61. Tyler Bridges, "Chávez, Lula promote competing visions," *The Miami Herald*, August 10, 2007.

62. "Cancilleres de Argentina y Venezuela preparan próxima reunión bilateral," Agence France Presse, May 4, 2007.

63. "Chávez llegó a Argentina para acto 'antiimperialista' y acuerdo con Kirchner," Agence France Presse, March 9, 2007.

64. Interview with Victor Bronstein, April 7, 2007

CHAPTER 2

1. Interview with Emir Sader, April 10, 2007
2. "Venezuela's Chávez Announces World Bank Debt Has Been Paid Off," venezuelanalysis.com, April 15 2007, http://www.venezuelanalysis.com/news.php?newsno=2270 (accessed September 4, 2007).
3. Greg Palast, "Hugo Chávez," venezuelanalysis.com, September 16, 2006, http://www.venezuelanalysis.com/articles.php?artno=1818 (accessed September 4, 2007).
4. Natalie Obiko Pearson and Ian James, "Venezuela Funding To Latin America Challenges US Spending," Dow Jones International News, August 26, 2007.
5. Juan Forero, "Venezuela Tries To Create Its Own Kind of Socialism; Chávez Taps Oil Wealth in Effort to Build System That Favors 'Human Necessities,'" *The Washington Post*, August 6, 2007.
6. Cristina Marcano, "Esperan la definición del socialismo chavista," *Reforma*, January 7, 2007.
7. Bernd Debusmann, "FEATURE-In Venezuela, obstacles to 21st Century socialism," Reuters, June 20, 2007.
8. Forero, "Venezuela Tries To Create Its Own Kind of Socialism-Chávez."
9. Interview with Edgardo Lander, June 22, 2006
10. Cleto Sojo, "Venezuela's Chávez Closes World Social Forum with Call to Transcend Capitalism," venezualanalysis.com, January 31, 2005, http://www.venezuelanalysis.com/news.php?newsno=1486 (accessed September 2, 2007).
11. Greg Wilpert, "Chávez Says Americas Summit Will Serve to Bury FTAA," venezuelanalysis.com, November 4, 2005, http://www.venezuelanalysis.com/news.php?newsno=1806 (accessed September 2, 2007).
12. Edison López, "Thousands Protest Free Trade Talks in Ecuador," Associated Press, November 1, 2002, posted at Common Dreams Web site, http://www.commondreams.org/headlines02/1101–05.htm (accessed September 2, 2007).
13. Larry Rohter, "Ecuador, Swept by Inflation and Unrest, Brakes the Economy," *The New York Times*, March 13, 1999.
14. "Ecuador/IMF/Mahuad –2: Reiterates Dollarization Possibility," Dow Jones News Service, April 15, 1999.
15. "Ecuador to defend agriculture in FTA talks with US: official," Xinhua News Agency, May 25, 2005.
16. Interview with William Waters, March 10, 2007
17. "'No end' to Ecuador trade protest," BBC News Web site, March 15, 2006, http://news.bbc.co.uk/2/hi/americas/4807900.stm (accessed September 2, 2007)

18. "Ecuador protests 'will continue,'" March 16, 2006, BBC News Web site, http://news.bbc.co.uk/2/hi/americas/4814422.stm (accessed September 2, 2007).

19. Nadia Martínez, "Adiós, World Bank!" *Foreign Policy in Focus*, May 4, 2007, http://www.fpif.org/fpiftxt/4200 (accessed September 3, 2007).

20. Gonzalo Solano, "Ecuador Candidate Defends Chávez Ties," Associated Press, September 26, 2006.

21. "Ecuador economy: Social-security amendment threatens public finances," Economist Intelligence Unit – ViewsWire, July 19, 2005.

22. Gail Hurley, "Calling in Ecuador's Debt," Guardian Weekly Global Network, August 20, 2007, http://www.guardianweekly.co.uk/?page =editorial&id=113&catID=7 (accessed September 4, 2007).

23. "Ecuador's Rafael Correa, Tightening his grip," *The Economist*, April 19th 2007, http://www.economist.com/world/la/displaystory.cfm?story_ id=9040321 (accessed September 4, 2007).

24. "Ecuador rejects U.S. free trade pact," *Business Week*, December 10, 2006, posted at Institute For Agriculture and Trade Policy, http:// www.iatp.org/tradeobservatory/headlines.cfm?refID=96647 (accessed September 4, 2007).

25. Interview with Arze.

26. Hugh O'Shaughnessy, "Castro's free medicine wins friends and influence," *Irish Times*, May 21, 2007.

27. Charlotte Dennett and Gerard Colby, *Thy Will Be Done: The Conquest of The Amazon, Nelson Rockefeller and the Age of Oil* (New York: Harper Collins, 1995), 525–6, 528–9, 530–33.

28. Ronald Bruce St John, "Evo Morales No Che Guevara," *Foreign Policy in Focus*, January 9, 2006, http://www.fpif.org/fpiftxt/3021 (accessed September 1, 2007).

29. America Vera-Zavala, "Evo Morales Has Plans for Bolivia," *In These Times*, December 18, 2005, http://www.inthesetimes.com/article/2438/ (accessed September 1, 2007).

30. Interview with Rafael Dausá, March 22, 2007

31. O'Shaughnessy, "Castro's free medicine."

32. "Venezuelan BANDES To Open Offices in Nicaragua, Ecuador," *Latin America News Digest*, May 25, 2007.

33. Luis Carlos Niño, "Ecuador Proposes New Regional Monetary Fund," *Global Insight Daily Analysis*, April 5, 2007.

34. Richard Knee, "Chile reaches out," *The Florida Shipper*, June 25, 2007.

35. Sue Branford and Bernardo Kucinski, *The Debt Squads: The U.S., The Banks, and Latin America* (London: Zed Books, 1988), 85.

36. Interview with Manuel Cabieses, March 28, 2007

37. Interview with Jaime Bazán, March 26, 2007

38. "DJ USTR: Troubled By Chile Intellectual Ppty Law 'Deficiencies,'" Dow Jones Commodities Service, April 3, 2007.

39. Ben Shankland, "Chilean Government Takes Steps Towards IP Rehabilitation, as Generics Gain Market Share," *Global Insight Daily Analysis*, April 19, 2007.

40. Nikolas Kozloff, "Chile: A Country Geographically Located in South America, 'By Accident,'" Z Net, April 12, 2007, http://www.zmag.org/content/showarticle.cfm?SectionID=20&ItemID=12556 (accessed May 11, 2007).

41. Branford and Kucinski, *The Debt Squads*, 80.

42. James Brooke, "Workers' Advocate, a Front-Runner in Brazil, Shows He Thinks Like a Boss," *The New York Times*, April 30, 1989.

43. Nikolas Kozloff, "In Conversation: As South America Drifts Left, Wither Brazil?, Paulo Fontes with Nikolas Kozloff," *Brooklyn Rail*, March, 2007, http://www.brooklynrail.org/2007/3/express/as-south-america-drifts-left-wither-braz (accessed October 14, 2007)

44. "America Relationship," *US Fed News*, June 19, 2007.

45. Daniel Howden, "The Two Faces of São Paulo," *The Independent*, March 12, 2007.

46. Rafael Ruíz Harrell, "La Ciudad y el Crimen / Ciudades sin control," *Reforma*, January 22, 2007.

47. Tyler Bridges, "Chávez, Lula promote competing visions," *The Miami Herald*, August 10, 2007.

48. Bridges, "Chávez, Lula promote competing visions."

CHAPTER 3

1. "In South America, China and the U.S. Battle it Out," Gonzalo Sánchez Paz interviewed by Nikolas Kozloff, February 10, 2007, Z Net, http://www.zmag.org/content/showarticle.cfm?ItemID=12086 (accessed October 15, 2007)

2. Kelly Hearn, "US military presence in Paraguay irks neighbors; The Pentagon denies desire for a permanent base, but there are many skeptics," *The Christian Science Monitor*, December 2, 2005.

3. Benjamin Dangl, "U.S. Military in Paraguay Prepares to 'Spread Democracy,'" *Toward Freedom*, September 15, 2005, http://www.toward-freedom.com/home/index.php?option=content&task=view&id=593 (accessed September 10, 2007).

4. "Venezuela citizens train to fight U.S. Reserves expanded over fears of attack," *The Washington Times*, October 18, 2005.

5. Cleto Sojo, "U.S. Military Presence near Venezuela Raises Concerns," March 1, 2005, http://www.venezuelanalysis.com/news.php?newsno=1528 (accessed September 4, 2007)

6. Interview with Domingo Irwin, March 2, 2007

7. Phil Gunson, "Venezuela: A Latin Enigma; The recall vote may show whether Hugo Chávez is a new version of Fidel Castro or Daniel Ortega," *Newsweek International*, August 16, 2004.

8. Gunson, "Venezuela: A Latin Enigma"; Ian James, "Socialism a Hard Sell for Some Venezuelans," Associated Press, September 5, 2005.

9. "Venezuelan ideologue explains the fundamentals of 21st century socialism," BBC Monitoring Americas, January 21, 2007.

10. "Militares ecuatorianos construirán vías con fondos para pagar deuda externa," Agence France Presse, February 27, 2007; interview with Alberto Molina, March 9, 2007

11. "Ecuadoran armed forces concerned by possible civilian defence minister," BBC Monitoring Americas, December 12, 2006; interview with Molina.

12. Jeanneth Valdivieso, "Ecuador Names 1st Female Defense Chief," Associated Press, December 27, 2006, posted at Washington Post Web site, http://www.washingtonpost.com/wp-dyn/content/article/2006/12/27/AR2006122701366.html (accessed September 3, 2007).

13. Hilary Burke, "Women defense ministers chip at Latin America's macho image," Reuters News, January 31, 2007.

14. Jeanneth Valdivieso, "Ecuador Names 1st Female Defense Chief," Associated Press, December 27, 2006, posted at *The Washington Post* Web site, http://www.washingtonpost.com/wp-dyn/content/article/2006/12/27/AR2006122701366.html (accessed September 3, 2007).

15. Kintto Lucas, "Ecuador: Suspicions Surround Defense Minister's Death," Inter Press Service, January 26, 2007.

16. "Ecuador army chief sacked over errors leading to defense minister's death," Xinhua News Agency, February 3, 2007.

17. "Ecuador army chief sacked over errors leading to defense minister's death," Xinhua News Agency, February 3, 2007.

18. Interview with García. March 8, 2007.

19. Jeanneth Valdivieso, "Troubled U.S. Presence on Ecuador Coast," Associated Press, February 6, 2007.

20. "Ecuador: US says Manta not part of Plan Colombia," *Latinnews Daily*, March 1, 2007.

21. Valdivieso, "Troubled U.S. Presence on Ecuador Coast."

22. "Ecuador: US says Manta not part of Plan Colombia." *Latinnews Daily*, March 1, 2007.

23. Lucas, "Ecuador: Suspicions."

24. Interview with Gualdemar Jiménez, March 8, 2007

25. "Ecuador: US says Manta not part of Plan Colombia." *Latinnews Daily*, March 1, 2007.

26. "Time Running Out For US' Lone South American Military Post," *Dow Jones International News*, February 6, 2007.

27. Valdivieso, "Troubled U.S. Presence on Ecuador Coast."

28. "Time Running Out," Dow Jones International News.

29. Interview with Mónica Almeida, March 8, 2007

30. Interview with Manuel Cabieses, March 28, 2007

31. Mark Almberg, "Chile's brutal past," Morning Star Online, June 21, 2007

32. Interview with Guillermo Holzmann, March 31, 2007

33. Bill Cormier, "Women come to S. America's defense," Associated Press, January 31, 2007.

34. "Slaking a thirst for justice—Human rights," *The Economist*, April 14, 2007.

35. Bill Cormier, "Women come to S. America's defense," Associated Press, January 31, 2007.

36. Interview with Rut Diamint, April 9, 2007

37. "Argentina: Kirchner curtails autonomy of service chiefs," *Latin American Weekly Report*, June 20, 2006.

38. "Argentina: Tension grows between government and military," *Latinnews Daily*, June 6, 2006.

39. "Argentina: Kirchner curtails autonomy of service chiefs."

40. "Argentina: Tension grows."

41. Interview with Diamint.

42. "Argentina Sending Troops to Rights Class," Associated Press, May 2, 2007.

43. Interview with Andrea Chiappini, April 11, 2007

44. David Pion-Berlin, "Will soldiers follow? Economic integration and regional security in the Southern Cone," *Journal of Interamerican Studies & World Affairs*, April 1, 2000, Volume 42, Issue 1.

45. Interview with Chiappini.

46. Interview with Irwin; Martín Arostegui, Chávez seeks anti-U.S. military alliance, *Washington Times*, August 2, 2006, http://www.washington-times.com/world/20060801–104047–5464r_page2.htm (accessed May 19, 2007).

47. "Sabre-rattling, posturing and . . ." *Latin American Special Reports*, May 3, 2007.

48. Interview with Bertha García, March 8, 2007

49. Tyler Bridges, "Bolivia-Venezuela military deal raises red flags," *The Miami Herald*, October 29, 2006.

50. "Kirchner reshapes his cabinet in his image," *Latin American Brazil & Southern Cone Report*, December 20, 2005.

51. "Argentina, Chile create "unprecedented" joint peacekeeping force," EFE News Service, December 4, 2006.

52. "President Aristide Says 'I Was Kidnapped' 'Tell The World It Is A Coup," *Democracy Now!*, introduction to report on Web site, March 1st, 2004, http://www.democracynow.org/article.pl?sid=04/03/01/1521216 (accessed July 14, 2007).

53. "Préval calls for peace, dialogue in inaugural address," EFE News Service, May 14, 2006.

54. February 2006, Haiti (MINUSTAH), UN Security Council Report, http://www.securitycouncilreport.org/site/c.glKWLeMTIsG/b.1387811 /k.D542/February_2006BRHaiti_MINUSTAH.htm (accessed May 19, 2007).

55. "Brazilian general heading UN troops in Haiti wants out," Agence France Presse, June 17, 2005.
56. Mario Osava, "Haiti: General's Death Revives Debate on Brazil's Peace-keeping Role," January 12, 2006, http://www.ipsnews.net/news.asp ?idnews=31750 (accessed July 14, 2007).

CHAPTER 4

1. "In Conversation: Hugo Chávez and Latin American Populism," by Nikolas Kozloff and Steve Stein, *Brooklyn Rail*, Dec 2006/Jan 2007, http://brooklynrail.org/2006/12/express/hugo-Chávez (accessed October 17, 2007)
2. Tom Haines, "The Power of Art: Venezuelans Use a Big Canvas for Their Political Sentiments," *The Boston Globe*, December 28, 2003.
3. Sara Miller Llana, "Backstory: Venezuela's cultural revolution," *The Christian Science Monitor*, January 17, 2007.
4. "Benito Irady presidirá Fundef," Agencia Bolivariana de Noticias, May 23, 2005, http://www.abn.info.ve/go_news5.php?articulo=8680&lee=5 (accessed July 18, 2007).
5. Ian James, "Socialism a Hard Sell for Some Venezuelans," Associated Press, September 5, 2005.
6. Óscar Contardo, "Chávez y su revolución," *El Mercurio*, April 1, 2007.
7. Llana, "Backstory."
8. Juan Forero, "Chávez calls the tune on Venezuela charts," *The New York Times*, October 4, 2005.
9. Contardo, "Chávez y su revolución."
10. "El Perro y la Rana presentó primeros 12 libros de colección Entreverados," Agencia Bolivariana de Noticias, May 10, 2007, http://www.abn.info.ve/go_news5.php?articulo=91439&lee=18, El Perro y La Rana Web site, http://www.elperroylarana.gob.ve/, Silvio Camacho, "Huge interest for Marxist ideas at the Caracas Book Fair," In Defense of Marxism (Web site of the International Marxist Tendency), November 13, 2006, http://www.marxist.com/marxist-caracas-book-fair131106-5.htm (all accessed October 17, 2007)
11. David Bushnell (ed), *El Libertador, Writings of Simón Bolívar* (Oxford University Press, 2003), xxvii, xxviii, xlv-xlviii, Alicia Torres, "Chávez's Ace-Venezuelan Leader Taps Bolívar Myths, Cults," Pacific News Service, Feb 27, 2003, http://news.pacificnews.org/news/view_article.html?article_id=347658bbc7bdecb9b0b75e34e188850d (accessed October 17, 2007)
12. "Venezuela lanza una ofensiva cinematográfica," *La República*, August 10, 2006.
13. Llana, "Backstory Chávez."
14. C. Hernández, "An entertaining war," *El País*—English Edition, June 7, 2006.

15. Aldo Rodríguez Villouta, "Chávez starts up movie studio to counter Hollywood hegemony," EFE News Service, September 4, 2006.
16. Hernández, "An entertaining war."
17. Contardo, "Chávez y su revolución."
18. Interview with Lorena Almarza, February 27, 2007
19. Villouta, "Chávez starts up movie studio."
20. Andreína Martínez Santiso, "Plataforma del Cine y el Audiovisual anunció sus proyectos para 2007," *El Nacional*, February 9, 2007.
21. Humberto Márquez, "Venezuela: Petrodollars for Local Film Industry," Inter Press Service, January 15, 2007.
22. Marion Barbel, "Election 2006: President Calls For Single Revolutionary Party in Venezuela," *Global Insight Daily Analysis*, September 11, 2006.
23. Laura Weffer Cifuentes, "Una biblioteca revolucionaria alimenta el verbo presidencial," *El Nacional*, June 18, 2006.
24. Anna Marie De La Fuente, "Glover letter gets guilds in trouble; Cnac instructed to cut ties with guilds," *Daily Variety*, June 4, 2007.
25. Llana, "Backstory Chávez."
26. Anna Marie De La Fuente, "Venezuela lays down law; But tough tactics can't stop H'wood," *Daily Variety*, September 3, 2006.
27. Llana, "Backstory." Chávez
28. De La Fuente, "Venezuela lays down law."
29. Márquez, "Venezuela: Petrodollars."
30. Ian James, "Venezuela School for Poor Controversial," Associated Press, July 28, 2005.
31. Ian James, "Reading, writing and revolution: Free Venezuelan university stresses politics, socialism and Hugo Chávez," Associated Press, July 29, 2005.
32. James, "Venezuela School for Poor."
33. James, "Reading, writing and revolution."
34. James, "Venezuela School for Poor."
35. Monte Reel, "Chávez Educates Masses at a University in His Image," *The Washington Post*, May 25, 2006
36. Reel, "Chávez Educates Masses."
37. James, "Reading, writing and revolution."
38. "Professor at heart of a south American dream," *Lincolnshire Echo*, November 21, 2006.
39. Reel, "Chávez Educates Masses."
40. "Professor at heart of a south American dream," *Lincolnshire Echo*.
41. "El ALBA cultural se expande," *La República*, April 4, 2007.

CHAPTER 5

1. Jeanneth Valdivieso, "Correa recibe respaldo indígena en Ecuador," AP Spanish Worldstream, September 30, 2006.

2. "Correa, un cristiano amigo de Chávez que promete revolucionar a Ecuador," Agence France Presse, October 15, 2006.

3. Brooke Larson, *Trials of Nation Making: Liberalism, Race, and Ethnicity in the Andes, 1810–1910*, (Cambridge: Cambridge University Press, 2004), http://books.google.com/books?hl=en&lr=&id=FeTXZFUH-ykC&oi=fnd&pg=PR9&dq=ecuador+indians+colonial+period+racism&ots=4xhHYwzoPX&sig=wLXuLD3jBpzlwTFY62VwKB_n5pQ#PPA106,M1, Allen Gerlach, *Indians, Oil and Politics: A Recent History of Ecuador* (Scholarly Resources, 2003), 21, 22, 28

4. Monte Hayes, "Leftist nationalist assumes presidency in Ecuador, promising major change," Associated Press, January 15, 2007.

5. Interview with Marc St.-Upéry, March 5, 2007

6. "Ecuador: Indigenous movement seems to be changing course," Latin American Special Reports, July 12, 2007.

7. "Bolivia: Morales backtracks to save constituent assembly," Latin American Special Reports, March 1, 2007.

8. "Bolivia: Morales backtracks to save constituent assembly," Latin American Special Reports, March 1, 2007.

9. "Bolivia president-elect Morales blessed by native priests in ancient temple," *The Canadian Press*, January 21, 2006.

10. Fiona Smith, "Bolivian President-elect declares struggle against poverty at Indian leadership ceremony," Associated Press, January 21, 2006.

11. "Bolivia president-elect Morales blessed by native priests in ancient temple," *The Canadian Press*, January 21, 2006.

12. Smith, "Bolivian President-elect declares struggle."

13. Jeremy Mumford, "Coca Politics in Bolivia: Coca Growers Have Turned the 'Sacred Leaf' into a National Symbol," *The Boston Globe*, September 28, 2003.

14. Steve Boggan, "Coca is a way of life," *The Guardian*, February 9, 2006.

15. "Bolivia's Morales authorizes coca leaf sales by producers," BBC Monitoring Americas, June 22, 2006.

16. "US doubts figures on Bolivia coca," *Morning Star Online*, April 26, 2007.

17. "U.S. claims allies are falling short in war on drugs," *Winnipeg Free Press*, March 2, 2007.

18. Dan Keane, "Reid in South America calls for improved U.S.-Bolivia relations," Associated Press, December 29, 2006.

19. Interview with Martín Condori Flores, March 21, 2007

20. "Bolivia minister wants coca fed to school children," Reuters News, February 10, 2006, "World Briefing | Americas: Bolivia: Coca Leaf, Juice And Muffin Or Toast," *New York Times*, February 11, 2006, http://query.nytimes.com/gst/fullpage.html?res=9E06EFD7153EF932A25751C0A9609C8B63&n=Top%2FReference%2FTimes%20Topics%2FSubjects%2FC%2FCalcium (accessed October 18, 2007)

21. Interview with Xavier Albó, March 19, 2007

22. Interview with Magdalena Cajías, March 21, 2007
23. Interview with Magdalena Cajías, March 21, 2007
24. Raúl Pierri, "South America: Aymara Rage Explodes," Inter Press Service, May 3, 2004.
25. Jack Chang, "Indigenous worldview: Bolivia's president accused of racist politics," *Charleston Gazette*, August 20, 2006.
26. Burton Bollag, "Bolivia's Indian Majority Goes to College," *Chronicle of Higher Education*, July 14, 2006.
27. Bollag, "Bolivia's Indian Majority."
28. Interview with Victor Hugo Cárdenas, March 21, 2007
29. "Oposición advierte de riesgos sobre la democracia de Bolivia," Agence France Presse, October 9, 2006.
30. José de Córdoba and David Luhnow, "A Dash of Mysticism: Governing Bolivia The Aymara Way—Reading Forefathers' Wrinkles Doesn't Require Books; The Future Lies Behind," *The Wall Street Journal*, July 6, 2006.
31. Chang, "Indigenous worldview."
32. De Córdoba and Luhnow, "A Dash of Mysticism."
33. De Córdoba and Luhnow, "A Dash of Mysticism."
34. "Bolivia to discard 'colonialist' approach to schooling," EFE News Service, July 11, 2006.
35. Interview with Daniel Buarque, April 18, 2007
36. "Anti-globalization forum starts in Brazil to counter Davos summit," Agence France Presse, January 26, 2005.
37. "In Conversation: As South America Drifts Left, Wither Brazil? Paulo Fontes with Nikolas Kozloff," *Brooklyn Rail*, March 2007, http://www.brooklynrail.org/2007/3/express/as-south-america-drifts-left-wither-braz (accessed October 18, 2007)
38. Mala Htun, "Playing Brazil's Race Card," *Foreign Policy 86*, November 1, 2005 (Factiva)
39. Mac Margolis, "Culture for The Masses," *Newsweek International*, Latin America Edition, February 3, 2003.
40. Peter Culshaw, "Features—The Arts—'Brazil has a new energy'," *The Daily Telegraph*, July 1, 2003.
41. Margolis, "Culture for The Masses."
42. Culshaw, "Brazil has a new energy."

CHAPTER 6

1. Sarah Wagner, "Women in Bolivarian Venezuela, pt.1, Women and Venezuela's Bolivarian Revolution," venezuelanalysis.com, January 15, 2005, http://www.venezuelanalysis.com/articles.php?artno=1353 (accessed August 12, 2007)
2. Dawn Gable, "Civil Society, Social Movements, and Participation in Venezuela's Fifth Republic," venezuelanalysis.com, February 9, 2004,

http://www.venezuelanalysis.com/analysis/350 (accessed October 19, 2007)

3. Juan Forero, "Chávez's Grip Tightens As Rivals Boycott Vote," *New York Times*, December 5, 2005, http://www.nytimes.com/2005/12/05 /international/americas/05venez.html?_r=1&n=Top/Reference/Times% 20Topics/People/F/Forero,%20Juan&oref=slogin (accessed October 19, 2007), "Media Advisory: U.S. Papers Hail Venezuelan Coup as Pro-Democracy Move," Fairness and Accuracy in Reporting, April 18, 2002, http://www.fair.org/index.php?page=1867 (accessed October 19, 2007), Coral Wynter, "Book Review: Creating A Caring Economy, Nora Castañeda and the Women's Development Bank of Venezuela," *Green Left Weekly*, February 21, 2006, posted at venezuelanalysis.com Web site, http://www.venezuelanalysis.com/articles.php?artno=1677 (accessed August 12, 2007)

4. Albor Ruíz, "Latin Women's Mission of Peace," *New York Daily News*, January 26, 2006.

5. "The bank that likes to say yes–if you're a woman: Diane Taylor talks to the founder of a unique financial institution," *The Guardian*, March 24, 2005 (Factiva)

6. *Banmujer* magazine, Ministerio para la economía popular, Año 5, No. 9, marzo 2006.

7. "The bank that likes to say yes—if you're a woman," *The Guardian*, March 24, 2005.

8. Banmujer calendar, 2006.

9. Sarah Wagner, "Women in Bolivarian Venezuela, pt.2, The Bolivarian Response to the Feminization of Poverty in Venezuela," February 5, 2005 http://www.venezuelanalysis.com/articles.php?artno=1369 (accessed August 12, 2007).

10. *Banmujer* magazine, Ministerio para la economía popular, Año 4, No. 8, Caracas, diciembre 2005, Año 5, No. 9, marzo 2006.

11. Humberto Márquez, "Step Back Renews Women's Drive to Move Forward in Venezuela," Inter Press Service, June 17, 2006, posted at venezuelanalysis.com Web site, http://www.venezuelanalysis.com/articles.php?artno=1753 (accessed August 29, 2007).

12. Humberto Márquez, "Step Back Renews Women's Drive to Move Forward in Venezuela," Inter Press Service, June 17, 2006, posted at venezuelanalysis.com Web site, http://www.venezuelanalysis.com/articles.php?artno=1753 (accessed August 29, 2007).

13. Nikolas Kozloff, "Hugo Chávez's Holy War," Z Net, March 11, 2007, http://www.zmag.org/content/showarticle.cfm?ItemID=12302 (accessed October 19, 2007)

14. "The bank that likes to say yes," *The Guardian*, March 24, 2005.

15. Wagner, "Women in Bolivarian Venezuela."

16. Wagner, "Women in Bolivarian Venezuela."

17. Interview with Mariño Alvarado, June 20, 2006

18. Alice O'Keeffe, "Chávez: From hero to tyrant," *New Statesman*, July 16, 2007.

19. Silene Ramírez, "Venezuela launches effort to solve housing crisis," Reuters, May 17, 2005.

20. Ahiana Figueroa, "En 8 años se invirtieron Bs 11,6 billones para construir sólo 204.065 viviendas," *El Nacional*, April 3, 2007.

21. Interview with F.frén Figuera, June 23, 2006

22. Karem Racines Arévalo, "Vargas está menos vulnerable," *El Nacional*, March 29, 2007 (Factiva)

23. "105 familias de Quebrada Seca esperan por vivienda," *El Nacional*, March 14, 2007.

24. Steven Dudley, "Hospital funding chasm follows political division," *The Miami Herald*, November 22, 2006,

25. "Venezuela: médicos piden más sueldo y protestan por cubanos," AP Spanish Worldstream, July 15, 2005.

26. Kozloff, "Chávez's Holy War," "Chávez: We'll give health, education expertise to ALBA countries," EFE News Service, April 29, 2007.

27. Rebecca Trotzky Sirr, "Talking Dirty About Revolution: Sexual Health and Gender Inequality in Venezuela," Upside Down World, August 15, 2007, http://upsidedownworld.org/main/content/view/852/1/ (accessed August 28, 2007).

28. Ben Shankland, "Cuban Doctors' Return Home Clouds Outlook for Venezuelan Healthcare," *Global Insight Daily Analysis*, February 13, 2007.

29. Dudley, "Hospital funding chasm."

30. Dudley, "Hospital funding chasm."

31. "Cuban Doctors Staff Venezuela's Free Clinics," *NPR: Day to Day*, December 1, 2006.

32. "Venezuela: médicos piden más sueldo y protestan por cubanos," AP Spanish Worldstream, July 15, 2005.

33. "Cuban Doctors," *NPR: Day to Day.*

34. Kozloff, "Chávez's Holy War"

35. Adam Easton, "Venezuela struggles to cope with Aids," BBC News Web site, July 6, 2002, http://news.bbc.co.uk/2/hi/americas/2103040.stm (accessed August 28, 2007).

36. Humberto Márquez, "Health—Venezuela: Gov't Imports Generic AIDS Drugs From India," Inter Press Service, June 7, 2004.

37. Aldo Rodríguez Villouta, "Aquatic weed returns to Venezuelan lakeside town," EFE News Service, February 22, 2006.

38. Yensi Rivero, "Environment—Venezuela: Freshwater Weed Strangling Lake Maracaibo," Inter Press Service, June 7, 2004.

39. Aldo Rodríguez Villouta, "Aquatic weed returns to Venezuelan lakeside town," EFE News Service, February 22, 2006 (Factiva)

40. Rivero, "Environment—Venezuela."

41. "Chávez jura 'salvar' lago de Maracaibo de planta invasora," AP Spanish, June 23, 2004.

42. Dámaso Jiménez, "Recolección de lemna en lago de Maracaibo lleva in-
     vertidos Bs 41 mil millones," *El Nacional*, November 23, 2004.
43. Nikolas Kozloff, "Hugo Chávez: Environmental Hypocrite or Ecologi-
     cal Savior?" venezuelanalysis.com, February 1, 2007, http://www.
     venezuelanalysis.com/articles.php?artno=1948 (accessed September 13,
     2007).
44. "Hugo Chávez's Achilles Heel, An Interview with Jorge Hinestroza,"
     venezuelanalysis, October 9, 2006, http://www.venezuelanalysis.com/
     analysis/1997 (accessed October 19, 2007)
45. E-mail to author from Elio Ríos, August 16, 2007,
46. "Venezuela's Lake Maracaibo threatened by aquatic plant overgrowth,"
     EFE News Service, June 11, 2004.
47. "Chávez jura 'salvar' lago de Maracaibo de planta invasora," AP Spanish,
     June 23, 2004.
48. "Chávez tiene otros seis años para inventar nuevo modelo de socialismo,"
     Agence France Presse, December 4, 2006.
49. "Venezuelan ideologue explains the fundamentals of 21st century social-
     ism," BBC Monitoring Americas, January 21, 2007.
50. Interview with Rafael Uzcátegui, Media Coordinator of Provea, July 1,
     2006
51. "In Conversation: Hugo Chávez and Latin American Populism, by
     Nikolas Kozloff and Steve Stein," *Brooklyn Rail*, December 2006/January
     2007, http://www.brooklynrail.org/2006/12/express/hugo-chavez (ac-
     cessed October 19, 2007)
52. Interview with Umberto Silvio Beltrán, August 1, 2006
53. Cristóbal Valencia Ramírez, "Venezuela's Bolivarian Revolution: Who
     Are The Chavistas?" in Steve Ellner and Miguel Tinker Salas (eds),
     Venezuela: Hugo Chávez and the Decline of an "Exceptional Democracy"
     (Rowman and Littlefield, 2007), 128.
54. Marion Lloyd, "Venezuela Breaking Down on Class Lines," *Boston Globe*,
     December 29, 2002.
55. Interview with Beltrán.
56. "In Conversation: Hugo Chávez and Latin American Populism"
57. "Venezuelan ideologue," BBC Monitoring Americas.
58. "Venezuelan ideologue," BBC Monitoring Americas.
59. Juan Forero, "Venezuela Tries To Create Its Own Kind of Socialism" *The
     Washington Post*, August 6, 2007.
60. Bernd Debusmann, "In Venezuela, obstacles to 21st Century socialism,"
     Reuters, June 20, 2007.
61. "Venezuela's Chávez Denies Plans To Seize Property," Dow Jones Com-
     modities Service, January 29, 2007.
62. José Zambrano, "Che Guevara Essay Contest Criticized," Inter Press
     Service, November 8, 2000.
63. "Cristo, Bolívar, Che y Chávez son los íconos del 'socialismo del siglo
     XXI,'" Agence France Presse, November 30, 2006.

64. "Venezuelan president claims 'knockout' of President Bush," BBC Monitoring Americas, March 14, 2007.

65. "Venezuelan official says education is motor for socialism in his country," Associated Press, January 30, 2007 (Factiva)

66. Monte Reel, "Chávez Educates Masses at a University in His Image," *The Washington Post*, May 25, 2006.

67. Debusmann, "In Venezuela, obstacles to 21st Century socialism."

68. Forero, "Venezuela Tries To Create Its Own Kind of Socialism."

CHAPTER 7

1. Interview with Marc Saint-Upéry, March 5, 2007

2. Kintto Lucas, "Ecuador: Tortuoso Camino a La Constituyente," Inter Press Service, February 1, 2007.

3. "Ecuador: El movimiento indígena apoyará a Correa 'en todo lo que signifique cambio', pero no incondicionalmente," Europa Press—Servicio Internacional, June 4, 2007.

4. Interview with Manuel Castro, March 20, 2007

5. "Ecuador: Bucaram returns," *Economist* Intelligence Unit—Country Monitor, April 4, 2005.

6. "Ecuador: El movimiento indígena," Europa Press.

7. Interview with William Waters, March 10, 2007

8. Interview with Efrén Icaza, March 11, 2007

9. Amy E. Robertson, "Ecuador invites world to save its forest," *The Christian Science Monitor*, June 5, 2007.

10. "Ecuador says continues to analyze rejoining OPEC," Reuters, June 19, 2007.

11. Robertson, "Ecuador invites world to save its forest."

12. Judy Rebick, "Peaceful revolution is taking shape," *The Toronto Star*, August 8, 2006.

13. "Morales' victory likely to help Bolivia's indigenous movement," Xinhua News Agency, December 20, 2005.

14. Tom Hennigan, "Poncho revolutionaries rise up to topple leaders and shake continent," *The Times*, June 11, 2005.

15. José de Córdoba and David Luhnow, "A Dash of Mysticism: Governing Bolivia The Aymara Way—Reading Forefathers' Wrinkles Doesn't Require Books; The Future Lies Behind," *The Wall Street Journal*, July 6, 2006.

16. De Córdoba and Luhnow, "A Dash of Mysticism."

17. Rebick, "Peaceful revolution."

18. De Córdoba and Luhnow, "A Dash of Mysticism."

19. Interview with Martín Condori Flores, March 21, 2007

20. "Bolivia: Morales radicalises YPFB," *Latin American Weekly Report*, February 1, 2007.

21. Dan Keane, "Morales' Gas Nationalization Complete," Associated Press, October 28, 2006, posted at *San Francisco Chronicle* Web site, http://

sfgate.com/cgi-bin/article.cgi?f=/n/a/2006/10/28/international/i2329
29D30.DTL&hw=Morales&sn=001&sc=1000   (accessed   August   1,
2007).

22. Peter Howard Wertheim, "Bolivia decrees foreigners may not export
     products," *The Oil and Gas Journal*, May 21, 2007.
23. Interview with Carlos Arze, March 23, 2007
24. "Bolivia: Morales radicalises YPFB."

CHAPTER 8

1. Albor Ruíz, "Latin Women's Mission of Peace," *New York Daily News*,
    January 26, 2006.
2. "Chile: President Discusses About Her Objective To Improve Health-
    care Quality," *US Fed News*, August 2, 2006.
3. "Chile Police Disperse Hundreds Of Student Protesters," Dow Jones In-
    ternational News, October 18, 2006.
4. "Chile Pres Proposes Education Reform After Student Protests," Dow
    Jones International News, April 9, 2007.
5. Patrick Fitzgerald, "Stanford: Chile's students emerge as remarkably po-
    tent political force," *The Stanford Daily*, U-Wire, May 30, 2007.
6. "Chile Pres Proposes Education Reform," Dow Jones International News.
7. "Chile: Bachelet gives education top billing," *Latin American Weekly Re-
    port*, May 24, 2007.
8. Fitzgerald "Chile's students."
9. Fitzgerald "Chile's students."
10. Daniela Estrada, "Amnesty Condemns Attacks on Mapuche Indians,"
    Inter Press Service, May 25, 2007.
11. "Argentina Piquetero Leaders See Minor Gains In Elections," Dow
    Jones International News, October 25, 2005.
12. "Argentina risk: Political stability risk," *Economist* Intelligence Unit—
    Risk Briefing, January 25, 2007.
13. Marcela Valente, "Politics—Argentina: Spending Cuts Spark Loud
    Protests," Inter Press Service, August 8, 2001. De la Rúa finally resigned
    after violent protests, spurred by an ongoing recession and a freeze on
    bank deposits. See "Argentina risk: Political stability risk," Economist
    Intelligence Unit—Risk Briefing, January 25, 2007.
14. Interview with Andrés Ruggeri, April 2, 2007
15. Interview with Guillermo Pflujer, April 2, 2007; "Foreigners on Edge in
    Argentina as Election Nears," *Platt's Oilgram News*, Vol. 71, No. 179,
    September 15, 1993.
16. Interview with Pflujer.
17. "Worker-managed companies thriving in Argentina's boom," Indo-Asian
    News Service, July 14, 2007.
18. Marie Trigona, "Workers' Power in Argentina: Reinventing Working
    Culture," *Monthly Review*, Vol. 59. No. 3, July 1, 2007.

19. "Worker-managed companies thriving in Argentina's boom," Indo-Asian News Service, July 14, 2007.

20. "Worker-managed companies."

21. Interview with Ramón Lucero, April 9, 2007

22. Sue Branford, "Lula critics expelled from Brazilian Workers Party," *Red Pepper*, February 2004, http://www.redpepper.org.uk/Feb2004/x-Feb-2004-Lula.html (accessed August 5, 2007).

23. Branford, "Lula critics expelled."

24. James Petras, "Lula's 'Workers' Regime' Plummets in Stew of Corruption," Counterpunch, July 30 / 31, 2005, http://www.counterpunch.org/petras08012005.html (accessed August 5, 2007).

25. "Lula–Brazil's Lost Leader," Council on Hemispheric Affairs, June 21st, 2006 http://www.coha.org/2006/06/21/lula-brazils-lost-leader/ (accessed August 6, 2007).

26. Branford, "Lula critics expelled."

27. Petras, "Lula's 'Workers' Regime' Plummets."

28. "Social movements take to the streets," *Gazeta Mercantil*, July 18, 2006.

29. Interview with Valter Pomar, April 17, 2007

30. "Agrarian reform in Brazil, This land is anti-capitalist land," *The Economist* print edition, April 26, 2007 http://www.economist.com/world/la/displaystory.cfm?story_id=9079861 (accessed August 7, 2007).

31. Jason Mark, "Brazil's MST: Taking Back the Land," *Multinational Monitor*, Jan./Feb. 2001, Vol. 22, No. 1–2, http://multinationalmonitor.org/mm2001/01jan-feb/corp2.html (accessed August 7, 2007) .

32. "Agrarian reform in Brazil."

33. "Brazil's problem is the neoliberal model, An interview with João Pedro Stédile of the Landless Workers Movement," Z Net, September 6, 2005, http://www.zmag.org/content/showarticle.cfm?ItemID=8684 (August 7, 2007).

34. Petras, "Lula's 'Workers' Regime' Plummets."

35. "In Conversation: As South America Drifts Left, Wither Brazil? Paulo Fontes with Nikolas Kozloff," *Brooklyn Rail*, March, 2007, http://www.brooklynrail.org/2007/3/express/as-south-america-drifts-left-wither-braz (accessed October 20, 2007)

36. Mario Osava, "/MAY DAY/ LABOUR-LATAM: Brazil an Exception to Trade Union Crisis," April 30, 2003, http://ipsnews.net/interna.asp?idnews=17912 (accessed August 7, 2007).

37. Rosa Maria Marques and Áquilas Mendes, "Lula and Social Policy: In the Service of Financial Capital," *Monthly Review*, Vol. 58, No. 8, February 2007, https://www.monthlyreview.org/0207marques2.htm.

38. "Lula–Brazil's Lost Leader," Council on Hemispheric Affairs, June 21, 2006 http://www.coha.org/2006/06/21/lula-brazils-lost-leader/ (accessed August 6, 2007).

39. Interview with Fontes.

40. Interview with Tarcisio Secoli, April 17, 2007; "U.S. Bankers Relieved by
     Collor Election Victory," Reuters News, December 21, 1989.

                              CHAPTER 9

1.   "Bolivia se incorpora formalmente como socio de Telesur," Agencia
     EFE—Servicio General, January 30, 2007.
2.   Interview with Carlos Correa, June 24, 2006
3.   "In Conversation: Hugo Chávez and Latin American Populism, by Steve
     Stein and Nikolas Kozloff," Brooklyn Rail, December 2006/January 2007,
     http://www.brooklynrail.org/2006/12/express/hugo-chavez   (accessed
     October 23, 2007)
4.   Interview with Greg Wilpert, February 28, 2007; Aporrea Website,
     Sobre Aporrea.org, undated, http://www.aporrea.org/nosotros.php, (ac-
     cessed August 15, 2007).
5.   Simon Romero, "Building a TV Station and a Platform for Leftists,
     THE SATURDAY PROFILE," The New York Times, June 16, 2007 (Fac-
     tiva)
6.   Bart Jones, "Hugo Chávez versus RCTV," The Los Angeles Times, May
     30, 2007, posted at venezuelanalysis.com Web site, http://www.vene-
     zuelanalysis.com/articles.php?artno=2054 (accessed August 8, 2007).
7.   Jones, "Hugo Chávez versus RCTV."
8.   Andrés Cañizález, "Media—Venezuela: Lack of Objectivity Faulted in
     Local Press," Inter Press Service, May 20, 2002.
9.   Simon Romero, "Building a TV Station and a Platform for Leftists," The
     New York Times, June 16, 2007.
10. Simon Romero, "Building a TV Station and a Platform for Leftists," The
     New York Times, June 16, 2007.
11. Jones, "Hugo Chávez versus RCTV."
12. Romero, "Building a TV Station."
13. Interview with Aram Aharonian, February 24, 2007
14. Romero, "Building a TV Station."
15. Interview with Aharonian.
16. Romero, "Building a TV Station."
17. "International TeleSUR Conference: Discussion on Media Ownership
     and the Right to Information," PR Newswire Europe, May 23, 2007.
18. Interview with Manuel Castro, March 20, 2007; Richard García and
     Alexis Ibarra, "La fiesta del Sol se vive en línea," El Mercurio, June 21,
     2006; Carmen Valdivieso Hulbert, "Inmigrantes andinos celebran la Fi-
     esta del Sol en Nueva York," Associated Press, July 3, 2007.
19. Interview with Mónica Almeida, March 8, 2007
20. "Ecuador's Assembly To Regulate Media Ownership–Pres Correa," Dow
     Jones International News, July 23, 2007.
21. "Presidente Correa plantea prohibir 'incesto' entre banca y prensa en
     Ecuador," Agence France Presse, June 12, 2007.

22. "Correa anuncia vigilancia para evitar concentración de medios de comunicación," Agencia EFE—Servicio General, April 10, 2007.
23. Interview with Efrén Icaza, March 11, 2007
24. "Ecuador's Assembly," Dow Jones International News.
25. "Presidente Correa plantea prohibir 'incesto'," Agence France Presse.
26. "Correa dice en caso similar a RCTV él cancelaría 'inmediatamente' licencia," Agencia EFE—Servicio General, July 11, 2007.
27. Interview with Icaza.
28. "Ecuador communication secretary denies government hostility toward journalists," BBC Monitoring Americas, May 22, 2007.
29. "Correa anuncia vigilancia" Agencia EFE—Servicio General.
30. "La señal de Telesur se inaugura en Ecuador," AP Spanish Worldstream, September 17, 2005.
31. "El Gobierno tiene dos opciones para instalar su canal de TV," *El Comercio*, February 25, 2007.
32. "Ecuador communication secretary," BBC Monitoring Americas.
33. "El Ecuador es dueño del 5 % del canal Telesur," *El Comercio*, August 31, 2007.
34. Carlos Valdéz, "Morales rejects worries over press freedom, promises community TV stations," Associated Press, March 19, 2007.
35. "Bolivia's Morales to have Chávez-style weekly radio show," EFE News Service, June 2, 2007.
36. Interview with Baldwin Montero, March 22, 2007
37. Carlos Valdéz, "Morales rejects worries over press freedom, promises community TV stations," Associated Press, March 19, 2007.
38. "Bolivia's Morales to have Chávez-style weekly radio show," EFE News Service, June 2, 2007.
39. Valdéz, "Morales rejects worries."
40. Interview with Montero.
41. "Periodistas venezolanos proponen crear 'periódico del sur' para Sudamérica," Agencia EFE—Servicio General, May 23, 2007.
42. Interviews with Paulo Fontes, January 20, 2007 and Daniel Buarque, April 18, 2007
43. Interview with Buarque.
44. "Lula conducts radio interviews of Brazil soccer stars," EFE News Service, August 23, 2004.
45. "Bolivia se incorpora formalmente como socio de Telesur," Agencia EFE—Servicio General, January 30, 2007.

CONCLUSION

1. Interview with Fermín Toro, March 3, 2007
2. "Bolivia to urge S. American integration at summit," Xinhua News Agency, December 6, 2006; "New Andean trade group head laments Venezuela loss," Reuters News, February 23, 2007;

3. "Bolivia to urge S. American integration," Xinhua News Agency.

4. José Luis Paniagua, "Cuba y Mercosur buscan mayor y más variado intercambio conjunto," Agencia EFE–Servicio Económico, November 2, 2006

5. "South American leaders agree to push for pan-continent trade group," Agence France Presse, July 21, 2006.

6. "South American leaders," Agence France Presse.

7. Andrés Oppenheimer, "Mercosur trade bloc in limbo," *The Miami Herald*, June 14, 2007.

8. Oppenheimer, "Mercosur trade bloc."

9. Oppenheimer, "Mercosur trade bloc."

10. Raúl Pierri, "Mercosur: Brazil Has Reassuring Words for its 'Little Brother,'" Inter Press Service, February 28, 2007.

11. "Mercosur: Honeyed words but limited solutions," *Latinnews Daily*, January 22, 2007.

12. "Argentina, Brazil seen leading push for South American unity," EFE News Service, March 19, 2007.

13. "Argentina, Brazil," EFE News Service.

14. Interview with Valter Pomar, April 17, 2007

15. Interview with Fermín Toro. According to Agence France Presse, Mercosur nations endorsed Venezuela's bid to get a non-permanent seat at the United Nations Security Council. "South American leaders agree to push for pan-continent trade group," Agence France Presse, July 21, 2006.

16. Baradan Kuppusamy, "Iraq dominates debate at non-aligned summit," *South China Morning Post*, February 24, 2003.

INDEX